R. Weber

MUCH ADO ABOUT

NOTHING

(a bit expurgated)
M A Faithfull 2004

EDITED BY

J. C. SMITH, M.A.

FORMERLY EXHIBITIONER OF TRINITY COLLEGE, OXFORD
EDITOR OF "AS YOU LIKE IT"

BLACKIE AND SON LIMITED
50 OLD BAILEY LONDON
GLASGOW AND BOMBAY

THE WARWICK SHAKESPEARE

General Editor—C. H. HERFORD, LITT.D.

Professor of English Language and Literature in the University of Manchester
Examiner in English to London University

As You Like It. Edited by J. C. SMITH, M.A.(Edin.), B.A.(Oxon.), formerly exhibitioner of Trinity College, Oxford; formerly Rector of Stirling High School. 1s. 6d.

Coriolanus. Edited by EDMUND K. CHAMBERS, M.A., formerly scholar of Corpus Christi College, Oxford; Editor of *English Pastorals*, *The Red Letter Shakespeare*, &c. 1s. 6d.

Cymbeline. Edited by A. J. WYATT, M.A., sometime scholar of Christ's College, Cambridge. 1s. 6d.

Hamlet. Edited by EDMUND K. CHAMBERS, M.A., Editor of *Coriolanus*, &c. 1s. 6d.

Henry the Fourth. PART I. Edited by F. W. MOORMAN, B.A., Ph.D., Assistant Professor of English Language and Literature, University of Leeds. 1s. 6d.

Henry the Fifth. Edited by G. C. MOORE SMITH, M.A., Professor of English Language and Literature in University of Sheffield. 1s. 6d.

Henry the Eighth. Edited by D. NICHOL SMITH, M.A., Reader in English, Oxford University; Editor of *King Lear*. 1s. 6d.

Julius Cæsar. Edited by ARTHUR D. INNES, M.A., formerly scholar of Oriel College, Oxford. 1s.

King John. Edited by G. C. MOORE SMITH, M.A., Editor of *Henry the Fifth*. 1s. 6d.

King Lear. Edited by D. NICHOL SMITH, M.A., Editor of *Henry the Eighth*. 1s. 6d.

Macbeth. Edited by EDMUND K. CHAMBERS, M.A., Editor of *Coriolanus*, *Hamlet*, &c. 1s.

Merchant of Venice, The. Edited by H. L. WITHERS, B.A., late Professor of Education, Owens College, Manchester; formerly scholar of Balliol College, Oxford. 1s. 6d.

Midsummer-Night's Dream, A. Edited by EDMUND K CHAMBERS, M.A. 1s. 6d.

Much Ado About Nothing. Edited by J. C. SMITH, M.A., Editor of *As You Like It*. 1s. 6d.

Richard the Second. Edited by Professor C. H. HERFORD, LITT.D., General Editor of the Series. 1s. 6d.

Richard the Third. Edited by GEORGE MACDONALD, M.A., LL.D., Balliol College, Oxford; formerly Classical Examiner in the University of Edinburgh. 1s. 6d.

Tempest, The. Edited by F. S. BOAS, M.A., LL.D., Inspector in English Literature to the L.C.C. Education Department. 1s. 6d.

Twelfth Night. Edited by ARTHUR D. INNES, M.A., Editor of *Julius Cæsar*. 1s. 6d.

CONTENTS

INTRODUCTION

I. HISTORY OF THE PLAY

§ 1. *Much Ado About Nothing* is first mentioned in the Stationers' Register under date August 4th, [1600],[1] when it is noted along with *As You Like it*, *Henry V*, and *Every Man in his Humour* as a book to be "stayed", *i.e.* not printed without further authority. The note (it is not a regular entry) points to an attempted piracy, against which a protest had been lodged. A few weeks later our play was published in a sixpenny quarto by Andrew Wise and William Aspley, being entered to them in the Register under date August 23rd. This Quarto presents a very good text, but was not revised by Shakespeare. It retains the name of a character, Innogen, who never appears. That it frequently marks exits too early, and in one place gives the names of the actors for those of the characters, are signs that it was printed from a playhouse copy supplemented by the actors' parts.[2] The Quarto was not re-issued, and *Much Ado* next appeared in print in the collected edition of Shakespeare's works known as the First Folio, 1623. The Folio text of *Much Ado* is a recension of the Quarto, whose characteristic errors it retains.[2]

Publication.

§ 2. The title page of the Quarto bears that the play had already "been sundry times publicly acted" by the Lord Chamberlain's servants (Shakespeare's company). The carelessness of printers has preserved the names of two of the original cast. William Kemp took the part of Dogberry and Richard

Early Stage History.

---

[1] The year is not given, but is inferred from the preceding entry and the subsequent publication of *Much Ado*.　　[2] See further the Appendix on the Text.

Cowley that of Verges. Kemp was the most famous low comedian of the day. In the character of Dogberry he was succeeded by Robert Armin, who in the dedication to his *Italian Tailor and his Boy* (1609) speaks of himself as one "who hath been writ down for an ass in his time, and pleads under *formâ pauperis* in it still, notwithstanding his constableship and office". Thanks to the comic characters, the play was very popular. Several of Dogberry's "derangements of epitaphs" passed at once into the language. The dramatic literature of the first decade of the seventeenth century contains many traces of *Much Ado*. In particular Heywood's *Fair Maid of the Exchange* (1607) teems with reminiscences. But the only recorded performance in Shakespeare's lifetime took place in the spring of 1613, when seven of Shakespeare's plays were produced at Court to grace the wedding festivities of the Princess Elizabeth. At some date prior to May 20th of that year *Much Ado* was presented before Prince Charles, the Princess Elizabeth, and the Elector Palatine, and a play called *Benedicte and Betteris* was presented (apparently) before the king. Probably this was but another name for *Much Ado*; two other plays were, for the same occasion, re-named *Sir John Falstaff* and *Hotspur*,[1] and long afterwards Charles I entered "Benedick and Beatrice" against the title of *Much Ado* in his copy of the Second Folio, recalling (it may be) this very performance. The revival of 1613 was under the management of John Heming, who afterwards helped to edit the First Folio. There is reason to think that the recension which he adopted in the First Folio was originally made for these Court performances of 1613.[2]

Two famous allusions attest the continued popularity of the play in Charles's reign. In the third edition of the *Anatomy of Melancholy* (1628) Burton cited Benedick and Beatrice as an instance of the power of familiarity to overcome dislike. And Leonard Digges declared:

---

[1] It has not hitherto been observed that the plays renamed *were already in print*; the others were still unpublished.   [2] See Appendix on the Text.

"let but Beatrice
And Benedick be seen, lo in a trice
The cockpit, galleries, boxes all are full".

These verses, though perhaps written in 1623, were not published till 1640. In 1642 the theatres were closed.

§ 3. When they were reopened after the Restoration several of Shakespeare's plays were revived in various mangled forms. *Much Ado* was one of the first to suffer adaptation. The old favourites Benedick and Beatrice were transferred by Davenant to his *Law against Lovers*, of which *Measure for Measure* supplied the staple. Pepys saw the play on Feb. 28th, 1661/2. Scraps of *Much Ado* also adorn J. Miller's *Universal Passion* (1736/7). But by that time Shakespeare had begun to enjoy his own again. In 1721 *Much Ado* was revived at Lincoln's Inn Fields with Ryan, Quin, and Mrs. Seymour in the cast. The statement of the play-bill "not acted thirty years" points to an earlier revival, of which no record has been found. Miller's play seems to have stimulated interest in *Much Ado*, which was acted three times towards the close of 1737. But it was not till 1748, when Garrick first appeared in his favourite rôle of Benedick, that the play finally took its place as one of the glories of the English stage. To the German stage it was introduced by Holtei and Devrient, but it has never been quite so popular in Germany as in England.

After the Restoration.

II. DATE OF COMPOSITION

§ 4. From the Stationers' Register we know that the play was written before August 1600; as it is not included by Meres in the full list of Shakespeare's comedies given in his *Treasury of Wit*, it was presumably written after September 1598. The two plays "stayed" along with it—*Henry V* and *As You Like It*—belong to the same period. Now in August 1600 *As You Like It* was apparently a new play, whereas

External Evidence.

Much Ado had been "sundry times publicly acted". On the other hand, the Epilogue to *2 Henry IV* promises to continue the story. The authenticity of the Epilogue may be doubted, but it is unlikely that Shakespeare would interrupt with an alien comedy the trilogy of which Henry V is the hero. The plays, then, were written in this order —*Henry V*, *Much Ado*, *As You Like It*. *Henry V* was finished after, but not long after, the departure of Essex for Ireland on March 27th, 1599.[1] This leaves the summer and autumn of 1599 for the composition of *Much Ado*.

§ 5. The play contains no recognizable allusion to any contemporary event. Critics have seen allusions to Essex's Irish campaign in i. 1. 8, and in i. 1. 45; to his rebellion in iii. 1. 9; and to Jonson's *Cynthia's Revels* in iii. 3. 116. But the first two allusions are unlikely, and the last two impossible. (See notes *ad locc.*)

Allusions.

§ 6. Considerations of style, tone, and characterization corroborate the external evidence. Vocabulary links the play to *2 Henry IV*, prose style to *As You Like It*. In point of versification it falls somewhere between *Richard II* and *Hamlet*. In point of structure it marks the maturity of Shakespeare's comic art. The comic plot is now, for the first time, so woven into the structure of the serious plot that the climax of the one forces the solution of the other. The moral tone of the play has been called immature by comparison *e.g.* with the *Merchant of Venice*. But this is only partially true. The moral crudeness was ingrained in his material, but Shakespeare's treatment of that material shows, by comparison with the *Merchant of Venice*, a growing consciousness of its crude morality. Finally, the character of Claudio is an intimate study of a young man by a man no longer in his first youth.[2]

Internal Evidence.

[1] *Henry V*, Chorus to act v, ll. 30 *seq.*
[2] Fleay takes a very different view of the date of composition. Comparing i. 1. 254, "The sixth of July", with ii. 1. 321, "Not till Monday, my dear son, which is hence a just seven-night", observing that these two remarks are made on the same day, and finding that July 6th fell on a Monday in 1590 and 1601 but in no year between, he concludes that *Much Ado* (though afterwards retouched) was

III. SOURCE OF THE PLOT

§ 7. "A lover deceived into thinking his betrothed unfaithful, by seeing a man at her chamber-window"—such is the kernel of the story. A similar incident has been detected[1] in the late Greek romance of *Chæreas and Callirhoe* (c. 400 A.D.). In Western literature it is found first in the famous Spanish romance of *Tirante the White* (c. 1400), which formed part of Don Quixote's library.[2] As the story of Ariodante and Genevra it appeared in Ariosto's *Orlando Furioso* (1516); and as the story of Phaon and Claribel in Spenser's *Faery Queen* (1590). With both of these versions Shakespeare was familiar. The *Orlando Furioso* had been translated by Harington in 1591: the Genevra episode had already been translated by Peter Beverley in 1565, and also (unless Harington was mistaken)[3] by Turbervil, and had formed the subject of a lost play acted in 1583.

Early Versions. Ariosto. Spenser.

§ 8. But in the main Shakespeare followed the version, not of Ariosto or of Spenser, but of the Italian novelist Bandello.[4] This is the story of Timbreo di Cardona as told by Bandello in 1554:—

Bandello.

originally written in 1590, and was the play referred to by Meres as *Love's Labour Won* (commonly supposed to have been a first draft of *All's Well*). Unfortunately, the same line of argument breaks down in the case of *Every Man in his Humour*, where dates supposed to point to 1607 are found in the Quarto of 1601, which reproduced the acting-version of 1598. Fleay's second argument is that Kemp, who played Dogberry, left the Lord Chamberlain's men in 1599, when they moved from the Curtain to the Globe. But the only evidence for this is the fact that Kemp played in *Every Man in his Humour* and did not play in *Every Man out of his Humour*. The same argument would prove that Shakespeare had left the company. Moreover, from the *Return from Parnassus*, iv. 3, it appears that Kemp was still with the Lord Chamberlain's men in 1601; while the gibes at the Stage Clown in the First Quarto of Hamlet (1603), if pointed at Kemp, show that his defection was recent. [1] *Jahrbuch*, xxxiv. 339.

[2] *Don Quixote*, pt. 1, c. 6. "In its way," says the licentiate, "it is the very best book in the world."

[3] The only evidence for Turbervil's version is Harington's casual mention of it. It is not in the *Tragical Tales*. "Turbervil's *Genevra*" is a figment of W. C. Hazlitt's.

[4] How Shakespeare made acquaintance with Bandello's story is uncertain. The "enriched" French version of Belle-Forest (1582) he does not seem to have used.

"In the year 1283, after the massacre of the Sicilian Vespers, King Piero of Arragon seized the throne of Sicily, and having defeated and captured Charles of Anjou, established his court at Messina. Here his favourite Timbreo di Cardona saw and loved Fenicia, the daughter of a decayed gentleman of the town, Lionato de' Lionati. At first he tried to get her for his mistress, but failing in this he approached her father by proxy and sought her hand in honourable marriage. They were betrothed. But Timbreo's brother-in-arms, Girondo, had also seen and loved Fenicia. To prevent the marriage he suborned a foolish youth, who told Timbreo that Fenicia was in the habit of receiving a friend of his three nights a week. For proof of this Timbreo, concealed in the garden, saw the aforesaid youth, with a servant of Girondo's disguised as a gentleman, and a third man carrying a ladder, approach Lionato's house at night. The supposed lover entered by a window in a deserted part of the house at which Fenicia used sometimes to sit by day. This was enough for Timbreo. The friend who had negotiated the engagement was sent to break off the match. Lionato thought that Timbreo had repented of marrying into so poor a family and had coined the story as a pretext. On hearing it Fenicia fell from swoon into swoon, reviving only when all thought her dead, and preparations had been made for her burial. It was resolved to send her away to an uncle's house in the country, and to proceed with the funeral as if she were dead indeed. Remorse now entered into Girondo. In the church, before Fenicia's tomb, he confessed his crime to Timbreo, proffered his poniard, and bade him take vengeance. But Timbreo forgave him, and together they went to Lionato, offering to undergo any penance he might

Relics of an earlier play are supposed to crop out in the name Innogen (see note on *Dramatis Personæ*), the entrance of the Bastard marked in Q. and F. at i. 1. 183, and the unexplained allusions in Beatrice's speech, ii. 1. 248-251. But the only external evidence to support this hypothesis is a notice in the Revels Accounts for 1574 of a "matter of panecia." (? Phenicia) showed by "my Lord of Leicester's men".

impose. Lionato asked merely that Timbreo should come to him if ever again he thought of marriage. This, after a year of mourning, Timbreo did, and was betrothed anew to Fenicia, who was now seventeen and had grown so much taller and more beautiful that Timbreo did not recognize her. The wedding took place at the uncle's house in the country, the bride's identity was disclosed, Girondo was made happy with the hand of her younger sister Belfiore, and the whole party returned in joy to Messina."

§ 9. This is plainly, in outline, the story of Hero and Claudio. For Ariosto and Spenser it will suffice to note the points at which Shakespeare seems to have preferred their version to Bandello's. In Ariosto, the villain bribes Genevra's maid (who is his mistress) to dress in Genevra's clothes and thus attired to be seen toying with him in Genevra's chamber. This suggested the part played by Margaret. Spenser makes the lady's supposed paramour "a groom of base degree", and the villain's motive envy or native malice— *(margin: Hints taken from Ariosto and Spenser.)*

> "He, either envying my toward good,
> Or of himself to treason ill disposed"—

hints developed in the characters of Borachio and Don John. This is all the recognizable material.[1]

IV. CRITICISM

§ 10. "A pretty comical matter", Harington calls this story of Genevra. The phrase sounds singularly inept. Yet Shakespeare has turned this "matter" into a pretty. if not a perfect comedy. In this section we shall try to follow the process of creation.

Shakespeare early found a congenial method. He made some false starts, as in *Love's Labour's Lost*, where he

---

[1] Attempts to affiliate *Much Ado* on *Die Schoene Phaenicia* of Jacob Ayrer (*ob.* 1605) are mistaken. It is true that both plays deal with the story of Timbreo, and that each has a comic sub-plot. But Furness has shown conclusively that Ayrer followed Belle-Forest's version, and Shakespeare did not. As for resemblances in the sub-plots—"there is a river in Macedon ; and there is also moreover a river at Monmouth . . . and there is salmons in both".

tried to work from the abstract; but his apprenticeship
to history confirmed him in a more excellent
way. Taking some *datum* of story, he set
himself to render it into dramatically effective
scenes, naturally transacted by probable characters, in
accordance with some general (comic or tragic) conception
of the significance of the story as an episode in human
life. In the present case he had a task of some difficulty.
The story of Timbreo is not very striking, nor very probable, nor obviously comic. Shakespeare had to make it
striking and probable, and yet to avoid a tragic solution.

The Dramatic Problem.

§ 11. A playwright must economize time, place, incident,
and character. Bandello's story wanders from Messina to
the country and back again. It spreads over
a year and more. It dallies with incidents
like the Sicilian Vespers which lie beyond the
scope of the action, and with characters like Re Piero and
his queen, who do nothing to forward it. Shakespeare
has confined the action to Messina, and to a few places
there. He has compressed it into nine days, of which
four are blank. Five separate scenes and five days
suffice. He has brought the preliminary action and the
preliminary characters directly into the service of his plot.
The war from which Don Pedro is returning has been
caused by the rebellion of his bastard brother. The elation
of victory helps to create the comic atmosphere, and the
pardoned rebel makes a serviceable villain. Don Pedro
becomes a gay bachelor, and takes on himself the rôle of
go-between. Antonio, retained to play the father, is made
a foil to Leonato. Lionato's wife is left out, though
apparently at the last moment.[1] But even omissions are
turned to account.

Dramatic Economy.

§ 12. Such economies as these every playwright must
practise, as part of the conditions of an art
which has to achieve its effects in small com-
pass. But Shakespeare succeeds beyond all
other playwrights in achieving condensation without

Dramatic Time.

---

[1] See note on *Dramatis Personæ.*

sacrificing breadth and perspective. He gives his characters a past, he exhibits their action as an episode in a larger social life. Don Pedro had passed through Messina on his way to the wars, so that when the play opens the heroes and heroines have already been some months acquainted. Feelings which have been so long in bud may well blossom fast "in summer's ripening breath". The relations of the characters are thus partially defined from the outset. Incidental references, sometimes unexplained, heighten the illusion of a lengthened intercourse. By similar means, by a few seemingly irrelevant touches, an environment is suggested for the action. An uncle of Claudio's is mentioned, but not introduced; a son of Antonio's is introduced, merely to pass over the stage. By rapid transitions from group to group of his characters, by the references of one group to the doings of another, he creates an extraordinary impression of simultaneous activity. His treatment of time is part of the same illusion. The first five scenes take place on a Monday, the last three acts on the Sunday, Monday, and Tuesday of the following week. But in the midst of scenes dated with such ostentatious precision comes a scene (ii. 3) which is not dated at all. In this scene Claudio's engagement and Beatrice's supposed infatuation are represented as at least several days old. Yet in iii. 2, which is supposed to fall on Sunday afternoon, Benedick has been showing signs of love-sickness for some days. The undated scene gives the imagination scope to conceive the development of feeling in these characters without retarding the dramatic march of the main action.

§ 13. The climax of the novel is the midnight episode. Here Shakespeare abandoned Bandello in favour of Ariosto's more plausible version. Various touches are added to heighten the probability —the night is dark, windy, and wet: the maid is addressed by Hero's name; and when Borachio descends from the ladder he is questioned and vouchsafes an ample disclosure. But even with these changes Shakespeare

The Dramatic Climax.

found it impossible to represent the scene effectively on the stage. On the other hand, he saw the dramatic possibilities of the repudiation so tamely transacted in Bandello; he resolved to report the midnight episode, giving no less than three accounts of it, and to make the repudiation scene the climax of his play. The result was the admirable Church Scene, worthy to be named with the Trial Scene in the *Merchant of Venice* as the most striking of its kind in all his comedies. The Church Scene, like the Trial Scene, is postponed to the Fourth Act, and the finale has to be curtailed. Timbreo's long repentance is replaced by a short lyric scene; as Girondo has gone Belfiore is superfluous; and for the elaborate wedding, the recognition, and the joyous return, we have some score of hasty verses.

§ 14. One of his problems is solved already. Shakespeare has secured dramatic effect. But he has secured it by means which leave the other problems no easier of solution. He has made his play striking. Can he make it probable, in accordance, that is, with the laws of comic probability? Above all, can he make it yield the pleasure (in Aristotelian phrase) "appropriate to" comedy? The Church Scene has strained feeling almost to breaking-point. It has imposed on the hero a rôle more odious and exaggerated than that of Timbreo. Timbreo conducts the repudiation like a gentleman, Claudio (by comparison) like a play-actor. Shakespeare has solved both problems, so far as they are soluble, by the new atmosphere which he has created, by the new incidents which he has added, and by the new interpretation which he has given of the characters of the hero and the heroine.

The atmosphere of the play can hardly be discussed apart from the characters—chiefly new characters—from whom it emanates. But even the original material, as we have seen, is made to diffuse an air of gaiety and irresponsibility at the outset. The horrid background of the Sicilian Vespers is expunged. The gentlemen have returned from a cheaply-bought victory to a house which welcomes them. The elation of victory is succeeded by the bustle of festivities, and the bustle of festivities by the excitement of a wedding. It is the height of summer, when mad blood is stirring: governor and governed are "good neighbours"; masters and men, maids and mistresses joke together "this busy time". The Prince leads the frolics; the old men take their part with boyish zest. The maid, who is to be the instrument of mischief, becomes (in defiance of prosaic likelihood) an innocent accomplice, the most boisterous of all the crew. Everything begins to end well.

§ 15. The plotter who is to disturb this gay company cannot be a part of it. Shakespeare refuses to make a villain of his hero's brother-in-arms or to make rivalry in love a motive for villainy.[1] He reconstructs the preliminaries to supply him with a villain, and to supply his villain with a motive. "Motiveless malignity" is a portent which he does not yet recognize, if indeed he ever did. The stain on Don John's birth has given him a spite against society, which he has just tried to gratify, and failed. His failure has redounded to the glory of Claudio, who has taken in his brother's favour, and in the favour of society, the place which the Bastard has forfeited. He shuns the company of his peers, whom he despises, and sulks apart with his creatures, waiting for a chance to bite. Unable to work his will, his spirit labours in devising mischief. He is agog for any stroke that will mortify his brother's favourite and wound his brother's host. Certainly the Bastard is a kind of devil: "er reizt und wirkt und muss als Teufel schaffen". But he is not a formidable devil, not a devil conceived in the spirit of tragedy. Unlike Richard, he cannot dissemble. Unlike Iago, he has confidants. One of these supplies the device which he has the will but not the wit to conceive. But Borachio's very name of "Drunkard" is a guarantee of failure.

The Complication—Don John.

---

[1] So in *Othello*. In the original (Cinthio's *Hecatommitti*, Dec. 3, Nov. 7), the *alfiero* (ancient) is actuated by a passion for Disdemona.

§ 16. A villain like Don John is incapable of repentance. The solution must therefore be sought elsewhere. It is left, as in Comedy it may legitimately be left, to chance. Borachio's advertised weakness makes the chance probable. The instruments of chance are conceived in the true comic spirit. An Elizabethan audience demanded that every comedy should contain scenes of pure clowning. The virtue which Shakespeare made of this necessity is the best proof of his constructive skill. For his serious plot he went to Italy, for his clowns he looked at home. "The humour of the constable in *A Midsummer-Night's Dream*", says Aubrey, confusing Dogberry with Bottom, "he happened to take at Grendon in Bucks." "At Grendon in Bucks", or elsewhere in England, he found such material for low comedy as Hardy finds in his Wessex clowns. But Shakespeare touched his clowns with the spirit of his comedy and forced them into the service of his plot. These homely watchmen diffuse an air of settled English security in which tragedy cannot breathe. They arrest the plotter before the plot has borne fruit. But to discover the solution before the climax would spoil all. Dogberry and Verges come to the rescue. Only such a pair could have failed to suspect the gravity of their information; only the pair of them could have kept Leonato so long in talk without giving him an inkling of it. His laxity and haste conspire with their stupidity; they go off elated to examine their prisoners, and the plot proceeds. But the tragic virus has been effectually counteracted.

The staple of this low comedy is nothing recondite. To murder the King's English is always enough to amuse an English audience; and the incompetent pomp of magistracy may sit comically even on a Scotsman. But the genial pomposity, the suspicious complacency, the racy muddle-headedness of Dogberry, doing violence to law and language "in the Prince's name", are beyond any but an English Bumble. Our poor rude nation hath not his fellow. Some of his verbal, certainly some of his legal

The Solution—Dogberry and the Watch.

blunders, had a keener relish for his contemporaries than they have for us. But enough is left to keep him fresh for ever.

§ 17. Here, then, is a complication which rises almost to tragedy, and a solution which borders on farce. To fuse these extremes, high comedy is introduced in the persons of Benedick and Beatrice. Hero is provided with a cousin, and Claudio with a brother-in-arms, both professed wits, and both sworn foes to love. At first they appear as the brightest points in the social background, radiating that spirit of *insouciance* which animates the first two acts. Presently these twin stars are detached from the background by a mutual attraction latent from the first, and are involved in an under-plot which is essentially a comic inversion of the main plot. As Claudio is deceived into thinking Hero false, they are entrapped into thinking each other fond.

High Comedy—Benedick and Beatrice.

The hero and heroine of this under-plot may have been suggested by the Girondo and Belfiore of the novel. But its central idea is one with which Shakespeare had already dealt, though more abstractly, in *Love's Labour's Lost.* The would-be self-sufficiency of sex, which forms the subject of that play, is re-embodied in Benedick and Beatrice. By their rival eminence in wit, as well as by their common contempt for a passion which they have never felt, they are obviously meant for each other, if they could be brought to see it. But the speck of vanity in each blinds them. Beatrice has been a little spoiled by an indulgent guardian and a retiring cousin. Her beauty and dancing spirits have attracted suitors whom she has routed with shafts of mockery. This laughing Diana has no prudish reverence for men. Her feeling for them is compounded of maidenly pride and intellectual contempt. They are her brothers, and as such she is ready for them; but the mystery of love-making excites her scorn. She has seen no man of whose wit she has a better opinion than of her own, or for whose manly qualities she would yield her proud freedom to call him lord and master. Such

is her state of mind until she crosses swords with Benedick.

Benedick is a soldier, a gentleman, and (as befits a
Paduan) something of a scholar. In camps and schools
he has preserved until manhood a boyish contempt for
women. No amorist himself, he views the amorous
follies of his friends with amused wonder· like other
heretics, he erects his incapacity into a creed, and
poses as invincible against all assaults of passion. To
exasperate Beatrice he gives himself lady-killing airs.
But he is neither a confirmed jester nor a convinced
misogynist. He acknowledges Beatrice's beauty; her
formidable wit he cannot deny. But the two have talked
themselves into an outrageous opposition, from which
they cannot advance without giving the lie to their pretensions. These pretensions make them fair game for
Comedy, and justify the ruse which leads each of them to
take the first step in the belief that it has been taken by
the other. But their vanity (to give it so harsh a name) is
only skin-deep, and the soundness of their hearts, which is
demonstrated even by the success of Don Pedro's trick,
is vindicated in the sequel. For it is Don John's plot, not
his brother's, which finally unites them and makes one
match where it aimed at ruining another. The repudiation of Hero awakens all that is generous in both their
natures; it leaves them together in a heat of emotion
which melts the barriers reared by wit and pride; it gives
Benedick a chance to show that real manliness which we
have hitherto had to take on trust; and it reveals to the
gallant girl the weakness of her womanhood and the need
of a man to champion her cause. Thus the climax of the
main plot forces on the solution of the under-plot, and
raises these charming characters from the position of
dupes, giving dignity to a love-scene which must otherwise have been rather ridiculous. Yet the Comic Nemesis
is complete. Beatrice turns for help to the man, of all
men, at whom she had scoffed most mercilessly; and for
love of her who was his aversion, Benedick, once loudly

sceptical of woman's virtue, draws his sword to defend a woman's honour.

The wit of this couple, extraordinarily gratifying to Shakespeare's contemporaries, has now lost some of its lustre. They are voluble chiefly on the one theme of marriage, and at one another's expense. Time, it may be granted, has rusted some of their repartees. They say nothing that lives in the memory as do the fantasias of Rosalind and Mercutio. But, though the expression of their mirth is thus limited and personal, they give us two things that age cannot wither. They represent a universal phase of that drawn battle between the sexes which gives zest to all comedy: and they are living creations of the comic spirit, born in a merry hour, sound and happy natures, a permanent addition to human gaiety. Their rippling speech, sparkling with alliteration and antithesis at every turn, is perhaps Shakespeare's most finished performance in comic prose.

§ 18. These new characters, with the atmosphere which they diffuse, go far to make the play a comedy, and lighten the task of rendering the main action probable and pleasing. We have seen that Shakespeare in his search for effect made that task harder *The Hero and the Heroine.* than he found it. Wounded self-esteem, at best, is difficult to express with dignity, and the indignation of the chaste male, however righteous, is rarely prepossessing. Above all, the theatricality of Claudio's revenge makes a hard part for a hero. He has to do what looks very like a dastardly thing without being thought a dastard. The solution is sought in a character which is one of Shakespeare's most interesting studies in the psychology of youth. From the messenger's opening eulogy to Benedick's parting taunt Claudio's youth is emphasized. His merits and his faults alike are those of youth. He is one of Nature's darlings, brave, and personally pure, with that poetic susceptibility to beauty in nature and in woman which is sometimes but the brief flower of adolescence; his quick self-respect and moral delicacy inspire at times a heady rhetoric, and his emotional speech is always melodious. But his mind and character are unformed. His wit always waits for a cue: he shows no discernment, taking Don John's word against his patron as he is presently to take it against his betrothed. He has no self-reliance, and little initiative; he confides his passion to one friend after another, and turns at every crisis to the Prince. He is preoccupied with his own emotions, chiefly with thoughts of fame and love. Fortune has conspired with Nature to favour him. He has distinguished himself early in the field, and won the signal favour of the Prince. It is spring-time with him. From thoughts of war he turns again to the Governor's fair daughter. But the Prince's favourite must be prudent. His first question to Don Pedro betrays an interest in Hero's dowry. His patron reassures him, and undertakes not only to make the match but to conduct the wooing. Plainly it is no grand passion that Don John seeks to ruin. Hero and Claudio should hardly be called lovers So far as the play shows, he says not a word to her till the betrothal, and but one formal sentence before the wedding-day. His love for her is an ideal sentiment, localized by expediency, but independent of knowledge and superior to any care for the welfare of its earthly object. When she is accused, there is no affectionate intimacy to set against the evidence of his senses or to countervail his resentment: he believes without hesitation and punishes without pity. Hero has wounded him doubly She has affronted his idea of woman and his esteem for himself—two very tender spots in a young man's mind. But neither the Hero whom he loved nor the Hero whom he repudiates is the real Hero. The inference Shakespeare would have us draw is that there is no harm done. Nor is there obviously much good done either, so far at least as these two are concerned. "Poor Claudio's" self-esteem is shattered by the revelation of Hero's innocence: he is as forward for reparation as he was for offence; but his midnight vigil restores him, and he emerges jaunty on his second wedding-day. Shake-

speare's resolute adherence to his comic scheme prevents
the hurried finale from exhibiting any real deepening of
feeling, any true reconciliation.

His task with the hero was to preserve our sympathy:
his task with the heroine is to keep it in check. Too
poignant sympathy with Hero would drive the Church
Scene into tragedy. Against this Shakespeare guards,
with the more ease inasmuch as the Heros of this world
did not yet attract him so much as the Beatrices. Hero
is indeed a "modest young lady", "a sweet and innocent
lady", with a shy beauty and a quiet charm of her own.
The sentiment of the play wells from her silence, as its
mirth and merriment radiate from Beatrice's speech. But
hers is not yet the deep and "gracious" silence of a Valeria:
extraordinarily silent in company, she has a mischievous
tongue at her friends' service; she can be testy with her
maid, and in moments of elation can talk of simple beauties
with a pretty fancy. For the rest, she is a good young
girl, with little mind or inclination of her own. She takes
a husband as her father pleases: she expects and accepts
Don Pedro, she is given to Claudio. Her repudiation is
painful and shameful enough, but at least it is not the
parting of fond hearts. Before Claudio's accusation she
stands helpless. When next she meets him, indeed, she
hastens to assert her innocence; but again the hurried
finale allows no further hint of any strength she may have
drawn from her ordeal.

§ 19. Brilliant and artful as this comedy is, it does not
entirely satisfy the modern reader. We do not take it to
our hearts as we do other plays of Shake-
speare's, less brilliant and much less artful.   Conclusion.
This dissatisfaction seems to be due partly to a sort of
conflict between Shakespeare's comic method and his
growing imaginative power, partly to a kind of moral
indulgence which he was apt to extend, especially to young
men of the type of Claudio. The vividness of his imaginative presentment, in fact, reveals the flaw ingrained in
his material: the main plot is essentially repugnant to

comic treatment.   Shakespeare uses all his art to maintain the comic scheme: but his need of effect, his imaginative force, his interest in character are too much for him.
He cuts too deep.   Yet he will not abandon the conventional solution, with the result that the gravity of his
climax clashes with the levity of his conclusion.   The
moral indignation which his climax excites he attempts
to satisfy by the promise of "brave punishments" for
the villain "to-morrow".   But his hero gets off, literally,
for an old song.   Yet his offence was not, on the face
of it, so very different from that for which Leontes is so
heavily punished.   But Claudio belongs to a type, not
altogether admirable in itself, which Nature (for her own
ends) often seems to favour.   And Shakespeare was like
Nature.   To these young men of his he was an indulgent
father.   But his tone was already growing sterner.
Claudio's faults, though condoned, are not ignored.   In
a year or two Shakespeare was to draw the character
of Bertram, and to say his last word on that subject—
and so to bid good-bye to Comedy.   In the play of
which Bertram is the hero, and in its unlucky companion *Measure for Measure*, the confused issues of the
conflict between convention and imagination became intolerable, and the irresistible growth of his native genius
drove Shakespeare into Tragedy.

MUCH ADO ABOUT NOTHING

DRAMATIS PERSONÆ

Don Pedro, prince of Arragon.

Don John, his bastard brother.

Claudio, a young lord of Florence.

Benedick, a young lord of Padua.

Leonato, governor of Messina.

Antonio, his brother.

Balthasar, attendant on Don Pedro.

Conrade,
Borachio, } followers of Don John.

Friar Francis.

Dogberry, a constable.

Verges, a headborough.

A Sexton.

A Boy.

Hero, daughter to Leonato.

Beatrice, niece to Leonato.

Margaret,
Ursula, } gentlewomen attending on Hero.

Messengers, Watch, Attendants, &c.

Scene: *Messina.*

MUCH ADO ABOUT NOTHING

ACT I

Scene I. *Before Leonato's house*

Enter Leonato, Hero, *and* Beatrice, *with a* Messenger

Leon. I learn in this letter that Don Pedro of Arragon comes this night to Messina.

Mess. He is very near by this: he was not three leagues off when I left him.

Leon. How many gentlemen have you lost in this action?

Mess. But few of any sort, and none of name.

Leon. A victory is twice itself when the achiever brings home full numbers. I find here that Don Pedro hath bestowed much honour on a young Florentine called Claudio.   11

Mess. Much deserved on his part and equally remembered by Don Pedro: he hath borne himself beyond the promise of his age, doing, in the figure of a lamb, the feats of a lion: he hath indeed better bettered expectation than you must expect of me to tell you how.

Leon. He hath an uncle here in Messina will be very much glad of it.

Mess. I have already delivered him letters, and there appears much joy in him; even so much that joy could not show itself modest enough without a badge of bitterness.   22

Leon. Did he break out into tears?

27

Mess. In great measure.

Leon. A kind overflow of kindness: there are no faces truer than those that are so washed. How much better is it to weep at joy than to joy at weeping!

Beat. I pray you, is Signior Mountanto returned from the wars or no?

Mess. I know none of that name, lady: there was none such in the army of any sort.   31

Leon. What is he that you ask for, niece?

Hero. My cousin means Signior Benedick of Padua.

Mess. O, he's returned; and as pleasant as ever he was.

Beat. He set up his bills here in Messina and challenged Cupid at the flight; and my uncle's fool, reading the challenge, subscribed for Cupid, and challenged him at the bird-bolt. I pray you, how many hath he killed and eaten in these wars? But how many hath he killed? for indeed I promised to eat all of his killing.   41

Leon. Faith, niece, you tax Signior Benedick too much; but he'll be meet with you, I doubt it not.

Mess. He hath done good service, lady, in these wars.

Beat. You had musty victual, and he hath holp to eat it: he is a very valiant trencher-man; he hath an excellent stomach.

Mess. And a good soldier too, lady.

Beat. And a good soldier to a lady: but what is he to a lord?   50

Mess. A lord to a lord, a man to a man; stuffed with all honourable virtues.

Beat. It is so, indeed; he is no less than a stuffed man: but for the stuffing,—well, we are all mortal.

Leon. You must not, sir, mistake my niece. There is a kind of merry war betwixt Signior Benedick and her: they never meet but there's a skirmish of wit between them.   57

Beat. Alas! he gets nothing by that. In our last conflict

four of his five wits went halting off, and now is the whole
man governed with one: so that if he have wit enough to
keep himself warm, let him bear it for a difference between
himself and his horse; for it is all the wealth that he hath
left, to be known a reasonable creature.   Who is his companion now?   He hath every month a new sworn brother.

Mess. Is't possible?

Beat. Very easily possible: he wears his faith but as
the fashion of his hat; it ever changes with the next
block.

Mess. I see, lady, the gentleman is not in your books. 69

Beat. No; an he were, I would burn my study.   But,
I pray you, who is his companion?   Is there no young
squarer now that will make a voyage with him to the
devil?

Mess. He is most in the company of the right noble
Claudio.

Beat. O Lord, he will hang upon him like a disease: he
is sooner caught than the pestilence, and the taker runs
presently mad.   God help the noble Claudio! if he have
caught the Benedick, it will cost him a thousand pound
ere a' be cured.   80

Mess. I will hold friends with you, lady.

Beat. Do, good friend.

Leon. You will never run mad, niece.

Beat. No, not till a hot January.

Mess. Don Pedro is approached.

Enter DON PEDRO, DON JOHN, CLAUDIO, BENEDICK,
and BALTHASAR

D. Pedro. Good Signior Leonato, you are come to meet
your trouble: the fashion of the world is to avoid cost, and
you encounter it.

Leon. Never came trouble to my house in the likeness of
your grace: for trouble being gone, comfort should remain;

but when you depart from me, sorrow abides, and happiness takes his leave.   92

D. Pedro. You embrace your charge too willingly. I think this is your daughter.

Leon. Her mother hath many times told me so.

Bene. Were you in doubt, sir, that you asked her?

Leon. Signior Benedick, no; for then were you a child.

D. Pedro. You have it full, Benedick: we may guess by this what you are, being a man. Truly, the lady fathers herself. Be happy, lady; for you are like an honourable father.   101

Bene. If Signior Leonato be her father, she would not have his head on her shoulders for all Messina, as like him as she is.

Beat. I wonder that you will still be talking, Signior Benedick: nobody marks you.

Bene. What, my dear Lady Disdain! are you yet living?

Beat. Is it possible disdain should die while she hath such meet food to feed it as Signior Benedick? Courtesy itself must convert to disdain, if you come in her presence.

Bene. Then is courtesy a turncoat. But it is certain I am loved of all ladies, only you excepted: and I would I could find in my heart that I had not a hard heart; for, truly, I love none.   114

Beat. A dear happiness to women: they would else have been troubled with a pernicious suitor. I thank God and my cold blood, I am of your humour for that: I had rather hear my dog bark at a crow than a man swear he loves me.

Bene. God keep your ladyship still in that mind! so some gentleman or other shall 'scape a predestinate scratched face.   122

Beat. Scratching could not make it worse, an t' were such a face as yours were.

Bene. Well, you are a rare parrot-teacher.

Beat. A bird of my tongue is better than a beast of yours.

Bene. I would my horse had the speed of your tongue, and so good a continuer. But keep your way, a' God's name; I have done.   130

Beat. You always end with a jade's trick: I know you of old.

D. Pedro. That is the sum of all, Leonato. Signior Claudio and Signior Benedick, my dear friend Leonato hath invited you all. I tell him we shall stay here at the least a month; and he heartily prays some occasion may detain us longer. I dare swear he is no hypocrite, but prays from his heart. *dramatic irony*

Leon. If you swear, my lord, you shall not be forsworn. [*To Don John*] Let me bid you welcome, my lord: being reconciled to the prince your brother, I owe you all duty.   142

D. John. I thank you: I am not of many words, but I thank you.

Leon. Please it your grace lead on?

D. Pedro. Your hand, Leonato; we will go together.

[*Exeunt all except Benedick and Claudio*

Claud. Benedick, didst thou note the daughter of Signior Leonato?

Bene. I noted her not; but I looked on her.

Claud. Is she not a modest young lady?   150

Bene. Do you question me, as an honest man should do, for my simple true judgement; or would you have me speak after my custom, as being a professed tyrant to their sex?

Claud. No; I pray thee speak in sober judgement.

Bene. Why, i' faith, methinks she's too low for a high praise, too brown for a fair praise and too little for a great praise: only this commendation I can afford her, that were she other than she is, she were unhandsome; and being no other but as she is, I do not like her. *in rank*

Claud. Thou thinkest I am in sport: I pray thee tell me
truly how thou likest her.   161

Bene. Would you buy her, that you inquire after her?

Claud. Can the world buy such a jewel?

Bene. Yea, and a case to put it into. But speak you
this with a sad brow? or do you play the flouting Jack,
to tell us Cupid is a good hare-finder, and Vulcan a rare
carpenter? Come, in what key shall a man take you, to
go in the song?

Claud. In mine eye she is the sweetest lady that ever
I looked on.   170

Bene. I can see yet without spectacles, and I see no
such matter: there's her cousin, an she were not possessed
with a fury, exceeds her as much in beauty as the first of
May doth the last of December. But I hope you have no
intent to turn husband, have you?

Claud. I would scarce trust myself, though I had sworn
the contrary, if Hero would be my wife.

Bene. Is't come to this? In faith, hath not the world
one man but he will wear his cap with suspicion? Shall
I never see a bachelor of threescore again? Go to, i'
faith; an thou wilt needs thrust thy neck into a yoke,
wear the print of it and sigh away Sundays. Look; Don
Pedro is returned to seek you.   183

Re-enter DON PEDRO

D. Pedro. What secret hath held you here, that you
followed not to Leonato's?

Bene. I would your grace would constrain me to tell.

D. Pedro. I charge thee on thy allegiance.

Bene. You hear, Count Claudio: I can be secret as a
dumb man; I would have you think so; but, on my allegiance, mark you this, on my allegiance. He is in love.
With who? now that is your grace's part. Mark how short
his answer is:—With Hero, Leonato's short daughter.   192

Claud. If this were so, so were it uttered.

Bene. Like the old tale, my lord: 'it is not so, nor 't was not so, but, indeed, God forbid it should be so'.

Claud. If my passion change not shortly, God forbid it should be otherwise.

D. Pedro. Amen, if you love her; for the lady is very well worthy.

Claud. You speak this to fetch me in, my lord.   200

D. Pedro. By my troth, I speak my thought.

Claud. And, in faith, my lord, I spoke mine.

Bene. And, by my two faiths and troths, my lord, I spoke mine.

Claud. That I love her, I feel.

D. Pedro. That she is worthy, I know.

Bene. That I neither feel how she should be loved nor know how she should be worthy, is the opinion that fire cannot melt out of me: I will die in it at the stake.

D. Pedro. Thou wast ever an obstinate heretic in the despite of beauty.   211

Claud. And never could maintain his part but in the force of his will.

Bene. That a woman conceived me, I thank her; that she brought me up, I likewise give her most humble thanks: but that I will have a recheat winded in my forehead, or hang my bugle in an invisible baldrick, all women shall pardon me. Because I will not do them the wrong to mistrust any, I will do myself the right to trust none; and the fine is, for the which I may go the finer, I will live a bachelor.   221

D. Pedro. I shall see thee, ere I die, look pale with love.

Bene. With anger, with sickness, or with hunger, my lord, not with love: prove that ever I lose more blood with love than I will get again with drinking, pick out mine eyes with a ballad-maker's pen and hang me up for the sign of blind Cupid.

(M 824)   3

D. Pedro. Well, if ever thou dost fall from this faith, thou wilt prove a notable argument.

Bene. If I do, hang me in a bottle like a cat and shoot at me, and he that hits me, let him be clapped on the shoulder, and called Adam.　　232

D. Pedro. Well, as time shall try:

‘In time the savage bull doth bear the yoke’.

Bene. The savage bull may; but if ever the sensible Benedick bear it, pluck off the bull's horns and set them in my forehead: and let me be vilely painted, and in such great letters as they write ‘Here is good horse to hire’, let them signify under my sign ‘Here you may see Benedick the married man’.　　240

Claud. If this should ever happen, thou wouldst be horn-mad.

D. Pedro. Nay, if Cupid have not spent all his quiver in Venice, thou wilt quake for this shortly.

Bene. I look for an earthquake too, then.

D. Pedro. Well, you will temporize with the hours. In the meantime, good Signior Benedick, repair to Leonato's: commend me to him and tell him I will not fail him at supper; for indeed he hath made great preparation.

Bene. I have almost matter enough in me for such an embassage; and so I commit you—　　251

Claud. To the tuition of God: From my house, if I had it,—

D. Pedro. The sixth of July: Your loving friend, Benedick.

Bene. Nay, mock not, mock not. The body of your discourse is sometime guarded with fragments, and the guards are but slightly basted on neither: ere you flout old ends any further, examine your conscience: and so I leave you.　　[*Exit*　260

Claud. My liege, your highness now may do me good.

D. Pedro. My love is thine to teach: teach it but how,
And thou shalt see how apt it is to learn
Any hard lesson that may do thee good.
  Claud. Hath Leonato any son, my lord?
  D. Pedro. No child but Hero; she's his only heir.
Dost thou affect her, Claudio?
  Claud.   O, my lord,
When you went onward on this ended action,
I look'd upon her with a soldier's eye,
That liked, but had a rougher task in hand   270
Than to drive liking to the name of love:
But now I am return'd and that war-thoughts
Have left their places vacant, in their rooms
Come thronging soft and delicate desires,
All prompting me how fair young Hero is,
Saying, I liked her ere I went to wars.
  D. Pedro. Thou wilt be like a lover presently
And tire the hearer with a book of words.
If thou dost love fair Hero, cherish it,
And I will break with her and with her father   280
And thou shalt have her.   Was 't not to this end
That thou began'st to twist so fine a story?
  Claud. How sweetly you do minister to love,
That know love's grief by his complexion!
But lest my liking might too sudden seem,
I would have salved it with a longer treatise.
  D. Pedro. What need the bridge much broader than the
    flood?
The fairest grant is the necessity.
Look, what will serve is fit: 't is once, thou lovest,
And I will fit thee with the remedy.   290
I know we shall have revelling to-night:
I will assume thy part in some disguise
And tell fair Hero I am Claudio,
And in her bosom I 'll unclasp my heart

And take her hearing prisoner with the force
And strong encounter of my amorous tale;
Then after to her father will I break;
And the conclusion is, she shall be thine.
In practice let us put it presently.   [*Exeunt*

SCENE II. *A room in Leonato's house*

Enter LEONATO *and* ANTONIO, *meeting*

Leon. How now, brother! Where is my cousin, your
son? hath he provided this music?

Ant. He is very busy about it. But, brother, I can tell
you strange news that you yet dreamt not of.

Leon. Are they good?

Ant. As the event stamps them : but they have a good
cover; they show well outward. The prince and Count
Claudio, walking in a thick - pleached alley in mine
orchard, were thus much overheard by a man of mine:
the prince discovered to Claudio that he loved my niece
your daughter and meant to acknowledge it this night in
a dance; and if he found her accordant, he meant to take
the present time by the top and instantly break with you
of it.   14

Leon. Hath the fellow any wit that told you this?

Ant. A good sharp fellow: I will send for him; and
question him yourself.

Leon. No, no; we will hold it as a dream till it appear
itself: but I will acquaint my daughter withal, that she may
be the better prepared for an answer, if peradventure this
be true. Go you and tell her of it. [*Enter attendants.*]
Cousins, you know what you have to do. O, I cry you
mercy, friend; go you with me, and I will use your skill.
Good cousin, have a care this busy time.   [*Exeunt* 24

SCENE III.   *The same*

Enter DON JOHN *and* CONRADE

Con. What the good-year, my lord! why are you thus out of measure sad?

D. John. There is no measure in the occasion that breeds; therefore the sadness is without limit.

Con. You should hear reason.

D. John. And when I have heard it, what blessing brings it?

Con. If not a present remedy, at least a patient suffer-ance.   9

D. John. I wonder that thou, being, as thou sayest thou art, born under Saturn, goest about to apply a moral medicine to a mortifying mischief. I cannot hide what I am: I must be sad when I have cause and smile at no man's jests, eat when I have stomach and wait for no man's leisure, sleep when I am drowsy and tend on no man's business, laugh when I am merry and claw no man in his humour.

Con. Yea, but you must not make the full show of this till you may do it without controlment. You have of late stood out against your brother, and he hath ta'en you newly into his grace; where it is impossible you should take true root but by the fair weather that you make your-self: it is needful that you frame the season for your own harvest.   24

D. John. I had rather be a canker in a hedge than a rose in his grace, and it better fits my blood to be dis-dained of all than to fashion a carriage to rob love from any: in this, though I cannot be said to be a flattering honest man, it must not be denied but I am a plain-deal-ing villain. I am trusted with a muzzle and enfranchised with a clog; therefore I have decreed not to sing in my

cage. If I had my mouth, I would bite; if I had my
liberty, I would do my liking: in the meantime let me be
that I am and seek not to alter me.   34

Con. Can you make no use of your discontent?

D. John. I make all use of it, for I use it only.   Who
comes here?

Enter BORACHIO

What news, Borachio?

Bora. I came yonder from a great supper: the prince
your brother is royally entertained by Leonato; and I can
give you intelligence of an intended marriage.   41

D. John. Will it serve for any model to build mischief
on?   What is he for a fool that betroths himself to un-
quietness!

Bora. Marry, it is your brother's right hand.

D. John. Who? the most exquisite Claudio?

Bora. Even he.

D. John. A proper squire!   And who, and who? which
way looks he?

Bora. Marry, on Hero, the daughter and heir of
Leonato.   51

D. John. A very forward March-chick! How came you
to this?

Bora. Being entertained for a perfumer, as I was
smoking a musty room, comes me the prince and Claudio,
hand in hand, in sad conference: I whipt me behind the
arras; and there heard it agreed upon that the prince
should woo Hero for himself, and having obtained her,
give her to Count Claudio.

D. John. Come, come, let us thither: this may prove
food to my displeasure.   That young start-up hath all the
glory of my overthrow: if I can cross him any way, I bless
myself every way.   You are both sure, and will assist me?

Con. To the death, my lord.   64

D. John. Let us to the great supper: their cheer is the

greater that I am subdued.   Would the cook were of my mind!   Shall we go prove what's to be done?

Bora. We'll wait upon your lordship.   [*Exeunt*

ACT II

SCENE I.   *A hall in Leonato's house*

Enter LEONATO, ANTONIO, HERO, BEATRICE, *and others*

Leon. Was not Count John here at supper?

Ant. I saw him not.

Beat. How tartly that gentleman looks!   I never can see him but I am heart-burned an hour after.

Hero. He is of a very melancholy disposition.

Beat. He were an excellent man that were made just in the midway between him and Benedick: the one is too like an image and says nothing, and the other too like my lady's eldest son, evermore tattling.

Leon. Then half Signior Benedick's tongue in Count John's mouth, and half Count John's melancholy in Signior Benedick's face,—   12

Beat. With a good leg and a good foot, uncle, and money enough in his purse, such a man would win any woman in the world, if a' could get her good-will.

Leon. By my troth, niece, thou wilt never get thee a husband, if thou be so shrewd of thy tongue.

Ant. In faith, she's too curst.

Beat. Too curst is more than curst: I shall lessen God's sending that way; for it is said, 'God sends a curst cow short horns'; but to a cow too curst he sends none.   21

Leon. So, by being too curst, God will send you no horns.

Beat. Just, if he sends me no husband; for the which

blessing I am at him upon my knees every morning and evening. Lord, I could not endure a husband with a beard on his face: I had rather lie in the woollen.

Leon. You may light on a husband that hath no beard.

Beat. What should I do with him? dress him in my apparel and make him my waiting-gentlewoman? He that hath a beard is more than a youth, and he that hath no beard is less than a man: and he that is more than a youth is not for me, and he that is less than a man, I am not for him: therefore I will even take sixpence in earnest of the bear-ward, and lead his apes into hell.   35

Leon. Well, then, go you into hell?

Beat. No, but to the gate; and there will the devil meet me, like an old cuckold, with horns on his head, and say 'Get you to heaven, Beatrice, get you to heaven; here's no place for you maids': so deliver I up my apes, and away to Saint Peter for the heavens; he shows me where the bachelors sit, and there live we as merry as the day is long.

Ant. [*To Hero*] Well, niece, I trust you will be ruled by your father.   44

Beat. Yes, faith; it is my cousin's duty to make curtsy and say, 'Father, as it please you'. But yet for all that, cousin, let him be a handsome fellow, or else make another curtsy and say 'Father, as it please me'.

Leon. Well, niece, I hope to see you one day fitted with a husband.   50

Beat. Not till God make men of some other metal than earth. Would it not grieve a woman to be overmastered with a piece of valiant dust? to make an account of her life to a clod of wayward marl? No, uncle, I'll none: Adam's sons are my brethren; and, truly, I hold it a sin to match in my kindred.

Leon. Daughter, remember what I told you: if the prince do solicit you in that kind, you know your answer.   58

Beat. The fault will be in the music, cousin, if you be

not wooed in good time: if the prince be too important, tell him there is measure in everything and so dance out the answer. For, hear me, Hero: wooing, wedding, and repenting, is as a Scotch jig, a measure, and a cinque pace: the first suit is hot and hasty, like a Scotch jig, and full as fantastical; the wedding, mannerly-modest as a measure, full of state and ancientry; and then comes repentance and, with his bad legs, falls into the cinque pace faster and faster, till he sink into his grave.

Leon. Cousin, you apprehend passing shrewdly.

Beat. I have a good eye, uncle; I can see a church by daylight.   71

Leon. The revellers are entering, brother: make good room.   [*All put on their masks*

Enter DON PEDRO, CLAUDIO, BENEDICK, BALTHASAR, DON JOHN, BORACHIO, MARGARET, URSULA, *and others, masked*

D. Pedro. Lady, will you walk about with your friend?

Hero. So you walk softly and look sweetly and say nothing, I am yours for the walk; and especially when I walk away.

D. Pedro. With me in your company?

Hero. I may say so, when I please.

D. Pedro. And when please you to say so?   80

Hero. When I like your favour; for God defend the lute should be like the case!

D. Pedro. My visor is Philemon's roof; within the house is Jove.

Hero. Why, then, your visor should be thatched.

D. Pedro. Speak low, if you speak love.

                                                 [*Drawing her aside*

Balth. Well, I would you did like me.

Marg. So would not I, for your own sake; for I have many ill qualities.

Balth. Which is one?   90

Marg. I say my prayers aloud.

Balth. I love you the better: the hearers may cry, Amen.

Marg. God match me with a good dancer!

Balth. Amen.

Marg. And God keep him out of my sight when the dance is done!   Answer, clerk.

Balth. No more words: the clerk is answered.

Urs. I know you well enough; you are Signior Antonio.

Ant. At a word, I am not.

Urs. I know you by the waggling of your head.   100

Ant. To tell you true, I counterfeit him.

Urs. You could never do him so ill-well, unless you were the very man.   Here's his dry hand up and down: you are he, you are he.

Ant. At a word, I am not.

Urs. Come, come, do you think I do not know you by your excellent wit? can virtue hide itself?   Go to, mum, you are he: graces will appear, and there's an end.

Beat. Will you not tell me who told you so?

Bene. No, you shall pardon me.   110

Beat. Nor will you not tell me who you are?

Bene. Not now.

Beat. That I was disdainful, and that I had my good wit out of the 'Hundred Merry Tales':—well, this was Signior Benedick that said so.

Bene. What's he?

Beat. I am sure you know him well enough.

Bene. Not I, believe me.

Beat. Did he never make you laugh?

Bene. I pray you, what is he?   120

Beat. Why, he is the prince's jester: a very dull fool; only his gift is in devising impossible slanders: none but libertines delight in him; and the commendation is not in his wit, but in his villany; for he both pleases men and angers them, and then they laugh at him and beat him. I am sure he is in the fleet: I would I had boarded me.

Bene. When I know the gentleman, I'll tell him what you say.

Beat. Do, do: he'll but break a comparison or two on me; which, peradventure not marked or not laughed at, strikes him into melancholy; and then there's a partridge wing saved, for the fool will eat no supper that night. [*Music.*]   We must follow the leaders.   133

Bene. In every good thing.

Beat. Nay, if they lead to any ill, I will leave them at the next turning.

[*Dance.   Then exeunt all except Don John,
Borachio, and Claudio*

D. John. Sure my brother is amorous on Hero and hath withdrawn her father to break with him about it.   The ladies follow her and but one visor remains.

Bora. And that is Claudio: I know him by his bearing.

D. John. Are not you Signior Benedick?   141

Claud. You know me well: I am he.

D. John. Signior, you are very near my brother in his love: he is enamoured on Hero; I pray you dissuade him from her: she is no equal for his birth: you may do the part of an honest man in it.

Claud. How know you he loves her?

D. John. I heard him swear his affection.

Bora. So did I too; and he swore he would marry her to-night.   150

D. John. Come, let us to the banquet.

[*Exeunt Don John and Borachio*

Claud. Thus answer I in name of Benedick,
But hear these ill news with the ears of Claudio.
'T is certain so; the prince wooes for himself.
Friendship is constant in all other things
Save in the office and affairs of love:

Therefore all hearts in love use their own tongues;
Let every eye negotiate for itself
And trust no agent; for beauty is a witch
Against whose charms faith melteth into blood.   160
This is an accident of hourly proof,
Which I mistrusted not.   Farewell, therefore, Hero!

Re-enter BENEDICK

Bene. Count Claudio?
Claud. Yea, the same.
Bene. Come, will you go with me?
Claud. Whither?
Bene. Even to the next willow, about your own business,
county.   What fashion will you wear the garland of? about
your neck, like an usurer's chain? or under your arm, like
a lieutenant's scarf?   You must wear it one way, for the
prince hath got your Hero.   171
Claud. I wish him joy of her.
Bene. Why, that's spoken like an honest drovier: so they
sell bullocks.   But did you think the prince would have
served you thus?
Claud. I pray you, leave me.
Bene. Ho! now you strike like the blind man: 't was the
boy that stole your meat, and you'll beat the post.
Claud. If it will not be, I'll leave you.   [*Exit* 179
Bene. Alas, poor hurt fowl! now will he creep into
sedges.   But that my Lady Beatrice should know me,
and not know me! The prince's fool! Ha? It may be
I go under that title because I am merry.   Yea, but so
I am apt to do myself wrong; I am not so reputed: it is
the base, though bitter, disposition of Beatrice that puts
the world into her person, and so gives me out.   Well, I'll
be revenged as I may.

Re-enter DON PEDRO

D. Pedro. Now, signior, where's the count? did you see
him?   189

Bene. Troth, my lord, I have played the part of Lady
Fame. I found him here as melancholy as a lodge in a
warren: I told him, and I think I told him true, that your
grace had got the good will of this young lady; and I
offered him my company to a willow-tree, either to make
him a garland, as being forsaken, or to bind him up a rod,
as being worthy to be whipped.

D. Pedro. To be whipped! What's his fault?

Bene. The flat transgression of a school-boy, who, being
overjoyed with finding a birds' nest, shows it his companion, and he steals it.   200

D. Pedro. Wilt thou make a trust a transgression? The
transgression is in the stealer.

Bene. Yet it had not been amiss the rod had been made,
and the garland too; for the garland he might have worn
himself, and the rod he might have bestowed on you, who,
as I take it, have stolen his birds' nest.

D. Pedro. I will but teach them to sing, and restore
them to the owner.

Bene. If their singing answer your saying, by my faith,
you say honestly.   210

D. Pedro. The Lady Beatrice hath a quarrel to you: the
gentleman that danced with her told her she is much
wronged by you.

Bene. O, she misused me past the endurance of a block!
an oak but with one green leaf on it would have answered
her; my very visor began to assume life and scold with
her. She told me, not thinking I had been myself, that I
was the prince's jester, that I was duller than a great
thaw; huddling jest upon jest with such impossible conveyance upon me that I stood like a man at a mark, with

a whole army shooting at me.   She speaks poniards, and
every word stabs: if her breath were as terrible as her
terminations, there were no living near her; she would
infect to the north star.   I would not marry her, though
she were endowed with all that Adam had left him before
he transgressed: she would have made Hercules have
turned spit, yea, and have cleft his club to make the fire
too.   Come, talk not of her: you shall find her the infernal
Ate in good apparel.   I would to God some scholar would
conjure her; for certainly, while she is here, a man may
live as quiet in hell as in a sanctuary; and people sin upon
purpose, because they would go thither; so, indeed, all
disquiet, horror, and perturbation follows her.   233

D. Pedro. Look, here she comes.

Re-enter CLAUDIO, BEATRICE, HERO, *and* LEONATO

Bene. Will your grace command me any service to the
world's end?   I will go on the slightest errand now to
the Antipodes that you can devise to send me on; I will
fetch you a tooth-picker now from the furthest inch of
Asia, bring you the length of Prester John's foot, fetch you
a hair off the great Cham's beard, do you any embassage
to the Pigmies, rather than hold three words' conference
with this harpy.   You have no employment for me?   242

D. Pedro. None, but to desire your good company.

Bene. O God, sir, here's a dish I love not: I cannot
endure my Lady Tongue.   [*Exit*

D. Pedro. Come, lady, come; you have lost the heart of
Signior Benedick.

Beat. Indeed, my lord, he lent it me awhile; and I gave
him use for it, a double heart for his single one: marry,
once before he won it of me with false dice, therefore your
grace may well say I have lost it.   251

D. Pedro. You have put him down, lady, you have put
him down.

Beat. So I would not he should do me, my lord. I have brought Count Claudio, whom you sent me to seek.

D. Pedro. Why, how now, count! wherefore are you sad?

Claud. Not sad, my lord.

D. Pedro. How then? sick?

Claud. Neither, my lord.   260

Beat. The count is neither sad, nor sick, nor merry, nor well; but civil count, civil as an orange, and something of that jealous complexion.

D. Pedro. I' faith, lady, I think your blazon to be true; though, I 'll be sworn, if he be so, his conceit is false. Here, Claudio, I have wooed in thy name, and fair Hero is won: I have broke with her father, and his good will obtained: name the day of marriage, and God give thee joy!   269

Leon. Count, take of me my daughter, and with her my fortunes: his grace hath made the match, and all grace say Amen to it.

Beat. Speak, count, 't is your cue.

Claud. Silence is the perfectest herald of joy: I were but little happy, if I could say how much. Lady, as you are mine, I am yours: I give away myself for you and dote upon the exchange.

Beat. Speak, cousin: or, if you cannot, stop his mouth with a kiss, and let not him speak neither.

D. Pedro. In faith, lady, you have a merry heart.   280

Beat. Yea, my lord; I thank it, poor fool, it keeps on the windy side of care. My cousin tells him in his ear that he is in her heart.

Claud. And so she doth, cousin.

Beat. Good Lord, for alliance! Thus goes every one to the world but I, and I am <u>sunburnt</u>; I may sit in a corner and cry heigh-ho for a husband!   = I am left out in the cold

D. Pedro. Lady Beatrice, I will get you one.

cp. Lear. Kent say I am turned out in the warm sun.

Beat. I would rather have one of your father's getting. Hath your grace ne'er a brother like you? Your father got excellent husbands, if a maid could come by them.   291

D. Pedro. Will you have me, lady?

Beat. No, my lord, unless I might have another for working-days: your grace is too costly to wear every day. But, I beseech your grace, pardon me: I was born to speak all mirth and no matter.

D. Pedro. Your silence most offends me, and to be merry best becomes you; for, out a' question, you were born in a merry hour.   299

Beat. No, sure, my lord, my mother cried; but then there was a star danced, and under that was I born. Cousins, God give you joy!

Leon. Niece, will you look to those things I told you of?

Beat. I cry you mercy, uncle.   By your grace's pardon.
                                                      [*Exit*

D. Pedro. By my troth, a pleasant-spirited lady.

Leon. There 's little of the melancholy element in her, my lord: she is never sad but when she sleeps, and not ever sad then; for I have heard my daughter say, she hath often dreamed of unhappiness and waked herself with laughing.   310

D. Pedro. She cannot endure to hear tell of a husband.

Leon. O, by no means: she mocks all her wooers out of suit.

D. Pedro. She were an excellent wife for Benedick.

Leon. O Lord, my lord, if they were but a week married, they would talk themselves mad.

D. Pedro. County Claudio, when mean you to go to church?

Claud. To-morrow, my lord: time goes on crutches till love have all his rites.   320

Leon. Not till Monday, my dear son, which is hence

a just seven-night; and a time too brief, too, to have all things answer my mind.

D. Pedro. Come, you shake the head at so long a breathing: but, I warrant thee, Claudio, the time shall not go dully by us. I will in the interim undertake one of Hercules' labours; which is, to bring Signior Benedick and the Lady Beatrice into a mountain of affection, th' one with th' other. I would fain have it a match, and I doubt not but to fashion it, if you three will but minister such assistance as I shall give you direction. 331

Leon. My lord, I am for you, though it cost me ten nights' watchings.

Claud. And I, my lord.

D. Pedro. And you too, gentle Hero?

Hero. I will do any modest office, my lord, to help my cousin to a good husband. 337

D. Pedro. And Benedick is not the unhopefullest husband that I know. Thus far can I praise him; he is of a noble strain, of approved valour and confirmed honesty. I will teach you how to humour your cousin, that she shall fall in love with Benedick; and I, with your two helps, will so practise on Benedick that, in despite of his quick wit and his queasy stomach, he shall fall in love with Beatrice. If we can do this, Cupid is no longer an archer: his glory shall be ours, for we are the only love-gods. Go in with me, and I will tell you my drift.   [*Exeunt* 347

SCENE II.   *The same*

Enter DON JOHN *and* BORACHIO

D. John. It is so; the Count Claudio shall marry the daughter of Leonato.

Bora. Yea, my lord; but I can cross it.

D. John. Any bar, any cross, any impediment will be

medicinable to me: I am sick in displeasure to him, and whatsoever comes athwart his affection ranges evenly with mine.   How canst thou cross this marriage?

Bora. Not honestly, my lord; but so covertly that no dishonesty shall appear in me.

D. John. Show me briefly how.   10

Bora. I think I told your lordship a year since, how much I am in the favour of Margaret, the waiting gentle-woman to Hero.

D. John. I remember.

Bora. I can, at any unseasonable instant of the night, appoint her to look out at her lady's chamber window.

D. John. What life is in that, to be the death of this marriage?   18

Bora. The poison of that lies in you to temper.   Go you to the prince your brother; spare not to tell him that he hath wronged his honour in marrying the renowned Claudio—whose estimation do you mightily hold up—to a contaminated stale, such a one as Hero.

D. John. What proof shall I make of that?

Bora. Proof enough to misuse the prince, to vex Claudio, to undo Hero and kill Leonato.   Look you for any other issue?

D. John. Only to despite them, I will endeavour any thing.   29

Bora. Go, then; find me a meet hour to draw Don Pedro and the Count Claudio alone: tell them that you know that Hero loves me; intend a kind of zeal both to the prince and Claudio, as,—in love of your brother's honour, who hath made this match, and his friend's reputation, who is thus like to be cozened with the semblance of a maid,—that you have discovered thus.   They will scarcely believe this without trial: offer them instances; which shall bear no less likelihood than to see me at her chamber window, hear me call Margaret Hero, hear Margaret term me Claudio;

and bring them to see this the very night before the intended wedding,—for in the meantime I will so fashion the matter that Hero shall be absent,—and there shall appear such seeming truth of Hero's disloyalty that jealousy shall be called assurance and all the preparation overthrown.

45

D. John. Grow this to what adverse issue it can, I will put it in practice. Be cunning in the working this, and thy fee is a thousand ducats.

Bora. Be you constant in the accusation, and my cunning shall not shame me.

50

D. John. I will presently go learn their day of marriage.

[*Exeunt*

SCENE III. *Leonato's orchard*

Enter BENEDICK

Bene. Boy!

Enter BOY

Boy. Signior?

Bene. In my chamber-window lies a book: bring it hither to me in the orchard.

Boy. I am here already, sir.

Bene. I know that; but I would have thee hence, and here again. [*Exit Boy.*] I do much wonder that one man, seeing how much another man is a fool when he dedicates his behaviours to love, will, after he hath laughed at such shallow follies in others, become the argument of his own scorn by falling in love: and such a man is Claudio. I have known when there was no music with him but the drum and the fife; and now had he rather hear the tabor and the pipe: I have known when he would have walked ten mile a-foot to see a good armour; and now will he lie ten nights awake, carving the fashion of a new doublet. He was wont to speak plain and to the

purpose, like an honest man and a soldier; and now is
he turned orthography; his words are a very fantastical
banquet, just so many strange dishes.   May I be so converted and see with these eyes?   I cannot tell; I think
not: I will not be sworn but love may transform me to an
oyster; but I'll take my oath on it, till he have made
an oyster of me, he shall never make me such a fool.
One woman is fair, yet I am well; another is wise, yet I
am well; another virtuous, yet I am well; but till all
graces be in one woman, one woman shall not come in
my grace.   Rich she shall be, that's certain; wise, or I'll
none; virtuous, or I'll never cheapen her; fair, or I'll never
look on her; mild, or come not near me; noble, or not I for
an angel; of good discourse, an excellent musician, and
her hair shall be of what colour it please God.   Ha! the
prince and Monsieur Love!   I will hide me in the arbour. 33
                                                     [*Withdraws*

Enter DON PEDRO, CLAUDIO, *and* LEONATO

D. Pedro.   Come, shall we hear this music?
Claud.   Yea, my good lord.   How still the evening is,
As hush'd on purpose to grace harmony!
D. Pedro.   See you where Benedick hath hid himself?
Claud.   O, very well, my lord: the music ended,
We'll fit the kid-fox with a pennyworth.

Enter BALTHASAR *with Music*

D. Pedro.   Come, Balthasar, we'll hear that song again.
Balth.   O, good my lord, tax not so bad a voice   41
To slander music any more than once.
D. Pedro.   It is the witness still of excellency
To put a strange face on his own perfection.
I pray thee, sing, and let me woo no more.
Balth.   Because you talk of wooing, I will sing;
Since many a wooer doth commence his suit

To her he thinks not worthy, yet he wooes,
Yet will he swear he loves.

   D. Pedro.   Now, pray thee, come;
Or, if thou wilt hold longer argument,   50
Do it in notes.

   Balth.   Note this before my notes;
There's not a note of mine that's worth the noting.

   D. Pedro. Why, these are very crotchets that he speaks;
Notes, notes, forsooth, and nothing.   [*Air*

   Bene. Now, divine air! now is his soul ravished! Is it not strange that sheep's guts should hale souls out of men's bodies? Well, a horn for my money, when all's done.

The Song

   Balth.   Sigh no more, ladies, sigh no more,
        Men were deceivers ever,   60
   One foot in sea and one on shore,
        To one thing constant never:
   Then sigh not so, but let them go,
        And be you blithe and bonny,
   Converting all your sounds of woe
        Into Hey nonny, nonny.

   Sing no more ditties, sing no moe,
        Of dumps so dull and heavy;
   The fraud of men was ever so,
        Since summer first was leavy: 70
        Then sigh not so, &c.

   D. Pedro. By my troth, a good song.

   Balth. And an ill singer, my lord.

   D. Pedro. Ha, no, no, faith; thou singest well enough for a shift.

   Bene. An he had been a dog that should have howled thus, they would have hanged him: and I pray God his

bad voice bode no mischief.   I had as lief have heard the
night-raven, come what plague could have come after it.   79

D. Pedro. Yea, marry, dost thou hear, Balthasar?   I
pray thee, get us some excellent music; for to-morrow
night we would have it at the Lady Hero's chamber-
window.

Balth. The best I can, my lord.

D. Pedro. Do so: farewell. [*Exit Balthasar.*] Come
hither, Leonato.   What was it you told me of to-day, that
your niece Beatrice was in love with Signior Benedick?

Claud. O, ay: stalk on, stalk on; the fowl sits.   I did
never think that lady would have loved any man.   89

Leon. No, nor I neither; but most wonderful that she
should so dote on Signior Benedick, whom she hath in all
outward behaviours seemed ever to abhor.

Bene. Is 't possible?   Sits the wind in that corner?

Leon. By my troth, my lord, I cannot tell what to think
of it but that she loves him with an enraged affection; it
is past the infinite of thought.

D. Pedro. May be she doth but counterfeit.

Claud. Faith, like enough.

Leon. O God, counterfeit!   There was never counterfeit
of passion came so near the life of passion as she discovers
it.   101

D. Pedro. Why, what effects of passion shows she?

Claud. Bait the hook well; this fish will bite.

Leon. What effects, my lord?   She will sit you, you
heard my daughter tell you how.

Claud. She did, indeed.

D. Pedro. How, how, I pray you?   You amaze me: I
would have thought her spirit had been invincible against
all assaults of affection.

Leon. I would have sworn it had, my lord; especially
against Benedick.   111

Bene. I should think this a gull, but that the white-bearded fellow speaks it: knavery cannot, sure, hide himself in such reverence.

Claud. He hath ta'en the infection: hold it up.

D. Pedro. Hath she made her affection known to Benedick?

Leon. No; and swears she never will: that's her torment.

Claud. 'T is true, indeed; so your daughter says: 'Shall I,' says she, 'that have so oft encountered him with scorn, write to him that I love him?'   122

Leon. This says she now when she is beginning to write to him; for she'll be up twenty times a night, and there will she sit in her smock till she have writ a sheet of paper: my daughter tells us all.

Claud. Now you talk of a sheet of paper, I remember a pretty jest your daughter told us of.

Leon. O, when she had writ it and was reading it over, she found Benedick and Beatrice between the sheet?   130

Claud. That.

Leon. O, she tore the letter into a thousand halfpence; railed at herself, that she should be so immodest to write to one that she knew would flout her; 'I measure him', says she, 'by my own spirit; for I should flout him, if he writ to me; yea, though I love him, I should'.

Claud. Then down upon her knees she falls, weeps, sobs, beats her heart, tears her hair, prays, curses; 'O sweet Benedick! God give me patience!'   139

Leon. She doth indeed; my daughter says so: and the ecstasy hath so much overborne her that my daughter is sometime afeard she will do a desperate outrage to herself: it is very true.

D. Pedro. It were good that Benedick knew of it by some other, if she will not discover it.

Claud. To what end? He would make but a sport of it and torment the poor lady worse.

D. Pedro. An he should, it were an alms to hang him. She's an excellent sweet lady; and, out of all suspicion, she is virtuous.   150

Claud. And she is exceeding wise.

D. Pedro. In every thing but in loving Benedick.

Leon. O, my lord, wisdom and blood combating in so tender a body, we have ten proofs to one that blood hath the victory. I am sorry for her, as I have just cause, being her uncle and her guardian.

D. Pedro. I would she had bestowed this dotage on me: I would have daffed all other respects and made her half myself. I pray you, tell Benedick of it, and hear what a' will say.   160

Leon. Were it good, think you?

Claud. Hero thinks surely she will die; for she says she will die, if he love her not, and she will die, ere she make her love known, and she will die, if he woo her, rather than she will bate one breath of her accustomed crossness.

D. Pedro. She doth well: if she should make tender of her love, 't is very possible he 'll scorn it; for the man, as you know all, hath a contemptible spirit. *contemptuous*

Claud. He is a very proper man.

D. Pedro. He hath indeed a good outward happiness. 170

Claud. Before God! and, in my mind, very wise.

D. Pedro. He doth indeed show some sparks that are like wit.

Claud. And I take him to be valiant.

D. Pedro. As Hector, I assure you: and in the managing of quarrels you may say he is wise; for either he avoids them with great discretion, or undertakes them with a most Christian-like fear.

Leon. If he do fear God, a' must necessarily keep peace: if he break the peace, he ought to enter into a quarrel with fear and trembling.   181

D. Pedro. And so will he do; for the man doth fear

God, howsoever it seems not in him by some large jests he will make. Well, I am sorry for your niece. Shall we go seek Benedick, and tell him of her love?

Claud. Never tell him, my lord: let her wear it out with good counsel.

Leon. Nay, that's impossible: she may wear her heart out first.   189

D. Pedro. Well, we will hear further of it by your daughter: let it cool the while. I love Benedick well; and I could wish he would modestly examine himself, to see how much he is unworthy so good a lady.

Leon. My lord, will you walk? dinner is ready.

Claud. If he do not dote on her upon this, I will never trust my expectation.

D. Pedro. Let there be the same net spread for her; and that must your daughter and her gentlewomen carry. The sport will be, when they hold one an opinion of another's dotage, and no such matter: that's the scene that I would see, which will be merely a dumb-show. Let us send her to call him in to dinner.   202

[*Exeunt Don Pedro, Claudio, and Leonato*

Bene. [*Coming forward*] This can be no trick: the conference was sadly borne. They have the truth of this from Hero. They seem to pity the lady: it seems her affections have their full bent. Love me! why, it must be requited. I hear how I am censured: they say I will bear myself proudly, if I perceive the love come from her; they say too that she will rather die than give any sign of affection. I did never think to marry: I must not seem proud: happy are they that hear their detractions and can put them to mending. They say the lady is fair; 'tis a truth, I can bear them witness; and virtuous; 'tis so, I cannot reprove it; and wise, but for loving me; by my troth, it is no addition to her wit, nor no great argument of her folly, for I will be horribly in love with her. I may

chance have some odd quirks and remnants of wit broken
on me, because I have railed so long against marriage:
but doth not the appetite alter? a man loves the meat in
his youth that he cannot endure in his age.   Shall quips
and sentences and these paper bullets of the brain awe a
man from the career of his humour?   No, the world must
be peopled.   When I said I would die a bachelor, I did
not think I should live till I were married.   Here comes
Beatrice.   By this day! she's a fair lady: I do spy some
marks of love in her.   226

Enter BEATRICE

Beat. Against my will I am sent to bid you come in to
dinner.

Bene. Fair Beatrice, I thank you for your pains.

Beat. I took no more pains for those thanks than you
take pains to thank me: if it had been painful, I would
not have come.   232

Bene. You take pleasure then in the message?

Beat. Yea, just so much as you may take upon a knife's
point and choke a daw withal.   You have no stomach,
signior: fare you well.   [*Exit*

Bene. Ha! 'Against my will I am sent to bid you
come in to dinner'; there's a double meaning in that. 'I
took no more pains for those thanks than you took pains
to thank me'; that's as much as to say, Any pains that I
take for you is as easy as thanks.   If I do not take pity
of her, I am a villain; if I do not love her, I am a Jew.   I
will go get her picture.   [*Exit* 243

ACT III

Scene I.   *Leonato's garden*

Enter Hero, Margaret, *and* Ursula

Hero. Good Margaret, run thee to the parlour;
There shalt thou find my cousin Beatrice
Proposing with the prince and Claudio:
Whisper her ear and tell her, I and Ursula
Walk in the orchard and our whole discourse
Is all of her; say that thou overheard'st us;
And bid her steal into the pleached bower,
Where honeysuckles, ripen'd by the sun,
Forbid the sun to enter, like favourites,
Made proud by princes, that advance their pride   10
Against that power that bred it: there will she hide her,
To listen our propose.   This is thy office;
Bear thee well in it and leave us alone.

Marg. I'll make her come, I warrant you, presently.
                                                          [*Exit*

Hero. Now, Ursula, when Beatrice doth come
As we do trace this alley up and down,
Our talk must only be of Benedick.
When I do name him, let it be thy part
To praise him more than ever man did merit:
My talk to thee must be how Benedick   20
Is sick in love with Beatrice.   Of this matter
Is little Cupid's crafty arrow made,
That only wounds by hearsay.

Enter Beatrice, *behind*

                                        Now begin;
For look where Beatrice, like a lapwing, runs
Close by the ground, to hear our conference.

Urs. The pleasant'st angling is to see the fish

Cut with her golden oars the silver stream,
And greedily devour the treacherous bait:
So angle we for Beatrice: who even now
Is couched in the woodbine coverture.   30
Fear you not my part of the dialogue.

    Hero. Then go we near her, that her ear lose nothing
Of the false sweet bait that we lay for it.

                            [Approaching the bower

No, truly, Ursula, she is too disdainful;
I know her spirits are as coy and wild
As haggerds of the rock.

    Urs.   But are you sure
That Benedick loves Beatrice so entirely?

    Hero. So says the prince and my new-trothed lord.

    Urs. And did they bid you tell her of it, madam?

    Hero. They did entreat me to acquaint her of it;   40
But I persuaded them, if they loved Benedick,
To wish him wrestle with affection,
And never to let Beatrice know of it.

    Urs. Why did you so?   Doth not the gentleman
Deserve as full as fortunate a bed
As ever Beatrice shall couch upon?

    Hero. O god of love!   I know he doth deserve
As much as may be yielded to a man:
But Nature never framed a woman's heart
Of prouder stuff than that of Beatrice;   50
Disdain and scorn ride sparkling in her eyes,
Misprising what they look on, and her wit
Values itself so highly that to her
All matter else seems weak: she cannot love,
Nor take no shape nor project of affection,
She is so self-endeared.

    Urs.   Sure, I think so;
And therefore certainly it were not good
She knew his love, lest she make sport at it.

Hero. Why, you speak truth.   I never yet saw man,
How wise, how noble, young, how rarely featured,   60
But she would spell him backward: if fair-faced,
She would swear the gentleman should be her sister;
If black, why, Nature, drawing of an antique,
Made a foul blot; if tall, a lance ill-headed;
If low, an agate very vilely cut;
If speaking, why, a vane blown with all winds;
If silent, why, a block moved with none.
So turns she every man the wrong side out
And never gives to truth and virtue that
Which simpleness and merit purchaseth.   70
    Urs. Sure, sure, such carping is not commendable.
    Hero. No, not to be so odd and from all fashions
As Beatrice is, cannot be commendable:
But who dare tell her so?   If I should speak,
She would mock me into air; O, she would laugh me
Out of myself, press me to death with wit.
Therefore let Benedick, like cover'd fire,
Consume away in sighs, waste inwardly:
It were a better death than die with mocks,
Which is as bad as die with tickling.   80
    Urs. Yet tell her of it: hear what she will say.
    Hero. No; rather I will go to Benedick
And counsel him to fight against his passion.
And, truly, I'll devise some honest slanders
To stain my cousin with: one doth not know
How much an ill word may empoison liking.
    Urs. O, do not do your cousin such a wrong.
She cannot be so much without true judgement—
Having so swift and excellent a wit
As she is prized to have—as to refuse   90
So rare a gentleman as Signior Benedick.
    Hero. He is the only man of Italy,
Always excepted my dear Claudio.

Urs. I pray you, be not angry with me, madam,
Speaking my fancy: Signior Benedick,
For shape, for bearing, argument and valour,
Goes foremost in report through Italy.

Hero. Indeed, he hath an excellent good name.

Urs. His excellence did earn it, ere he had it.
When are you married, madam?   100

Hero. Why, every day, to-morrow.   Come, go in:
I 'll show thee some attires, and have thy counsel
Which is the best to furnish me to-morrow.

Urs. She 's limed, I warrant you: we have caught her,
    madam.

Hero. If it proves so, then loving goes by haps:
Some Cupid kills with arrows, some with traps.

                               [*Exeunt Hero and Ursula*

Beat. [*Coming forward*] What fire is in mine ears?   Can
    this be true?
Stand I condemn'd for pride and scorn so much?
Contempt, farewell! and maiden pride, adieu!
No glory lives behind the back of such.   110
And, Benedick, love on; I will requite thee,
    Taming my wild heart to thy loving hand:
If thou dost love, my kindness shall incite thee
    To bind our loves up in a holy band;
For others say thou dost deserve, and I
Believe it better than reportingly.   [*Exit*

Scene II.   *A room in Leonato's house*

Enter Don Pedro, Claudio, Benedick, *and* Leonato

D. Pedro. I do but stay till your marriage be consummate, and then go I toward Arragon.

Claud. I 'll bring you thither, my lord, if you 'll vouchsafe me.

D. Pedro. Nay, that would be as great a soil in the new

gloss of your marriage as to show a child his new coat and
forbid him to wear it. I will only be bold with Benedick
for his company; for, from the crown of his head to the
sole of his foot, he is all mirth: he hath twice or thrice cut
Cupid's bow-string and the little hangman dare not shoot
at him; he hath a heart as sound as a bell and his tongue
is the clapper, for what his heart thinks his tongue speaks. 12

Bene. Gallants, I am not as I have been.

Leon. So say I: methinks you are sadder.

Claud. I hope he be in love.

D. Pedro. Hang him, truant! there's no true drop of
blood in him, to be truly touched with love: if he be sad,
he wants money.

Bene. I have the toothache.

D. Pedro. Draw it.   20

Bene. Hang it!

Claud. You must hang it first, and draw it afterwards.

D. Pedro. What! sigh for the toothache?

Leon. Where is but a humour or a worm.

Bene. Well, every one can master a grief but he that
has it.

Claud. Yet say I, he is in love.

D. Pedro. There is no appearance of fancy in him, unless
it be a fancy that he hath to strange disguises; as, to be
a Dutchman to-day, a Frenchman to-morrow, or in the
shape of two countries at once, as, a German from the
waist downward, all slops, and a Spaniard from the hip
upward, no doublet. Unless he have a fancy to this
foolery, as it appears he hath, he is no fool for fancy, as
you would have it appear he is.   35

Claud. If he be not in love with some woman, there is
no believing old signs: a' brushes his hat a' mornings;
what should that bode?

D. Pedro. Hath any man seen him at the barber's?

Claud. No, but the barber's man hath been seen with

him, and the old ornament of his cheek hath already
stuffed tennis-balls.   42

Leon. Indeed, he looks younger than he did, by the loss
of a beard.

D. Pedro. Nay, a' rubs himself with civet: can you smell
him out by that?

Claud. That's as much as to say, the sweet youth's in
love.

D. Pedro. The greatest note of it is his melancholy.

Claud. And when was he wont to wash his face?   50

D. Pedro. Yea, or to paint himself? for the which, I
hear what they say of him.

Claud. Nay, but his jesting spirit; which is now crept
into a lute-string and now governed by stops.

D. Pedro. Indeed, that tells a heavy tale for him: conclude, conclude he is in love.

Claud. Nay, but I know who loves him.

D. Pedro. That would I know too: I warrant, one that
knows him not.

Claud. Yes, and his ill conditions; and, in despite of all,
dies for him.   61

D. Pedro. She shall be buried with her face upwards.

Bene. Yet is this no charm for the toothache. Old
signior, walk aside with me: I have studied eight or nine
wise words to speak to you, which these hobby-horses
must not hear.   [*Exeunt Benedick and Leonato*

D. Pedro. For my life, to break with him about Beatrice.

Claud. 'T is even so. Hero and Margaret have by this
played their parts with Beatrice; and then the two bears
will not bite one another when they meet.   70

Enter DON JOHN

D. John. My lord and brother, God save you!

D. Pedro. Good den, brother.

D. John. If your leisure served, I would speak with you.

D. Pedro. In private?

D. John. If it please you: yet Count Claudio may hear; for what I would speak of concerns him.

D. Pedro. What's the matter?

D. John. [*To Claudio*] Means your lordship to be married to-morrow?

D. Pedro. You know he does.   80

D. John. I know not that, when he knows what I know.

Claud. If there be any impediment, I pray you discover it.

D. John. You may think I love you not: let that appear hereafter, and aim better at me by that I now will manifest. For my brother, I think he holds you well, and in dearness of heart hath holp to effect your ensuing marriage;—surely suit ill spent and labour ill bestowed.

D. Pedro. Why, what's the matter?

D. John. I came hither to tell you; and, circumstances shortened, for she has been too long a talking of, the lady is disloyal.   92

Claud. Who, Hero?

D. John. Even she; Leonato's Hero, your Hero, every man's Hero.

Claud. Disloyal?

D. John. The word is too good to paint out her wickedness; I could say she were worse: think you of a worse title, and I will fit her to it. Wonder not till further warrant: go but with me to-night, you shall see her chamber-window entered, even the night before her wedding-day: if you love her then, to-morrow wed her; but it would better fit your honour to change your mind. 103

Claud. May this be so?

D. Pedro. I will not think it.

D. John. If you dare not trust that you see, confess not that you know: if you will follow me, I will show you enough; and when you have seen more and heard more, proceed accordingly.

Claud. If I see any thing to-night why I should not marry her to-morrow, in the congregation, where I should wed, there will I shame her.   112

D. Pedro. And, as I wooed for thee to obtain her, I will join with thee to disgrace her.

D. John. I will disparage her no farther till you are my witnesses: bear it coldly but till midnight, and let the issue show itself.

D. Pedro. O day untowardly turned!

Claud. O mischief strangely thwarting!

D. John. O plague right well prevented! so will you say when you have seen the sequel.   [*Exeunt* 121

Scene III. *A street*

Enter Dogberry *and* Verges *with the* Watch

Dog. Are you good men and true?

Verg. Yea, or else it were pity but they should suffer salvation, body and soul.

Dog. Nay, that were a punishment too good for them, if they should have any allegiance in them, being chosen for the prince's watch.

Verg. Well, give them their charge, neighbour Dogberry.

Dog. First, who think you the most desartless man to be constable?   10

First Watch. Hugh Otecake, sir, or George Seacole; for they can write and read.

Dog. Come hither, neighbour Seacole. God hath blessed you with a good name: to be a well-favoured man is the gift of fortune; but to write and read comes by nature.

Sec. Watch. Both which, master constable,—   17

Dog. You have: I knew it would be your answer. Well, for your favour, sir, why, give God thanks, and make no boast of it; and for your writing and reading, let that appear when there is no need of such vanity. You are thought here to be the most senseless and fit man for the constable of the watch; therefore bear you the lantern. This is your charge: you shall comprehend all vagrom men; you are to bid any man stand, in the prince's name.

Sec. Watch. How if a' will not stand?   26

Dog. Why, then, take no note of him, but let him go; and presently call the rest of the watch together and thank God you are rid of a knave.

Verg. If he will not stand when he is bidden, he is none of the prince's subjects.   31

Dog. True, and they are to meddle with none but the prince's subjects. You shall also make no noise in the streets; for for the watch to babble and to talk is most tolerable and not to be endured.

Watch. We will rather sleep than talk: we know what belongs to a watch.

Dog. Why, you speak like an ancient and most quiet watchman; for I cannot see how sleeping should offend: only, have a care that your bills be not stolen. Well, you are to call at all the ale-houses, and bid those that are drunk get them to bed.   42

Watch. How if they will not?

Dog. Why, then, let them alone till they are sober: if they make you not then the better answer, you may say they are not the men you took them for.

Watch. Well, sir.

Dog. If you meet a thief, you may suspect him, by virtue of your office, to be no true man; and, for such kind of men, the less you meddle or make with them, why, the more is for your honesty.   51

Watch. If we know him to be a thief, shall we not lay hands on him?

Dog. Truly, by your office, you may; but I think they that touch pitch will be defiled: the most peaceable way for you, if you do take a thief, is to let him show himself what he is and steal out of your company.

Verg. You have been always called a merciful man, partner.

Dog. Truly, I would not hang a dog by my will, much more a man who hath any honesty in him.   61

Verg. If you hear a child cry in the night, you must call to the nurse and bid her still it.

Watch. How if the nurse be asleep and will not hear us?

Dog. Why, then, depart in peace, and let the child wake her with crying; for the ewe that will not hear her lamb when it baes will never answer a calf when he bleats.

Verg. 'T is very true.

Dog. This is the end of the charge:—you, constable, are to present the prince's own person: if you meet the prince in the night you may stay him.   71

Verg. Nay, by 'r lady, that I think a' cannot.

Dog. Five shillings to one on 't, with any man that knows the statues, he may stay him: marry, not without the prince be willing; for, indeed, the watch ought to offend no man; and it is an offence to stay a man against his will.

Verg. By 'r lady, I think it be so.

Dog. Ha, ah, ha! Well, masters, good night: an there be any matter of weight chances, call up me: keep your fellows' counsels and your own; and good night. Come, neighbour.   82

Watch. Well, masters, we hear our charge: let us go sit here upon the church-bench till two, and then all to bed.

Dog. One word more, honest neighbours. I pray you, watch about Signior Leonato's door; for the wedding being there to-morrow, there is a great coil to-night. Adieu: be vigitant, I beseech you.

[*Exeunt Dogberry and Verges*

Enter BORACHIO *and* CONRADE

Bora. What, Conrade!

Watch. [*Aside*] Peace! stir not.   90

Bora. Conrade, I say!

Con. Here, man; I am at thy elbow.

Bora. Mass, and my elbow itched; I thought there would a scab follow.

Con. I will owe thee an answer for that: and now forward with thy tale.

Bora. Stand thee close, then, under this pent-house, for it drizzles rain; and I will, like a true drunkard, utter all to thee.   99

Watch. [*Aside*] Some treason, masters: yet stand close.

Bora. Therefore know I have earned of Don John a thousand ducats.

Con. Is it possible that any villany should be so dear?

Bora. Thou shouldst rather ask if it were possible any villany should be so rich; for when rich villains have need of poor ones, poor ones may make what price they will.

Con. I wonder at it.

Bora. That shows thou art unconfirmed. Thou knowest that the fashion of a doublet, or a hat, or a cloak, is nothing to a man.   110

Con. Yes, it is apparel.

Bora. I mean, the fashion.

Con. Yes, the fashion is the fashion.

Bora. Tush! I may as well say the fool's the fool. But seest thou not what a deformed thief this fashion is?

Watch. [*Aside*] I know that Deformed; a' has been a vile thief this seven year; a' goes up and down like a gentleman: I remember his name.

Bora. Didst thou not hear somebody?

Con. No; 't was the vane on the house.   120

Bora. Seest thou not, I say, what a deformed thief this fashion is? how giddily a' turns about all the hot bloods between fourteen and five-and-thirty? sometimes fashioning them like Pharaoh's soldiers in the reechy painting, sometime like god Bel's priests in the old church-window, sometime like the shaven Hercules in the smirched worm-eaten tapestry, where his codpiece seems as massy as his club?

Con. All this I see; and I see that the fashion wears out more apparel than the man. But art not thou thyself giddy with the fashion too, that thou hast shifted out of thy tale into telling me of the fashion?   132

Bora. Not so, neither: but know that I have to-night wooed Margaret, the Lady Hero's gentlewoman, by the name of Hero: she leans me out at her mistress' chamber-window, bids me a thousand times good-night,—I tell this tale vilely:—I should first tell thee how the prince, Claudio and my master, planted and placed and possessed by my master Don John, saw afar off in the orchard this amiable encounter.   140

Con. And thought they Margaret was Hero?

Bora. Two of them did, the prince and Claudio; but the devil my master knew she was Margaret; and partly by his oaths, which first possessed them, partly by the dark night, which did deceive them, but chiefly by my villany, which did confirm any slander that Don John had made, away went Claudio enraged; swore he would meet her, as he was appointed, next morning at the temple, and there, before the whole congregation, shame her with what he saw o'er night and send her home again without a husband.

First Watch. We charge you, in the prince's name, stand!   152

Sec. Watch. Call up the right master constable. We

have here recovered the most dangerous piece of lechery that ever was known in the commonwealth.

First Watch. And one Deformed is one of them: I know him; a' wears a lock.

Con. Masters, masters,—

Sec. Watch. You'll be made bring Deformed forth, I warrant you.   160

Con. Masters,—

First Watch. Never speak: we charge you let us obey you to go with us.

Bora. We are like to prove a goodly commodity, being taken up of these men's bills.

Con. A commodity in question, I warrant you. Come, we'll obey you.   [*Exeunt*

SCENE IV.   *Hero's apartment*

Enter HERO, MARGARET, *and* URSULA

Hero. Good Ursula, wake my cousin Beatrice, and desire her to rise.

Urs. I will, lady.

Hero. And bid her come hither.

Urs. Well.   [*Exit*

Marg. Troth, I think your other rabato were better.

Hero. No, pray thee, good Meg, I'll wear this.

Marg. By my troth, 's not so good; and I warrant your cousin will say so.

Hero. My cousin's a fool, and thou art another: I'll wear none but this.   11

Marg. I like the new tire within excellently, if the hair were a thought browner; and your gown's a most rare fashion, i' faith. I saw the Duchess of Milan's gown that they praise so.

Hero. O, that exceeds, they say.

Marg. By my troth, 's but a night-gown in respect of

yours: cloth o' gold, and cuts, and laced with silver, set with pearls, down sleeves, side sleeves, and skirts, round underborne with a bluish tinsel: but for a fine, quaint, graceful and excellent fashion, yours is worth ten on 't.   21

Hero. God give me joy to wear it! for my heart is exceedingly heavy.

Marg. 'T will be heavier soon by the weight of a man.

Hero. Fie upon thee! art not ashamed?

Marg. Of what, lady? of speaking honourably? Is not marriage honourable in a beggar? Is not your lord honourable without marriage? I think you would have me say, 'saving your reverence, a husband': an bad thinking do not wrest true speaking, I 'll offend nobody: is there any harm in 'the heavier for a husband'? None, I think, an it be the right husband and the right wife; otherwise 't is light, and not heavy: ask my Lady Beatrice else; here she comes.   35

Enter BEATRICE

Hero. Good morrow, coz.

Beat. Good morrow, sweet Hero.

Hero. Why, how now? do you speak in the sick tune?

Beat. I am out of all other tune, methinks.

Marg. Clap 's into 'Light o' love'; that goes without a burden: do you sing it, and I 'll dance it.   41

Beat. Ye light o' love, with your heels! then, if your husband have stables enough, you 'll see he shall lack no barns.

Marg. O illegitimate construction! I scorn that with my heels.

Beat. 'T is almost five o'clock, cousin; 't is time you were ready. By my troth, I am exceeding ill: heigh-ho!

Marg. For a hawk, a horse, or a husband?

Beat. For the letter that begins them all, H.   50

Marg. Well, an you be not turned Turk, there's no more sailing by the star.

Beat. What means the fool, trow?

Marg. Nothing I; but God send every one their heart's desire!

Hero. These gloves the count sent me; they are an excellent perfume.

Beat. I am stuffed, cousin; I cannot smell.

Marg. A maid, and stuffed! there's goodly catching of cold.   60

Beat. O, God help me! God help me! how long have you professed apprehension?

Marg. Ever since you left it. Doth not my wit become me rarely?

Beat. It is not seen enough, you should wear it in your cap. By my troth, I am sick.

Marg. Get you some of this distilled Carduus Benedictus, and lay it to your heart: it is the only thing for a qualm.

Hero. There thou prickest her with a thistle.

Beat. Benedictus! why Benedictus? you have some moral in this Benedictus.   71

Marg. Moral! no, by my troth, I have no moral meaning; I meant, plain holy-thistle. You may think perchance that I think you are in love: nay, by'r lady, I am not such a fool to think what I list, nor I list not to think what I can, nor indeed I cannot think, if I would think my heart out of thinking, that you are in love or that you will be in love or that you can be in love. Yet Benedick was such another, and now is he become a man: he swore he would never marry, and yet now, in despite of his heart, he eats his meat without grudging: and how you may be converted I know not, but methinks you look with your eyes as other women do.   83

Beat. What pace is this that thy tongue keeps?

Marg. Not a false gallop.

Re-enter URSULA

Urs. Madam, withdraw: the prince, the count, Signior Benedick, Don John, and all the gallants of the town, are come to fetch you to church.

Hero. Help to dress me, good coz, good Meg, good Ursula.
                                                    [*Exeunt* 90

SCENE V.   *Another room in Leonato's house*

Enter LEONATO, *with* DOGBERRY *and* VERGES

Leon. What would you do with me, honest neighbour?

Dog. Marry, sir, I would have some confidence with you that decerns you nearly.

Leon. Brief, I pray you; for you see it is a busy time with me.

Dog. Marry, this it is, sir.

Verg. Yes, in truth it is, sir.

Leon. What is it, my good friends?

Dog. Goodman Verges, sir, speaks a little off the matter: an old man, sir, and his wits are not so blunt as, God help, I would desire they were; but, in faith, honest as the skin between his brows.   12

Verg. Yes, I thank God I am as honest as any man living that is an old man and no honester than I.

Dog. Comparisons are odorous: palabras, neighbour Verges.

Leon. Neighbours, you are tedious.

Dog. It pleases your worship to say so, but we are the poor duke's officers; but truly, for mine own part, if I were as tedious as a king, I could find it in my heart to bestow it all of your worship.   21

Leon. All thy tediousness on me, ah?

Dog. Yea, an 't were a thousand pound more than 't is; for I hear as good exclamation on your worship as of any

man in the city; and though I be but a poor man, I am
glad to hear it.

Verg. And so am I.

Leon. I would fain know what you have to say.

Verg. Marry, sir, our watch to-night, excepting your
worship's presence, ha' ta'en a couple of as arrant knaves
as any in Messina.   31

Dog. A good old man, sir; he will be talking: as they
say, When the age is in, the wit is out: God help us! it is
a world to see.   Well said, i' faith, neighbour Verges: well,
God 's a good man; an two men ride of a horse, one must
ride behind.   An honest soul, i' faith, sir; by my troth he
is, as ever broke bread; but God is to be worshipped; all
men are not alike; alas, good neighbour!

Leon. Indeed, neighbour, he comes too short of you.

Dog. Gifts that God gives.   40

Leon. I must leave you.

Dog. One word, sir: our watch, sir, have indeed com-
prehended two aspicious persons, and we would have
them this morning examined before your worship.

Leon. Take their examination yourself and bring it me:
I am now in great haste, as it may appear unto you.

Dog. It shall be suffigance.

Leon. Drink some wine ere you go: fare you well.

Enter a Messenger

Mess. My lord, they stay for you to give your daughter
to her husband.   50

Leon. I 'll wait upon them: I am ready.

[Exeunt Leonato and Messenger

Dog. Go, good partner, go, get you to Francis Seacole;
bid him bring his pen and inkhorn to the gaol: we are now
to examination these men.

Verg. And we must do it wisely.

Dog. We will spare for no wit, I warrant you; here 's

that shall drive some of them to a noncome: only get the learned writer to set down our excommunication and meet me at the gaol.   [*Exeunt*

ACT IV

Scene I.   *A church*

Enter Don Pedro, Don John, Leonato, Friar Francis, Claudio, Benedick, Hero, Beatrice, *and attendants*

Leon. Come, Friar Francis, be brief; only to the plain form of marriage, and you shall recount their particular duties afterwards.

Friar. You come hither, my lord, to marry this lady.

Claud. No.

Leon. To be married to her: friar, you come to marry her.

Friar. Lady, you come hither to be married to this count.

Hero. I do.   9

Friar. If either of you know any inward impediment why you should not be conjoined, I charge you, on your souls, to utter it.

Claud. Know you any, Hero?

Hero. None, my lord.

Friar. Know you any, count?

Leon. I dare make his answer, none.

Claud. O, what men dare do! what men may do! what men daily do, not knowing what they do!

Bene. How now! interjections? Why, then, some be of laughing, as, ah, ha, he!   20

Claud. Stand thee by, friar. Father, by your leave:
Will you with free and unconstrained soul
Give me this maid, your daughter?

Leon. As freely, son, as God did give her me.

Claud. And what have I to give you back, whose worth
May counterpoise this rich and precious gift?

D. Pedro. Nothing, unless you render her again.

Claud. Sweet prince, you learn me noble thankfulness.
There, Leonato, take her back again:
Give not this rotten orange to your friend;   30
She's but the sign and semblance of her honour.
Behold how like a maid she blushes here!
O, what authority and show of truth
Can cunning sin cover itself withal!
Comes not that blood as modest evidence
To witness simple virtue?   Would you not swear,
All you that see her, that she were a maid,
By these exterior shows?   But she is none:
She knows the heat of a luxurious bed;
Her blush is guiltiness, not modesty.   40

Leon. What do you mean, my lord?

Claud.   Not to be married,
Not to knit my soul to an approved wanton.

Leon. Dear my lord, if you, in your own proof,
Have vanquish'd the resistance of her youth,
And made defeat of her virginity,—

Claud. I know what you would say: if I have known her,
You will say she did embrace me as a husband,
And so extenuate the 'forehand sin:
No, Leonato,
I never tempted her with word too large;   50
But, as a brother to his sister, show'd
Bashful sincerity and comely love.

Hero. And seem'd I ever otherwise to you?

Claud. Out on thee!   Seeming! I will write against it:
You seem to me as Dian in her orb,
As chaste as is the bud ere it be blown;
But you are more intemperate in your blood

Than Venus, or those pamper'd animals
That rage in savage sensuality.

   Hero. Is my lord well, that he doth speak so wide?   60
   Leon. Sweet prince, why speak not you?
   D. Pedro.   What should I speak?
I stand dishonour'd, that have gone about
To link my dear friend to a common stale.

   Leon. Are these things spoken, or do I but dream?
   D. John. Sir, they are spoken, and these things are true.
   Bene. This looks not like a nuptial.
   Hero.   True? O God!
   Claud. Leonato, stand I here?
Is this the prince? is this the prince's brother?
Is this face Hero's? are our eyes our own?

   Leon. All this is so: but what of this, my lord?   70
   Claud. Let me but move one question to your daughter;
And, by that fatherly and kindly power
That you have in her, bid her answer truly.

   Leon. I charge thee do so, as thou art my child.
   Hero. O, God defend me! how am I beset!
What kind of catechising call you this?

   Claud. To make you answer truly to your name.
   Hero. Is it not Hero? Who can blot that name
With any just reproach?

   Claud.   Marry, that can Hero;
Hero itself can blot out Hero's virtue.   80
What man was he talk'd with you yesternight
Out at your window betwixt twelve and one?
Now, if you are a maid, answer to this.

   Hero. I talk'd with no man at that hour, my lord.
   D. Pedro. Why, then are you no maiden. Leonato,
I am sorry you must hear: upon mine honour,
Myself, my brother, and this grieved count
Did see her, hear her, at that hour last night
Talk with a ruffian at her chamber-window;

Who hath indeed, most like a liberal villain,   90
Confess'd the vile encounters they have had
A thousand times in secret.

   D. John. Fie, fie! they are not to be named, my lord,
Not to be spoke of;
There is not chastity enough in language
Without offence to utter them.   Thus, pretty lady,
I am sorry for thy much misgovernment.

   Claud. O Hero, what a Hero hadst thou been,
If half thy outward graces had been placed
About thy thoughts and counsels of thy heart!   100
But fare thee well, most foul, most fair! farewell,
Thou pure impiety and impious purity!   *oxymoron*
For thee I'll lock up all the gates of love,
And on my eyelids shall conjecture hang,
To turn all beauty into thoughts of harm,
And never shall it more be gracious.

   Leon. Hath no man's dagger here a point for me?
                                        [*Hero swoons*

   Beat. Why, how now, cousin! wherefore sink you down?

   D. John. Come, let us go.   These things, come thus to
      light,
Smother her spirits up.   110
              [*Exeunt Don Pedro, Don John, and Claudio*

   Bene. How doth the lady?

   Beat.   Dead, I think.   Help, uncle!
Hero! why, Hero!   Uncle!   Signior Benedick!   Friar!

   Leon. O Fate! take not away thy heavy hand.
Death is the fairest cover for her shame
That may be wish'd for.

   Beat.   How now, cousin Hero!

   Friar. Have comfort, lady.

   Leon. Dost thou look up?

   Friar. Yea, wherefore should she not?

   Leon. Wherefore!   Why, doth not every earthly thing

Cry shame upon her?   Could she here deny   120
The story that is printed in her blood?
Do not live, Hero; do not ope thine eyes:
For, did I think thou wouldst not quickly die,
Thought I thy spirits were stronger than thy shames,
Myself would, on the rearward of reproaches,
Strike at thy life.   Grieved I, I had but one?
Chid I for that at frugal nature's frame?
O, one too much by thee!   Why had I one?
Why ever wast thou lovely in my eyes?
Why had I not with charitable hand   130
Took up a beggar's issue at my gates,
Who smirched thus and mired with infamy,
I might have said 'No part of it is mine;
This shame derives itself from unknown loins'?
But mine and mine I loved and mine I praised
And mine that I was proud on, mine so much
That I myself was to myself not mine,
Valuing of her,—why, she, O, she is fallen
Into a pit of ink, that the wide sea
Hath drops too few to wash her clean again   140
And salt too little which may season give
To her foul-tainted flesh!
    Bene.   Sir, sir, be patient.
For my part, I am so attired in wonder,
I know not what to say.
    Beat.   O, on my soul, my cousin is belied!
    Bene.   Lady, were you her bedfellow last night?
    Beat.   No, truly not; although, until last night,
I have this twelvemonth been her bedfellow.
    Leon.   Confirm'd, confirm'd!   O, that is stronger made
Which was before barr'd up with ribs of iron!   150
Would the two princes lie, and Claudio lie,
Who loved her so, that, speaking of her foulness,
Wash'd it with tears?   Hence from her! let her die.

Friar. Hear me a little; for I have only been
Silent so long and given way unto
This course of fortune . . .
By noting of the lady I have mark'd
A thousand blushing apparitions
To start into her face, a thousand innocent shames
In angel whiteness beat away those blushes;   160
And in her eye there hath appear'd a fire,
To burn the errors that these princes hold
Against her maiden truth. Call me a fool;
Trust not my reading nor my observations,
Which with experimental seal doth warrant
The tenour of my book; trust not my age,
My reverence, calling, nor divinity,
If this sweet lady lie not guiltless here
Under some biting error.

   Leon.   Friar, it cannot be.
Thou seest that all the grace that she hath left   170
Is that she will not add to her damnation
A sin of perjury; she not denies it:
Why seek'st thou then to cover with excuse
That which appears in proper nakedness?

   Friar. Lady, what man is he you are accused of?

   Hero. They know that do accuse me; I know none:
If I know more of any man alive
Than that which maiden modesty doth warrant,
Let all my sins lack mercy! O my father,
Prove you that any man with me conversed   180
At hours unmeet, or that I yesternight
Maintain'd the change of words with any creature,
Refuse me, hate me, torture me to death!

   Friar. There is some strange misprision in the
   princes.

   Bene. Two of them have the very bent of honour;
And if their wisdoms be misled in this,

The practice of it lives in John the bastard,
Whose spirits toil in frame of villanies.

Leon. I know not.   If they speak but truth of her,
These hands shall tear her; if they wrong her honour,   190
The proudest of them shall well hear of it.
Time hath not yet so dried this blood of mine,
Nor age so eat up my invention,
Nor fortune made such havoc of my means,
Nor my bad life reft me so much of friends,
But they shall find, awaked in such a kind,
Both strength of limb and policy of mind,
Ability in means and choice of friends
To quit me of them throughly.

Friar.   Pause awhile,
And let my counsel sway you in this case.   200
Your daughter here the princes left for dead:
Let her awhile be secretly kept in,
And publish it that she is dead indeed;
Maintain a mourning ostentation
And on your family's old monument
Hang mournful epitaphs and do all rites
That appertain unto a burial.

Leon. What shall become of this? what will this do?

Friar. Marry, this well carried shall on her behalf
Change slander to remorse; that is some good: *pity*   210
But not for that dream I on this strange course,
But on this travail look for greater birth.
She dying, as it must be so maintain'd,
Upon the instant that she was accused,
Shall be lamented, pitied and excused
Of every hearer: for it so falls out
That what we have we prize not to the worth
Whiles we enjoy it, but being lack'd and lost,
Why, then we rack the value, then we find
The virtue that possession would not show us   220

Whiles it was ours.   So will it fare with Claudio:
When he shall hear she died upon his words,
The idea of her life shall sweetly creep
Into his study of imagination,
And every lovely organ of her life
Shall come apparell'd in more precious habit,
More moving-delicate and full of life,
Into the eye and prospect of his soul,
Than when she lived indeed; then shall he mourn,
If ever love had interest in his liver,   230
And wish he had not so accused her,
No, though he thought his accusation true
Let this be so, and doubt not but success
Will fashion the event in better shape
Than I can lay it down in likelihood.
But if all aim but this be levell'd false,
The supposition of the lady's death
Will quench the wonder of her infamy:
And if it sort not well, you may conceal her,
As best befits her wounded reputation,   240
In some reclusive and religious life,
Out of all eyes, tongues, minds and injuries.
    Bene. Signior Leonato, let the friar advise you:
And though you know my inwardness and love
Is very much unto the prince and Claudio.
Yet, by mine honour, I will deal in this
As secretly and justly as your soul
Should with your body.
    Leon.   Being that I flow in grief,
The smallest twine may lead me.
    Friar. 'T is well consented: presently away;   250
For to strange sores strangely they strain the cure.
Come, lady, die to live: this wedding-day
Perhaps is but prolong'd: have patience and endure.
                    [*Exeunt all but Benedick and Beatrice*

Bene. Lady Beatrice, have you wept all this while?

Beat. Yea, and I will weep a while longer.

Bene. I will not desire that.

Beat. You have no reason; I do it freely.

Bene. Surely I do believe your fair cousin is wronged.

Beat. Ah, how much might the man deserve of me that
would right her! 260

Bene. Is there any way to show such friendship?

Beat. A very even way, but no such friend.

Bene. May a man do it?

Beat. It is a man's office, but not yours.

Bene. I do love nothing in the world so well as you: is
not that strange?

Beat. As strange as the thing I know not. It were as
possible for me to say I loved nothing so well as you: but
believe me not; and yet I lie not; I confess nothing, nor
deny nothing. I am sorry for my cousin. 270

Bene. By my sword, Beatrice, thou lovest me.

Beat. Do not swear, and eat it.

Bene. I will swear by it that you love me; and I will
make him eat it that says I love not you.

Beat. Will you not eat your word?

Bene. With no sauce that can be devised to it. I protest
I love thee.

Beat. Why, then, God forgive me!

Bene. What offence, sweet Beatrice?

Beat. You have stayed me in a happy hour: I was about
to protest I loved you. 280

Bene. And do it with all thy heart.

Beat. I love you with so much of my heart that none is
left to protest.

Bene. Come, bid me do any thing for thee.

Beat. Kill Claudio.

Bene. Ha! not for the wide world.

Beat. You kill me to deny it. Farewell.

Bene. Tarry, sweet Beatrice.

Beat. I am gone, though I am here: there is no love in you: nay, I pray you, let me go.   291

Bene. Beatrice,—

Beat. In faith, I will go.

Bene. We 'll be friends first.

Beat. You dare easier be friends with me than fight with mine enemy.

Bene. Is Claudio thine enemy?   297

Beat. Is he not approved in the height a villain, that hath slandered, scorned, dishonoured my kinswoman? O that I were a man! What, bear her in hand until they come to take hands; and then, with public accusation, uncovered slander, unmitigated rancour, — O God, that I were a man! I would eat his heart in the market-place.

Bene. Hear me, Beatrice,—

Beat. Talk with a man out at a window! A proper saying!

Bene. Nay, but, Beatrice,—

Beat. Sweet Hero! She is wronged, she is slandered, she is undone.

Bene. Beat—   310

Beat. Princes and counties! Surely, a princely testimony, a goodly count, Count Comfect; a sweet gallant, surely! O that I were a man for his sake! or that I had any friend would be a man for my sake! But manhood is melted into courtesies, valour into compliment, and men are only turned into tongue, and trim ones too: he is now as valiant as Hercules that only tells a lie and swears it. I cannot be a man with wishing, therefore I will die a woman with grieving.   319

Bene. Tarry, good Beatrice. By this hand, I love thee.

Beat. Use it for my love some other way than swearing by it.

Bene. Think you in your soul the Count Claudio hath wronged Hero?

Beat. Yea, as sure as I have a thought or a soul.

Bene. Enough, I am engaged; I will challenge him. I will kiss your hand, and so I leave you. By this hand, Claudio shall render me a dear account. As you hear of me, so think of me. Go, comfort your cousin: I must say she is dead: and so, farewell. [*Exeunt* 330

SCENE II. *A prison*

Enter DOGBERRY, VERGES, *and* Sexton, *in gowns; and the* Watch, *with* CONRADE *and* BORACHIO

Dog. Is our whole dissembly appeared?

Verg. O, a stool and a cushion for the sexton.

Sex. Which be the malefactors?

Dog. Marry, that am I and my partner.

Verg. Nay, that's certain; we have the exhibition to examine.

Sex. But which are the offenders that are to be examined? let them come before master constable.

Dog. Yea, marry, let them come before me. What is your name, friend?   10

Bora. Borachio.

Dog. Pray, write down, Borachio. Yours, sirrah?

Con. I am a gentleman, sir, and my name is Conrade.

Dog. Write down, master gentleman Conrade. Masters, do you serve God?

Con. }
Bora. } Yea, sir, we hope.

Dog. Write down, that they hope they serve God: and write God first; for God defend but God should go before such villains! Masters, it is proved already that you are little better than false knaves; and it will go near to be thought so shortly. How answer you for yourselves?   21

Con. Marry, sir, we say we are none.

Dog. A marvellous witty fellow, I assure you; but I will go about with him. Come you hither, sirrah; a word in your ear: sir, I say to you, it is thought you are false knaves.

Bora. Sir, I say to you we are none.

Dog. Well, stand aside. 'Fore God, they are both in a tale. Have you writ down, that they are none?

Sex. Master constable, you go not the way to examine: you must call forth the watch that are their accusers.   31

Dog. Yea, marry, that's the eftest way. Let the watch come forth. Masters, I charge you, in the prince's name, accuse these men.

First Watch. This man said, sir, that Don John, the prince's brother, was a villain.

Dog. Write down Prince John a villain. Why, this is flat perjury, to call a prince's brother villain.

Bora. Master constable,—

Dog. Pray thee, fellow, peace: I do not like thy look, I promise thee.   41

Sex. What heard you him say else?

Sec. Watch. Marry, that he had received a thousand ducats of Don John for accusing the Lady Hero wrongfully.

Dog. Flat burglary as ever was committed.

Verg. Yea, by mass, that it is.

Sex. What else, fellow?

First Watch. And that Count Claudio did mean, upon his words, to disgrace Hero before the whole assembly, and not marry her.   51

Dog. O villain! thou wilt be condemned into everlasting redemption for this.

Sex. What else?

Watch. This is all.

Sex. And this is more, masters, than you can deny. Prince John is this morning secretly stolen away; Hero was in this manner accused, in this very manner refused, and upon the grief of this suddenly died. Master constable, let these men be bound, and brought to Leonato's: I will go before and show him their examination. [*Exit* 61

Dog. Come, let them be opinioned.

Verg. Let them be in the hands—

Con. Off, coxcomb!

Dog. God 's my life, where 's the sexton? let him write down the prince's officer coxcomb. Come, bind them. Thou naughty varlet!

Con. Away! you are an ass, you are an ass.   68

Dog. Dost thou not suspect my place? dost thou not suspect my years? O that he were here to write me down an ass! But, masters, remember that I am an ass; though it be not written down, yet forget not that I am an ass. No, thou villain, thou art full of piety, as shall be proved upon thee by good witness. I am a wise fellow, and, which is more, an officer, and, which is more, a householder, and, which is more, as pretty a piece of flesh as any is in Messina, and one that knows the law, go to; and a rich fellow enough, go to; and a fellow that hath had losses, and one that hath two gowns and every thing handsome about him. Bring him away. O that I had been writ down an ass!   [*Exeunt* 81

ACT V

SCENE I.   *Before Leonato's house*

Enter LEONATO *and* ANTONIO

Ant. If you go on thus, you will kill yourself;
And 't is not wisdom thus to second grief
Against yourself.

   Leon.   I pray thee, cease thy counsel,
Which falls into mine ears as profitless
As water in a sieve: give not me counsel;
Nor let no comforter delight mine ear
But such a one whose wrongs do suit with mine.
Bring me a father that so loved his child,
Whose joy of her is overwhelm'd like mine,
And bid him speak of patience;   10
Measure his woe the length and breadth of mine
And let it answer every strain for strain,
As thus for thus and such a grief for such,
In every lineament, branch, shape, and form:
If such a one will smile and stroke his beard,
Bid sorrow wag, cry 'hem!' when he should groan,
Patch grief with proverbs, make misfortune drunk
With candle-wasters; bring him yet to me,
And I of him will gather patience.
But there is no such man: for, brother, men   20
Can counsel and speak comfort to that grief
Which they themselves not feel; but, tasting it,
Their counsel turns to passion, which before
Would give preceptial medicine to rage,
Fetter strong madness in a silken thread,
Charm ache with air and agony with words:
No, no; 't is all men's office to speak patience
To those that wring under the load of sorrow,

But no man's virtue nor sufficiency
To be so moral when he shall endure   30
The like himself.   Therefore give me no counsel:
My griefs cry louder than advertisement.

Ant. Therein do men from children nothing differ.

Leon. I pray thee, peace.   I will be flesh and blood;
For there was never yet philosopher
That could endure the toothache patiently,
However they have writ the style of gods
And made a push at chance and sufferance.

Ant. Yet bend not all the harm upon yourself;
Make those that do offend you suffer too.   40

Leon. There thou speak'st reason: nay, I will do so.
My soul doth tell me Hero is belied;
And that shall Claudio know; so shall the prince
And all of them that thus dishonour her.

Ant. Here comes the prince and Claudio hastily.

Enter DON PEDRO *and* CLAUDIO

D. Pedro. Good den, good den.

Claud.   Good day to both of you.

Leon. Hear you, my lords,—

D. Pedro.   We have some haste, Leonato.

Leon. Some haste, my lord! well, fare you well, my lord:
Are you so hasty now? well, all is one.

D. Pedro. Nay, do not quarrel with us, good old man.   50

Ant. If he could right himself with quarrelling,
Some of us would lie low.

Claud.   Who wrongs him?

Leon. Marry, thou dost wrong me; thou dissembler,
    thou:—
Nay, never lay thy hand upon thy sword;
I fear thee not.

Claud.   Marry, beshrew my hand,
If it should give your age such cause of fear:

In faith, my hand meant nothing to my sword.

   Leon. Tush, tush, man; never fleer and jest at me:
I speak not like a dotard nor a fool,
As under privilege of age to brag   60
What I have done being young, or what would do
Were I not old.   Know, Claudio, to thy head,
Thou hast so wrong'd mine innocent child and me
That I am forced to lay my reverence by
And, with grey hairs and bruise of many days,
Do challenge thee to trial of a man.
I say thou hast belied mine innocent child;
Thy slander hath gone through and through her heart,
And she lies buried with her ancestors;
O, in a tomb where never scandal slept,   70
Save this of hers, framed by thy villany!

   Claud. My villany?

   Leon.   Thine, Claudio; thine, I say.

   D. Pedro. You say not right, old man.

   Leon.   My lord, my lord,
I'll prove it on his body, if he dare,
Despite his nice fence and his active practice,
His May of youth and bloom of lustihood.

   Claud. Away! I will not have to do with you.

   Leon. Canst thou so daff me? Thou hast kill'd my
   child:
If thou kill'st me, boy, thou shalt kill a man.

   Ant. He shall kill two of us, and men indeed: 80
But that's no matter; let him kill one first;
Win me and wear me; let him answer me.
Come, follow me, boy; come, sir boy, come, follow me:
Sir boy, I'll whip you from your foining fence;
Nay, as I am a gentleman, I will.

   Leon. Brother,—

   Ant. Content yourself.   God knows I loved my niece;
And she is dead, slander'd to death by villains,

That dare as well answer a man indeed
As I dare take a serpent by the tongue: 90
Boys, apes, braggarts, Jacks, milksops!
   Leon.   Brother Antony,—
   Ant. Hold you content.   What, man! I know them, yea,
And what they weigh, even to the utmost scruple,—
Scambling, out-facing, fashion-monging boys,
That lie and cog and flout, deprave and slander,
Go anticly, show outward hideousness,
And speak off half a dozen dangerous words,
How they might hurt their enemies, if they durst;
And this is all.
   Leon. But, brother Antony,—
   Ant.   Come, 't is no matter: 100
Do not you meddle; let me deal in this.
   D. Pedro. Gentlemen both, we will not wake your
     patience.
My heart is sorry for your daughter's death:
But, on my honour, she was charged with nothing
But what was true and very full of proof.
   Leon. My lord, my lord,—
   D. Pedro. I will not hear you.
   Leon. No?   Come, brother; away! I will be heard.
   Ant. And shall, or some of us will smart for it.
                 [*Exeunt Leonato and Antonio*
   D. Pedro. See, see; here comes the man we went to
     seek.   110

Enter BENEDICK

   Claud. Now, signior, what news?
   Bene. Good day, my lord.
   D. Pedro. Welcome, signior: you are almost come to
part almost a fray.
   Claud. We had like to have had our two noses snapped
off with two old men without teeth.

D. Pedro. Leonato and his brother. What thinkest thou? Had we fought, I doubt we should have been too young for them.

Bene. In a false quarrel there is no true valour. I came to seek you both.   121

Claud. We have been up and down to seek thee; for we are high-proof melancholy and would fain have it beaten away. Wilt thou use thy wit?

Bene. It is in my scabbard: shall I draw it?

D. Pedro. Dost thou wear thy wit by thy side?

Claud. Never any did so, though very many have been beside their wit. I will bid thee draw, as we do the minstrels; draw, to pleasure us.

D. Pedro. As I am an honest man, he looks pale. Art thou sick, or angry?   131

Claud. What, courage, man! What though care killed a cat, thou hast mettle enough in thee to kill care.

Bene. Sir, I shall meet your wit in the career, an you charge it against me. I pray you choose another subject.

Claud. Nay, then, give him another staff: this last was broke cross.

D. Pedro. By this light, he changes more and more: I think he be angry indeed.

Claud. If he be, he knows how to turn his girdle.   140

Bene. Shall I speak a word in your ear?

Claud. God bless me from a challenge!

Bene. [*Aside to Claudio*] You are a villain; I jest not: I will make it good how you dare, with what you dare, and when you dare. Do me right, or I will protest your cowardice. You have killed a sweet lady, and her death shall fall heavy on you. Let me hear from you.

Claud. Well, I will meet you, so I may have good cheer.

D. Pedro. What, a feast, a feast?

Claud. I' faith, I thank him; he hath bid me to a calf's head and a capon; the which if I do not carve most

curiously, say my knife's naught.   Shall I not find a
woodcock too?   153

Bene. Sir, your wit ambles well; it goes easily.

D. Pedro. I'll tell thee how Beatrice praised thy wit the
other day.   I said, thou hadst a fine wit: 'True,' said she,
'a fine little one'.   'No,' said I, 'a great wit': 'Right,'
says she, 'a great gross one.'   'Nay,' said I, 'a good wit':
'Just,' said she, 'it hurts nobody.'   'Nay,' said I, 'the
gentleman is wise': 'Certain,' said she, 'a wise gentleman.'   'Nay,' said I, 'he hath the tongues': 'That I
believe,' said she, 'for he swore a thing to me on Monday
night, which he forswore on Tuesday morning; there's a
double tongue; there's two tongues.'   Thus did she, an
hour together, trans-shape thy particular virtues: yet at
last she concluded with a sigh, thou wast the properest
man in Italy.   167

Claud. For the which she wept heartily and said she
cared not.

D. Pedro. Yea, that she did; but yet, for all that, an if
she did not hate him deadly, she would love him dearly:
the old man's daughter told us all.

Claud. All, all; and, moreover, God saw him when he
was hid in the garden.

D. Pedro. But when shall we set the savage bull's horns
on the sensible Benedick's head?

Claud. Yea, and text underneath, 'Here dwells Benedick, the married man'?   178

Bene. Fare you well, boy: you know my mind.   I will
leave you now to your gossip-like humour: you break jests
as braggarts do their blades, which, God be thanked, hurt
not.   My lord, for your many courtesies I thank you: I
must discontinue your company: your brother the bastard
is fled from Messina: you have among you killed a sweet
and innocent lady.   For my Lord Lackbeard there, he and
I shall meet: and, till then, peace be with him.   [*Exit*

D. Pedro. He is in earnest.

Claud. In most profound earnest; and, I 'll warrant you, for the love of Beatrice.

D. Pedro. And hath challenged thee.   190

Claud. Most sincerely.

D. Pedro. What a pretty thing man is when he goes in his doublet and hose and leaves off his wit!

Claud. He is then a giant to an ape; but then is an ape a doctor to such a man.

D. Pedro. But, soft you, let me be: pluck up, my heart, and be sad.   Did he not say, my brother was fled?

Enter DOGBERRY, VERGES, *and the* Watch, *with* CONRADE *and* BORACHIO

Dog. Come you, sir: if justice cannot tame you, she shall ne'er weigh more reasons in her balance: nay, an you be a cursing hypocrite once, you must be looked to.   200

D. Pedro. How now? two of my brother's men bound! Borachio one!

Claud. Hearken after their offence, my lord.

D. Pedro. Officers, what offence have these men done?

Dog. Marry, sir, they have committed false report; moreover, they have spoken untruths; secondarily, they are slanders; sixth and lastly, they have belied a lady; thirdly, they have verified unjust things; and, to conclude, they are lying knaves.   209

D. Pedro. First, I ask thee what they have done; thirdly, I ask thee what 's their offence; sixth and lastly, why they are committed; and, to conclude, what you lay to their charge.

Claud. Rightly reasoned, and in his own division; and, by my troth, there 's one meaning well suited.

D. Pedro. Who have you offended, masters, that you are thus bound to your answer? this learned constable is too cunning to be understood: what's your offence? 218

Bora. Sweet prince, let me go no farther to mine answer: do you hear me, and let this count kill me. I have deceived even your very eyes: what your wisdoms could not discover, these shallow fools have brought to light; who in the night overheard me confessing to this man how Don John your brother incensed me to slander the Lady Hero, how you were brought into the orchard and saw me court Margaret in Hero's garments, how you disgraced her, when you should marry her: my villany they have upon record; which I had rather seal with my death than repeat over to my shame. The lady is dead upon mine and my master's false accusation; and, briefly, I desire nothing but the reward of a villain. 231

D. Pedro. Runs not this speech like iron through your
    blood?

Claud. I have drunk poison whiles he utter'd it.

D. Pedro. But did my brother set thee on to this?

Bora. Yea, and paid me richly for the practice of it.

D. Pedro. He is composed and framed of treachery:
And fled he is upon this villany.

Claud. Sweet Hero! now thy image doth appear
In the rare semblance that I loved it first. 239

Dog. Come, bring away the plaintiffs: by this time our sexton hath reformed Signior Leonato of the matter: and, masters, do not forget to specify, when time and place shall serve, that I am an ass.

Verg. Here, here comes master Signior Leonato, and the sexton too.

Re-enter LEONATO *and* ANTONIO, *with the* Sexton

Leon. Which is the villain? let me see his eyes,
That, when I note another man like him,
I may avoid him: which of these is he?

Bora. If you would know your wronger, look on me.

Leon. Art thou the slave that with thy breath hast kill'd
Mine innocent child?
Bora.   Yea, even I alone.   251
Leon. No, not so, villain; thou beliest thyself:
Here stand a pair of honourable men,
A third is fled, that had a hand in it.
I thank you, princes, for my daughter's death:
Record it with your high and worthy deeds:
'T was bravely done, if you bethink you of it.
Claud. I know not how to pray your patience;
Yet I must speak.   Choose your revenge yourself;
Impose me to what penance your invention   260
Can lay upon my sin: yet sinn'd I not
But in mistaking.
D. Pedro.   By my soul, nor I:
And yet, to satisfy this good old man,
I would bend under any heavy weight
That he 'll enjoin me to.
Leon. I cannot bid you bid my daughter live:
That were impossible: but, I pray you both,
Possess the people in Messina here
How innocent she died; and if your love
Can labour aught in sad invention,   270
Hang her an epitaph upon her tomb
And sing it to her bones, sing it to-night:
To-morrow morning come you to my house,
And since you could not be my son-in-law,
Be yet my nephew: my brother hath a daughter,
Almost the copy of my child that 's dead,
And she alone is heir to both of us:
Give her the right you should have given her cousin,
And so dies my revenge.
Claud.   O noble sir,
Your over-kindness doth wring tears from me!   280

I do embrace your offer; and dispose
For henceforth of poor Claudio.

Leon. To-morrow then I will expect your coming;
To-night I take my leave.   This naughty man
Shall face to face be brought to Margaret,
Who I believe was pack'd in all this wrong,
Hired to it by your brother.

Bora.   No, by my soul, she was not,
Nor knew not what she did when she spoke to me,
But always hath been just and virtuous
In any thing that I do know by her.   290

Dog. Moreover, sir, which indeed is not under white and
black, this plaintiff here, the offender, did call me ass: I
beseech you, let it be remembered in his punishment.   And
also, the watch heard them talk of one Deformed: they
say he wears a key in his ear and a lock hanging by it,
and borrows money in God's name, the which he hath
used so long and never paid that now men grow hard-
hearted and will lend nothing for God's sake: pray you,
examine him upon that point.

Leon. I thank thee for thy care and honest pains.   300

Dog. Your worship speaks like a most thankful and
reverend youth; and I praise God for you.

Leon. There's for thy pains.

Dog. God save the foundation!

Leon. Go, I discharge thee of thy prisoner, and I thank
thee.

Dog. I leave an arrant knave with your worship; which
I beseech your worship to correct yourself, for the example
of others.   God keep your worship!   I wish your worship
well; God restore you to health!   I humbly give you
leave to depart; and if a merry meeting may be wished,
God prohibit it!   Come, neighbour.   312

[*Exeunt Dogberry and Verges*

Leon. Until to-morrow morning, lords, farewell.

Ant. Farewell, my lords: we look for you to-morrow.

D. Pedro. We will not fail.

Claud.   To-night I 'll mourn with Hero.

Leon. [*To the Watch*] Bring you these fellows on.
    We 'll talk with Margaret,
How her acquaintance grew with this lewd fellow.

[*Exeunt severally*

SCENE II.   *Leonato's garden*

Enter BENEDICK *and* MARGARET, *meeting*

Bene. Pray thee, sweet Mistress Margaret, deserve well
at my hands by helping me to the speech of Beatrice.

Marg. Will you then write me a sonnet in praise of my
beauty?

Bene. In so high a style, Margaret, that no man living
shall come over it; for, in most comely truth, thou de-
servest it.

Marg. To have no man come over me! why, shall I
always keep below stairs?

Bene. Thy wit is as quick as the greyhound's mouth;
it catches.   11

Marg. And yours as blunt as the fencer's foils, which
hit, but hurt not.

Bene. A most manly wit, Margaret; it will not hurt
a woman: and so, I pray thee, call Beatrice: I give thee
the bucklers.

Marg. Give us the swords: we have bucklers of our own.

Bene. If you use them, Margaret, you must put in the
pikes with a vice; and they are dangerous weapons for
maids.   20

Marg. Well, I will call Beatrice to you, who I think
hath legs.

Bene. And therefore will come.   [*Exit Margaret*

[*Sings*]   The God of love,
                That sits above,
        And knows me, and knows me.
            How pitiful I deserve,—   27

I mean in singing; but in loving, Leander the good
swimmer, Troilus the first employer of pandars, and a
whole bookful of these quondam carpet-mongers, whose
names yet run smoothly in the even road of a blank verse,
why, they were never so truly turned over and over as my
poor self in love. Marry, I cannot show it in rhyme; I
have tried: I can find out no rhyme to 'lady' but 'baby',
an innocent rhyme; for 'scorn', 'horn', a hard rhyme; for
'school', 'fool', a babbling rhyme; very ominous endings:
no, I was not born under a rhyming planet, nor I cannot
woo in festival terms.   38

Enter BEATRICE

Sweet Beatrice, wouldst thou come when I called thee?
  Beat. Yea, signior, and depart when you bid me.
  Bene. O, stay but till then!
  Beat. 'Then' is spoken; fare you well now: and yet,
ere I go, let me go with that I came; which is, with knowing what hath passed between you and Claudio.
  Bene. Only foul words; and thereupon I will kiss thee.
  Beat. Foul words is but foul wind, and foul wind is but
foul breath, and foul breath is noisome; therefore I will
depart unkissed.   48
  Bene. Thou hast frighted the word out of his right sense,
so forcible is thy wit. But I must tell thee plainly, Claudio
undergoes my challenge; and either I must shortly hear
from him, or I will subscribe him a coward. And, I pray
thee now, tell me for which of my bad parts didst thou first
fall in love with me?
  Beat. For them all together; which maintained so politic

a state of evil that they will not admit any good part to intermingle with them.   But for which of my good parts did you first suffer love for me?

Bene. Suffer love! a good epithet!   I do suffer love indeed, for I love thee against my will.   60

Beat. In spite of your heart, I think; alas, poor heart! If you spite it for my sake, I will spite it for yours; for I will never love that which my friend hates.

Bene. Thou and I are too wise to woo peaceably.

Beat. It appears not in this confession: there's not one wise man among twenty that will praise himself.

Bene. An old, an old instance, Beatrice, that lived in the time of good neighbours.   If a man do not erect in this age his own tomb ere he dies, he shall live no longer in monument than the bell rings and the widow weeps.   70

Beat. And how long is that, think you?

Bene. Question: why, an hour in clamour and a quarter in rheum: therefore is it most expedient for the wise, if Don Worm, his conscience, find no impediment to the contrary, to be the trumpet of his own virtues, as I am to myself.   So much for praising myself, who, I myself will bear witness, is praiseworthy: and now tell me, how doth your cousin?

Beat. Very ill.

Bene. And how do you?   80

Beat. Very ill too.

Bene. Serve God, love me and mend.   There will I leave you too, for here comes one in haste.

Enter URSULA

Urs. Madam, you must come to your uncle.   Yonder's old coil at home: it is proved my Lady Hero hath been falsely accused, the prince and Claudio mightily abused; and Don John is the author of all, who is fled and gone. Will you come presently?

Beat. Will you go hear this news, signior? 89
Bene. I will live in thy heart, die in thy lap and be buried in thy eyes; and moreover I will go with thee to thy uncle's. [*Exeunt*

Scene III. *A church*

Enter Don Pedro, Claudio, *and three or four with tapers*

Claud. Is this the monument of Leonato?
A Lord. It is, my lord.
Claud. [*Reading out of a scroll*]

> Done to death by slanderous tongues
>   Was the Hero that here lies:
> Death, in guerdon of her wrongs,
>   Gives her fame which never dies.
> So the life that died with shame
> Lives in death with glorious fame.

> Hang thou there upon the tomb,
> Praising her when I am dumb. 10
Now, music, sound, and sing your solemn hymn.

Song

> Pardon, goddess of the night,
> Those that slew thy virgin knight;
> For the which, with songs of woe,
> Round about her tomb they go.
>   Midnight, assist our moan;
>   Help us to sigh and groan,
>   Heavily, heavily:
> Graves yawn and yield your dead,
> Till death be uttered, 20
>   Heavily, heavily.

Claud. Now, unto thy bones good night!
    Yearly will I do this rite.

D. Pedro. Good morrow, masters; put your torches out:
   The wolves have prey'd; and look, the gentle day,
Before the wheels of Phœbus, round about
   Dapples the drowsy east with spots of grey.
Thanks to you all, and leave us: fare you well.

Claud. Good morrow, masters: each his several way.

D. Pedro. Come, let us hence, and put on other weeds;
   And then to Leonato's we will go.   31

Claud. And Hymen now with luckier issue speed's
   Than this for whom we render'd up this woe. [*Exeunt*

SCENE IV. *A room in Leonato's house*

Enter LEONATO, ANTONIO, BENEDICK, BEATRICE, MAR-
GARET, URSULA, FRIAR FRANCIS, *and* HERO

Friar. Did I not tell you she was innocent?

Leon. So are the prince and Claudio, who accused her
Upon the error that you heard debated:
But Margaret was in some fault for this,
Although against her will, as it appears
In the true course of all the question.

Ant. Well, I am glad that all things sorts so well.

Bene. And so am I, being else by faith enforced
To call young Claudio to a reckoning for it.

Leon. Well, daughter, and you gentlewomen all,   10
Withdraw into a chamber by yourselves,
And when I send for you, come hither mask'd.
                        [*Exeunt Ladies*
The prince and Claudio promised by this hour
To visit me. You know your office, brother:
You must be father to your brother's daughter,
And give her to young Claudio.

Ant. Which I will do with confirm'd countenance.

Bene. Friar, I must entreat your pains, I think.

Friar. To do what, signior?

Bene. To bind me, or undo me; one of them.   20
Signior Leonato, truth it is, good signior,
Your niece regards me with an eye of favour.

Leon. That eye my daughter lent her: 't is most true.

Bene. And I do with an eye of love requite her.

Leon. The sight whereof I think you had from me,
From Claudio and the prince: but what's your will?

Bene. Your answer, sir, is enigmatical:
But, for my will, my will is your good will
May stand with ours, this day to be conjoin'd
In the state of honourable marriage: 30
In which, good friar, I shall desire your help.

Leon. My heart is with your liking.

Friar.   And my help.
Here comes the prince and Claudio.

Enter DON PEDRO *and* CLAUDIO, *and two or three others*

D. Pedro. Good morrow to this fair assembly.

Leon. Good morrow, prince; good morrow, Claudio:
We here attend you.   Are you yet determined
To-day to marry with my brother's daughter?

Claud. I'll hold my mind, were she an Ethiope.

Leon. Call her forth, brother; here's the friar ready.
                                        [*Exit Antonio*

D. Pedro. Good morrow, Benedick.   Why, what's the
    matter,
                                        40
That you have such a February face,
So full of frost, of storm and cloudiness?

Claud. I think he thinks upon the savage bull.
Tush, fear not, man; we'll tip the horns with gold
And all Europa shall rejoice at thee,
As once Europa did at lusty Jove,
When he would play the noble beast in love.

Bene. Bull Jove, sir, had an amiable low;
And some such strange bull leap'd your father's cow,

And got a calf in that same noble feat   50
Much like to you, for you have just his bleat.
   Claud. For this I owe you: here comes other reckonings

   Re-enter ANTONIO, *with the* Ladies *masked*

Which is the lady I must seize upon?
   Ant. This same is she, and I do give you her.
   Claud. Why, then she's mine.   Sweet, let me see your
    face.
   Leon. No, that you shall not, till you take her hand
Before this friar and swear to marry her.
   Claud. Give me your hand: before this holy friar,
I am your husband, if you like of me.
   Hero. And when I lived, I was your other wife: 60
                                  [Unmasking
And when you loved, you were my other husband.
   Claud. Another Hero!
   Hero.   Nothing certainer:
One Hero died defiled, but I do live,
And surely as I live, I am a maid.
   D. Pedro. The former Hero!   Hero that is dead!
   Leon. She died, my lord, but whiles her slander lived.
   Friar. All this amazement can I qualify;
When after that the holy rites are ended,
I'll tell you largely of fair Hero's death:
Meantime let wonder seem familiar,   70
And to the chapel let us presently.
   Bene. Soft and fair, friar.   Which is Beatrice?
   Beat. [*Unmasking*] I answer to that name.   What is
    your will?
   Bene. Do not you love me?
   Beat.   Why, no; no more than reason.
   Bene. Why, then your uncle and the prince and Claudio
Have been deceived; they swore you did.
   Beat. Do not you love me?

Bene.   Troth, no; no more than reason.

Beat. Why, then my cousin, Margaret and Ursula
Are much deceived; for they did swear you did.

Bene. They swore that you were almost sick for me.   80

Beat. They swore that you were well-nigh dead for me.

Bene. 'T is no such matter.   Then you do not love me?

Beat. No, truly, but in friendly recompense.

Leon. Come, cousin, I am sure you love the gentleman.

Claud. And I 'll be sworn upon 't that he loves her;
For here 's a paper written in his hand,
A halting sonnet of his own pure brain,
Fashion'd to Beatrice.

Hero.   And here 's another
Writ in my cousin's hand, stolen from her pocket,
Containing her affection unto Benedick.   90

Bene. A miracle! here 's our own hands against our
hearts.   Come, I will have thee; but, by this light, I take
thee for pity.

Beat. I would not deny you; but, by this good day, I
yield upon great persuasion; and partly to save your life,
for I was told you were in a consumption.

Bene. Peace! I will stop your mouth.   [*Kissing her* 97

D. Pedro. How dost thou, Benedick, the married man?

Bene. I 'll tell thee what, prince; a college of wit-crackers
cannot flout me out of my humour.   Dost thou think
I care for a satire or an epigram?   No: if a man will be
beaten with brains, a' shall wear nothing handsome about
him.   In brief, since I do purpose to marry, I will think
nothing to any purpose that the world can say against it;
and therefore never flout at me for what I have said
against it; for man is a giddy thing, and this is my conclusion.   For thy part, Claudio, I did think to have beaten
thee; but in that thou art like to be my kinsman, live
unbruised and love my cousin.   109

Claud. I had well hoped thou wouldst have denied

Beatrice, that I might have cudgelled thee out of thy single life, to make thee a double-dealer; which, out of question, thou wilt be, if my cousin do not look exceeding narrowly to thee.

Bene. Come, come, we are friends: let's have a dance ere we are married, that we may lighten our own hearts and our wives' heels.

Leon. We'll have dancing afterward.

Bene. First, of my word; therefore play, music. Prince, thou art sad; get thee a wife, get thee a wife: there is no staff more reverend than one tipped with horn. 121

Enter a Messenger

Mess. My lord, your brother John is ta'en in flight,
And brought with armed men back to Messina.

Bene. Think not on him till to-morrow: I'll devise thee brave punishments for him. Strike up, pipers. [*Dance*
[*Exeunt*

NOTES

Dramatis Personæ. (1) Significant names—

BEATRICE = Lat. *Beatrix*, she who blesses.

BENEDICK = Lat. *Benedictus*, he who is blessed.

BORACHIO = Spanish *Borrácho*, drunkard (Percival's Sp. Dict., 1599). The form Borachio, in the sense of 'drunkard', is found as a common noun in the *Devil's Charter* (1607), "Like a Borrachio armed all in sack", and became English for a century; cf. Congreve, *Way of the World*, iv. 2. As a proper name it recurs in Cyril Tourneur's *Atheist's Tragedy* (1612). See also Glossary, *s.v.*

DOGBERRY is from the berry of the dog-rose. VERGES is said to be the same as 'verjuice'. As a proper name Dogberry is found in documents of the time of Richard II; and Verges in the couplet, "Here lies Father Varges, Who died to save charges".

Significant names are regularly confined to comic and minor characters.

(2) Of the non-significant names, DON PEDRO and LEONATO are taken, with slight change, from the Re Piero and Lionato of the novel. The bastard DON JOHN seems to have had an historical prototype. In 1458 a bastard prince of the house of Arragon, named John, assumed the crown of Sicily.

The names of the gentle-folks, as usual, are (or might be) Italian; the maids and the constables are plain English. CONRADE, by his name, should be German; perhaps a free-lance, like Scott's Conrad of Wolfenstein, who has served Don John in his rebellion.

Both in Q. and F. the stage-direction to i. 1 reads "Enter Leonato, governor of Messina; Innogen, his wife", &c. Again, at ii. 1 we have "Enter Leonato, his brother, his wife", &c. But no speech is assigned to her in the course of the play. Halliwell takes it on himself to give her some unimportant speeches of Leonato's; but this is an impossible remedy. If Hero's mother took any part it must have been an important part. Other editors are content to say with Theobald, "It seems as if the poet had in his first Plan design'd such a Character; which, on a Survey of it, he found would be superfluous; and therefore he left it out ". We may go further, and say that Shakespeare has habitually avoided depicting the relation of mother and daughter. The relation of father and daughter he has often and nobly drawn; but almost all his heroines are motherless. Juliet and Anne Page are the exceptions that prove the rule; for nothing really passes between Anne Page and her mother, and there is no spiritual kinship between Juliet and Lady Capulet, the loveless wife of an elderly husband. In the present play Hero's motherless state makes a fresh claim on our sympathy. (The name Innogen belongs to the wife of Brutus in Holinshed, and recalls Imogen in *Cymbeline*; it is an odd coincidence that *her* husband's name is Leonatus.)

Act I—Scene I

The opening scene has two functions: (1) it explains the situation, (2) it starts the action. (1) An audience wants to know, first of all, "what it is all about"; this desire is satisfied in crude or decadent drama by the prologue—a direct address to the audience, traces of which survive in Shakespeare. But as a rule he gives the requisite information by purely dramatic means. The merits of such a represented prologue are naturalness and economy. The explanations must seem to arise naturally in dialogue between the speakers, and not be too obviously dragged in for the benefit of the audience. And they must be brief. (2) In his earlier comedies Shakespeare was content with this; later, he tried also to get his real action started in the course of the first scene. Here we may say that the 'prologue' ends with the entrance of Don Pedro and the lords. From this point the dialogue proceeds briskly, and by the end of the scene the relation of Beatrice and Benedick has been made clear, the course of Claudio's wooing well outlined, even the elements of danger indicated in the moody attitude of Don John.

The time is Monday.

1. The Angelos or Messenger came into English drama from Seneca; but this is the only place in which Shakespeare has made him the medium of his explanatory prologue.

Don Pedro. Q. and F. *Don Peter*, both here and l. 9. Elsewhere Don Pedro. See note on v. 1. 91.

5, 6. **this action.** What action? Presumably the battle in which Don John's rebellion has been quelled.

7. **sort**: either 'kind' or 'rank', probably the former. See l. 31 and Glossary.

8. Critics have seen in this a reference to Essex's campaign in Ireland, 1599. But Essex lost three-fourths of his men through sickness and desertion. See below, l. 40.

10. Claudio is thus speedily and favourably introduced. We learn that he is young, brave, and a favourite with the Prince. The form of Leonato's remark might be thought to imply that Claudio is a stranger to him; but l. 17 shows that this is not so. Leonato is fishing for further information.

14, 15. The antithesis and the alliteration are characteristic of the style of speech called 'Euphuism', introduced by Lyly's *Euphues* (1579), and caricatured by Shakespeare in Don Armado (*Love's Labour's Lost*), and by Scott in Sir Percie Shafton (*The Monastery*). The messenger speaks in this style throughout, and Leonato gives him as good. Observe the cross-alliteration, *f*igure, *l*amb, *f*eats, *l*ion. *also false natural history !*

15. bettered, surpassed.

17. This uncle of Claudio's is not again mentioned. But the reference is not therefore superfluous. This is one of those touches by which Shakespeare imparts such breadth to his pictures, making us feel that the action is not isolated, but an incident of the life of 'men in a world of men'.

an uncle . . . will be. Abbott (§ 244) calls this 'omission of the relative'. But historically the idiom is a relic of an earlier usage, out of which the relative clause grew. This is the so-called ἀπὸ κοινοῦ construction of one subject with two predicates, *e.g.* "There was a lad was born in Kyle" (cf. Kellner, §§ 111, 274). It is possible, however, that Shakespeare felt an omitted relative.

18. much, as adverb, was originally used, as now, only with participles.

21, 22. badge of bitterness, sorrow's livery. *Badge*, not simply a mark, but a mark of service, worn by menials on the sleeves of their liveries.

25. kind . . . kindness. There is a mild play on the original meaning of 'kind', *i.e.* natural; common in E.E. See Glossary.

28. Benedick's name is now introduced—appropriately, by Beatrice. **Signior Mountanto** she calls him, as it were 'Mr. Cut-and-thrust'. *Mountanto*=an 'upright blow or thrust' (Cotgrave), from Sp. *montánte*, a two-handed sword. Beatrice's question is one of those glimpses which Shakespeare loves to give into the past of his characters. This trait of his has been called 'epic'. He likes, so far as the conditions of his art allow, to set out his action on a background. We seem to have known his characters for a long time. Here, for instance, we gather that Benedick has been in Messina before, and has crossed swords with Beatrice; we gather also that her interest in him is not dead, and that she is longing to renew the duel.

! Which like the toad, ugly & venomous,
wears yet a precious jewel in his head ?

31. **sort** here = rank. See l. 7 above.

32, 33. Leonato's **niece** and Hero's **cousin** reveal the relationship between these characters.

34. **pleasant,** amusing; cf. 'pleasantry' and Fr. *plaisant.*

36. **set up his bills,** issued posters conveying a public challenge.

36, 37. **challenged Cupid at the flight.** Benedick describes himself as a 'professed tyrant to their sex', and Beatrice represents him as defying the very god of love.

37. **flight,** an arrow used at long ranges.

39. **bird-bolt,** an arrow with a flat head, used to shoot birds without tearing the plumage. Cupid's arrow is often called a bird-bolt; and the fools in great houses were allowed this harmless weapon—"a fool's bolt is soon shot". Q. and F. *burbolt*; corr. Theobald.

42, 43. For **tax** and **meet** see Glossary.

45. It is possible that Beatrice's gibe was suggested (unconsciously) by the word 'meet'. Similarly, in line 109, 'meet' suggests 'food'. This is the habit of punning grown automatic. Chalmers thinks that there is a reference to Essex's campaign in Ireland (1599), on which, as he states on Camden's authority, the troops suffered from scarcity of provisions. But Shakespeare's practice, his complimentary reference to this campaign in *Henry V* (act v, Chorus 30-33), and what we know of his friendship for Essex—all these considerations render such a gibe very improbable. Moreover, Chalmers's reference to Camden remains unverified.

47. **stomach.** There is a play on the word in the sense of 'appetite for the fray'. Cf. *Henry V*, iv. 3. 35, "he which hath no stomach to this fight".

51. A perfect definition of a soldier and a gentleman.

stuffed. The word, though Beatrice seizes on it, does not necessarily have any ludicrous association in E.E.

53. **a stuffed man,** a puppet, a man of straw. The idea that it means 'cuckold' (as in Lyly's *Midas,* v. 1) is utterly inappropriate. Wright refers it back to 'good trencherman'.

54. **we are all mortal:** evidently a cant phrase of the day, to judge from *Sir Giles Goosecap* (1606), "his only reason for everything is, because we are all mortal".

Q. and F., *but for the stuffing well*; corr. Theobald after Davenant.

59. **five wits:** sometimes = the five senses; here = the intellectual powers, called five to correspond with the senses.

60. with, O.E. *mid*, to introduce the instrument.

60, 61. wit enough to keep himself warm: a proverbial expression (like our 'sense enough to come in out of the rain'), as is proved by *The Puritan*, iii. 6, "The old beldam's saying, 'He's wisest that keeps himself warmest'".

61. difference: a term of heraldry: "extraordinary additaments, whereby persons of the same coat armour may be distinguished" (Sloan-Evans, *Grammar of British Heraldry*).

63. to be known a reasonable creature: probably 'his one wit is all he has to distinguish him from the brutes'. But the phrase may be nominative: 'to be known, &c., is all the wealth he has', and this is borne out by the punctuation of Q., which puts a comma at 'left'.

64. sworn brother: an allusion to the *fratres jurati* of chivalry, warriors who vowed to share each other's fortunes. Mr. Herford sees a survival of this in the German custom of *Bruderschaft.*

65. The Messenger, in spite of his emphatic praise of Benedick, begins to be shaken in his opinion by Beatrice's vigorous onslaught.

68. block, (1) the mould on which the hat was shaped; (2) the shape itself. It would appear that hats were then reblocked to keep in fashion. Cf. *Cynthia's Revels*, i. 1, where Amorphus says that his hat "will take any block".

69. not in your books, not in your good books, as we should say. The origin of the expression is obscure. Wright and Halliwell incline to refer it to visiting books which contained lists of friends and acquaintances; others to college registers (as a man still keeps his name 'on the books' of his college), or to lists of retainers. The modern phrase 'good books', 'bad books', would seem to point to a commercial origin; cf. 'bad debts'.

70. Q. and F., *and*; corr. Theobald. And so *passim*. See Glossary.

study, library; abstract for collective, as often in Latin.

72. squarer, brawler. 'To square' is still used for 'to spar'. Who but Beatrice could have said this? With her, every word is like a familiar gesture—"Is Signior Mountanto returned from the wars?" Every turn of phrase calls up her laughing face.

78. presently, at once; now=soon, but not at once. Several other words which in E.E. refer to the immediate future have now lost their sense of immediacy; *e.g.* 'anon', and even 'by and by' (used in *Matt.* xiii. 21 to translate εὐθύς). The meaning of 'presently' had changed by Wycherley's time; cf. *Plain Dealer*, iv. 2—

"*Vernish.* I will go presently.
  Olivia. Presently! instantly! I will not let you stay a jot."

The change of meaning is due to that habit of exaggeration which has led to the weakening of many strong words.

80. a', F., *he*; and so frequently.

81. The puzzled messenger thinks he had best conciliate this sarcastic lady, whereupon Beatrice at once drops her mirth and says with beautiful courtesy, "Do, good friend".

83. **You will never run mad**, *i.e.* from catching the Benedick (Wright). F., *You'l ne'er*.

85. **is approached.** In O.E. *be* was used to form the perfect of intransitive, *have* of transitive verbs (Kellner, § 348). In E.E. it is so used with verbs of motion; and still with 'come', 'go', and a few others.

86. **you are:** Q., *are you.*

90. The antithetic form of these courtesies again recalls the style of Lyly, whose influence on Elizabethan prose was incalculable and (on the whole) good. Cf. especially *Endimion*, ii. 1.

92. **his, its.** In O.E. *his* is both masc. and neuter. *Its* was only coming into vogue in Shakespeare's day. It does not occur in Spenser, nor in the Bible of 1611; ten times in Shakespeare, seldom in Bacon. Alexander Gil, the grammarian, does not recognize it (1619). It did not become general till the Restoration.

93. **charge,** burden imposed or accepted.

F. omits 'sir'.

98. **You have it full:** a metaphor, probably not from boxing, but from the tourney: cf. 'encounter', l. 88 above and 296 below—both in Don Pedro's mouth.

99, 100. **fathers herself,** shows who her father is.

105. **still,** always.

107. Benedick, with a start, affects to observe Beatrice for the first time, and hails her in language that recalls their former encounters.

109. **to feed it.** Note the change of gender. Beatrice follows Benedick in personifying 'Disdain', but does not keep up the personification.

110. **convert:** intrans. = turn. Note again the change of genders.

112. To exasperate Beatrice by a gibe at her sex, Benedick states his pretensions in the most outrageous fashion. This has the effect of marking their opposition strongly at the outset. But these lady-killing airs are make-believe.

113. Cf. *Merchant of Venice*, ii. 2. 29, "and, in my conscience, my conscience is but a kind of hard conscience".

115. A dear happiness, a precious piece of good-luck. *Dear* is thus used of anything 'heartfelt'; even of anything extreme in its kind, "your dearest speed", *1 Henry IV*, v. 5. 36.

117. of your humour, of your way of thinking. See Glossary.

121. predestinate. See note on iii. 2. 2.

124. as yours were. The subjunctive, if sound, seems due to the subjunctive on which it depends. This is familiar in Latin as the 'Subjunctive of Grammatical Dependence'.

129. a', for 'in', is supported by the text in so many places that I have ventured to keep it. Mod. edd. 'i''.

133. While this set of wit is being played, Don Pedro and Leonato have been talking apart.

F., *This*. Q. and F. put colon after 'all' and comma after 'Leonato'; corr. Cambridge editors.

135, 136. at the least a month. By iii. 2. 1, Don Pedro has changed his mind, or Shakespeare has forgotten this passage, "I do but stay till your marriage be consummate, and then go I toward Arragon". But see note there.

143. Don John's first words are characteristic in their surly bluntness. Shakespeare knew

> "These kind of knaves . . . which in this plainness
> Harbour more craft and more corrupter ends
> Than twenty silly ducking observants".
> —*Lear*, ii. 2. 107-9.

Richard III is a "plain man" (i. 3. 51) and Iago is "honest".

145. Please: subjunctive here used interrogatively, but originally jussive.

149. noted...not. Cf. play on *noting* and *nothing* in ii. 3. 54.

151. With the instinct of the reputed wit, Benedick suspects a trap. But, assured that Claudio is in earnest, he is free to jest. His misogyny must not be taken too seriously.

156. too brown reminds us that we are in Elizabeth's days, when fair hair was the fashion.

160 seq. Throughout the rest of this scene observe carefully the interchange of *you* and *thou*. 'Thou' is used intimately to friends, familiarly to servants, contemptuously to strangers, and solemnly (as being a little archaic) in the higher poetic style. Here Claudio, seeking sympathy, uses the intimate 'thou'. Benedick keeps him off with the common-sense 'you'; till assured of his serious case he drops (l. 181) into friendly contempt. Don Pedro's 'you' (184) is plural. He is addressed as a rule, even in intimate conversation, with the ceremonious 'you', but uses 'thou' both to Benedick and to Claudio, except in 198 and 246. The former case falls under the rule that 'you' is used in conditional sentences (Abbott, § 234); in the latter the change of pronoun is a hint that the Prince has done with banter and would be left alone with Claudio. He proceeds to address Benedick formally as 'good Signior Benedick'.

165. sad, serious. See Glossary.

flouting Jack, mocking knave. Jack, being the commonest of all names among the lower classes, came to be used in many European languages as a term of contempt; cf. v. i. 91. Benedick means simply "Are you joking? You will be telling me that blind Cupid is a hare-finder, and the God of Fire a good carpenter."

167, 168. to go in the song, so as to be in harmony with you.

169. Claudio's sentimental utterances fall naturally into an iambic rhythm approaching the regularity of metre.

172. As Beatrice had turned the conversation from Claudio to Benedick, so Benedick now turns it from Hero to Beatrice.

179. wear his cap with suspicion, with the suspicion of having horns under it. The invisible horns of the man whose wife is unfaithful are an unfailing subject of mirth in Shakespeare. The idea is said to have arisen from the story of Actæon, who was turned into a stag for spying on Diana bathing.

182. sigh away Sundays. The expression has a proverbial ring, but the exact meaning is doubtful. Perhaps, 'If you must, you must: marry, and be humdrum ever after'.

183. Q. and F., *Enter Don Pedro and John the Bastard.*

190. Benedick's 'allegiance' is as handy as Falstaff's 'instinct'.

193. Claudio avoids an admission and says evasively, "If I had told him such a secret, he would have disclosed it in such a manner".

194. This **old tale**, or something like it, was communicated to the Variorum Edition of 1821 by Mr. Blakeway, who had it from his great-aunt. The villain, Mr. Fox, is a kind of Bluebeard. One day Lady Mary visits his house in his absence.

Over the hall-door is written, "Be bold, be bold, but not too bold"; but she proceeds till she comes on a room full of skeletons. Out of a window she sees Mr. Fox dragging a lady towards the house, and hides under the stair. As his victim clutches at the banisters, Mr. Fox cuts off her hand, which falls into Lady Mary's lap. At dinner some days after Lady Mary tells her experience as if it were a dream. At every turn Mr. Fox interjects, "It is not so, nor it was not so, and God forbid it should be so", till she comes to the severed hand, where to his "It is not so, &c." she suddenly retorts, "But it is so, and it was so, and here the hand I have to shew", whereupon the guests cut Mr. Fox to pieces. The story appears in various forms. The first part, with the inscription, "Be bold, &c." resembles *Faerie Queen*, III. xi. 54. Other versions are "Jacke of Shrewsberrie" in the *Ingoldsby Legends* (referred to by Mr. Verity), and the Nurse's Tale of Captain Murderer in Dickens's *Uncommercial Traveller*.

196. "An ominous qualification", says Kreyssig.

200. to fetch me in, to entrap me. After his 'roasting' by Benedick, Claudio has no mind to expose himself to another from the Prince.

203. my two faiths and troths, my faith and troth to both of you.

212, 213. in the force of his will, by sheer obstinacy, alluding to the definition of heresy as a 'wilful choice' (αἵρεσις). But there is probably a play on the sense of 'lust' which 'will' often has in Shakespeare.

214–216. The fears which Benedick affects are those which Claudio is too ready to feel.

220. fine, conclusion. Lat. *finis*; now only in the phrase 'in fine'.

go the finer, be the better dressed. Cf. "wherein went he?" *i.e.* how was he dressed? (*As You Like It*, iii. 2. 234). The pun is obvious.

224 ff. A sentiment worthy of Henry V, with whom Benedick has a good deal in common, including his soldierly contempt for verse. *Ballad* in E.E. = song of any sort, often love-song. Cf. "a woeful ballad Made to his mistress' eyebrow" (*As You Like It*, ii. 7. 148).

In the physiology of the time, sighing was supposed to drain the blood from the heart. The contrary operation of 'fertile sherris' in enriching the blood is demonstrated at large by Falstaff, *2 Henry IV*, iv. 3. 92.

230. bottle, basket; cf. 'twiggen bottle', *Othello*, ii. 3. 152. A cat in a basket was used as a mark at archery practice.

231, 232. **clapped on the shoulder.** Is this an allusion to the *accolade*? The successful archer is to get the name of 'Adam', referring to the famous outlaw and archer, Adam Bell, the Robin Hood of the English border. See the ballad of *Adam Bel, Clym of the Cloughe*, and *Willyam of Cloudesle*, first printed about 1550. [So Theobald and others. But Adam Bell was scarcely so famous that his Christian name could be used as a synonym for 'archer'. Collier suggests that the winner was to be called *the first man*, *i.e.* Adam.]

234. A reminiscence of Kyd's *Spanish Tragedy*, ii. 1—

> "In time the savage bull sustains the yoke".

(Date about 1587.) None of his contemporaries amused Shakespeare so much as Kyd, and few influenced him more. This line of Kyd's, and the whole passage, is imitated from Watson's *Ecatompathia*, Sonnet 47 (pub. 1582)—

> "In time the bull is brought to weare the yoke",

which in turn is inspired by Ovid, probably *Ars Amandi*, i. 471—

> "Tempore difficiles veniunt ad aratra juvenci".

237. **vilely.** The spelling of Q. and F., *vildly* or *vildely*, no doubt represents the pronunciation. The adverb is only once spelt in Shakespeare without the epenthetic *d*; the adj. varies. Naturally the *d* would be kept longer between the two *l*'s.

244. **Venice:** then the capital of the *demi-monde*.

245. Meaning that nothing less would make him quake.

246. **temporize with the hours,** come to terms in (with) time.

252. **tuition:** in its Latin sense of 'protection'. A parody on the formal endings of letters.

254. For Fleay's inference from this, see Introduction, § 6.

257. **guarded,** trimmed. The latest use of the word in this sense which I have noticed is in *Villette*, chap. xli., "a surtout guarded with velvet".

258. **neither:** really a case of double negative, 'but slightly' being = 'not firmly'.

258, 259. **old ends,** 'tags'; *i.e.* the scrap of verse parodied by Don Pedro and the formal endings referred to on 252. Cf. Induction to *Volpone*, "Nor hales he in a gull old ends reciting".

261. On Benedick's departure the dialogue at once rises to the pitch of verse. See Prosody, § 5. The relations of Claudio and the Prince are prefigured by those of Bassanio and Antonio in *Merchant of Venice*. Cf. i. 1. 119, to end.

265, 266. Observe this question, and the answer. Shakespeare has here diverged from Bandello, who makes his Lionato a gentleman of decayed fortune. The change is deliberate, as his reiteration of the point shows. Thus, in i. 3. 50 Hero is described as "the daughter *and heir* of Leonato"; in ii. 1. 270-71 Leonato says, "Count, take of me my daughter, and with her my fortunes"; in v. 1. 275-77, "my brother hath a daughter, . . . And she alone is heir to both of us". So, too, Bassanio: "In Belmont is a lady richly left".

267. affect, care for. Lat. *affectare*, to aim at.

270, 271. Claudio is no Romeo. His passion can wait.

272. This is a case of "'that' omitted and then inserted". Cf. Abbott, § 285, rather than § 284.

278. book of words. Cf. v. 2. 30, "a whole bookful of these quondam carpet-mongers".

280, 281. F. omits "and with her father, And thou shalt have her".

280. break with her, broach the subject.

282. twist: cf. 'spin a yarn'. Perhaps suggested by the words, "you have this string of falsehoods tied", in Harington.

283. F., *do you*.

284. complexion, appearance. See Glossary.

286. salved, excused; **treatise,** story generally. Claudio, like Bassanio, would wind about Don Pedro's love with circumstance.

287-290. The same idea is expressed four times over. Line 287 does double duty, referring alike to Claudio's speech and to Don Pedro's answer. 'Why make a long story? The greatest kindness is to give a man what he wants.' This is repeated in 288 and applied in 289. Such variation is characteristic of Shakespeare's full style. Cf. v. 1. 24, and note there.

287. What need. The fact that *need* is never used for *needs* when an object follows seems to show that in such phrases it was felt as a noun. "What need (is there that) the bridge (be) broader?"

289. 'tis once, once for all.

294. unclasp. The metaphor, from opening a book, is a favourite with the bookish Shakespeare, but less appropriate in Don Pedro's mouth than the figure from the tilt-yard which comes in 296.

Scene 2

A short bustling scene like this is one of Shakespeare's favourite devices. Unimportant in itself, inserted between scenes of such marked and different importance as i. 1 and ii. 1, it seems to give us a glimpse behind the curtain, and, while showing little, produces the impression that we have seen a great deal. The preparation for Capulet's feast in *Romeo and Juliet*, i. 5, is a close parallel.

1. cousin, here = nephew. See Glossary. This nephew is not again mentioned any more than Claudio's uncle.

4. F. omits 'strange'.

6. Q. and F., *events*; corr. F 2.

8. mine: F., *my*.

9. orchard, garden; the original sense. O.E. *ortgeard*, *i.e.* wort-yard, vegetable garden.

F. omits 'much'.

The conference thus overheard is not the dialogue of the preceding scene, which takes place before Leonato's house, and which is possibly meant to be that reported by Borachio. The present conference implies, and helps to fill up, an interval of time between i. 1 and the next four scenes, which follow each other in rapid succession on the evening of Monday. On this point see introduction to Act ii.

10. discovered, disclosed. The report is incorrect; so, though less seriously, is Borachio's version. Nothing comes of this mistake, except that it shows how the Prince's plan might be misconceived, and so prepares us for Don John's machinations in Act ii. But the discrepancy is none the less intentional. Shakespeare had noted that no two reports of an occurrence are, as a rule, precisely the same, unless by collusion. Cf. *Othello*, i. 3. 5—

> " But though they jump not on a just account,
>   As in these cases, where the aim reports,
>   'T is oft with difference . . .".

These little discrepancies, like the two views in a stereoscope, help to create that sense of solidity of which Shakespeare is the greatest master.

12. accordant, agreeable. Only here in Shakespeare.

12, 13. take the present time by the top: a variant on 'take Time by the forelock'.

18, 19. appear itself. Here, and in *Cymbeline*, iii. 4. 148—
" That which to appear itself must not yet be "—the verb may

be transitive = show. Dyce's *approve* is plausible. In *Coriolanus*, iv. 3. 9 — "Your favour is well appeared by your tongue "—Steevens's *approved* is generally adopted.

22. Cousins, friends: addressed to the attendants, who might also be relations. See Glossary.

24. Good cousin: addressed apparently to Antonio's son.

Scene 3

While the supper for which we have seen preparation is in progress, Don John is sulking apart with one of his creatures. Lines 1 to 37 serve simply to display his character and circumstances, and to warn us of possible mischief. Borachio's information supplies the opportunity.

1. What the good-year: a petty malediction, like "What the deuce". For its origin see Glossary. The tone indicates at once the terms on which Don John stands with his inferiors.

7. brings: F., *bringeth*.

8. at least: F. *yet*.

8, 9. sufferance, endurance.

11. born under Saturn. In astrology a man's disposition is supposed to depend on the 'aspect' of the planets at his birth. A man 'born under Saturn' is saturnine; under Jupiter, jovial; under Mercury, mercurial.

11, 12. moral medicine, a medicine consisting in moralizing. This use of the adj. = defining genitive is common in E.E. Cf. iv. 1. 48, "forehand sin"= sin of anticipation; v. 1. 24, "preceptial medicine"= medicine consisting in precepts.

12. mortifying mischief, deadly disease. The double alliteration, the balanced adjectives, and the antithesis between 'medicine' and 'mischief' are all Euphuistic.

12–17. Egotism, naked and unashamed.

14. stomach: common in E.E. for 'appetite' both literal and metaphorical.

19. controlment, restraint.

20. stood out, been in rebellion. By reminding Don John of his position Conrade informs the audience of it. Note the strong iambic rhythm: his remonstrance nearly runs into blank verse.

22. F. omits 'true'.

25. Don John keeps up the metaphor of transplantation The contrast between the canker (dog-rose, see Glossary) and the rose is worked out in *Sonnet* liv.

26. it better fits my blood. At the root of Don John's misanthropy lies the consciousness of the stain on his birth, of which he still is perversely proud. He has no social equals; he herds with his inferiors. Mr. Hardy has made the same trait the basis of the character of his Sergeant Troy. (Others explain 'blood' as 'temper'.)

27. fashion a carriage, shape my behaviour.

28. Don John makes a virtue of the surliness which he has not the wit to conceal. Such a villain will hardly prove an Iago. Shakespeare's great villains, when they practise self-revelation, do so in soliloquy.

29. honest man: to be pronounced as one word. See on ii. 1. 177.

must not be denied but I am, *negari non potest quin.* There is virtually a double negative.

36. F., *I will make.*

39. came. Modern usage would require the perfect.

42. A characteristic question. Don John's malevolence is agog for action: *er muss als Teufel schaffen.* He does not yet know who is to be married.

model, ground-plan. Bullokar defines 'model' as 'the platform or form of anything'. For the converse cf. *The Puritan*, i. 2, "The perfect platform (*i.e.* model) of a troubled wight".

43. What is he for a fool: exactly the German *was für ein.* The view of marriage which Benedick affects, Don John holds in bitter earnest.

48. Both **proper** and **squire** are used ironically = 'a fine fellow'.

52. A very forward March-chick! If these words apply to Claudio they are a sneer at his presumption in aspiring to such an heiress. But I think that they refer to 'young' Hero (i. 1. 275), and that forward = precocious. A chicken hatched in March is typical rather of precocity than of presumption, and it is characteristic that Don John (especially after his eager question) should vent his gall on Hero as well.

55. smoking a musty room. Fumigation, especially with the smoke of juniper, was employed to cleanse a room that had not been used.

comes me. The singular verb is common where the plural subject follows and is as yet undetermined. *Me* here and in l. 56 is ethical dative.

56. F. omits *me.*

58. woo Hero for himself. Not quite correct. See note on scene 2. The conference in scene 1 took place *before* Leonato's house, but we may suppose that it was continued within-doors.

61. start-up. Shakespeare uses 'upstart' only as an adjective. This line, taken with i. 1. 9–16, seems to show clearly that the war from which the Prince is returning was caused by Don John's rebellion. Don John, like Iago, is ready to give himself reasons for his malice. Cf. also Bacon, *Essay IX*, 'Of Envy'.

62. cross, thwart. But the antithesis to 'bless' shows that there is a play on the word in the sense of making the sign of the cross in benediction.

63. sure, reliable.

65. The egotist thinks that others are thinking of him, and rejoicing in his discomfiture as he would in theirs.

Act II—Scene I

It has been shown that an interval of time elapses between Act i, scene 1, and Act i, scene 2; on the other hand, this scene follows immediately on Act i, scene 3. Similarly, there is an interval between scenes 2 and 3 of this Act, but no interval between Act iii, scene 5, and Act iv. Spedding (*N. S. S. Transactions*, 1877–79, pp. 20–24) suggested that the present arrangement was due to the need of preparing the stage for the two great set scenes, the masked dance here and the church scene in Act iv. I believe that Spedding is right; and, further, that the present arrangement (which dates from the Folio) was made for a court performance in 1613. No acts are marked in the Quarto. See Appendix on the Text. With this long and brilliant scene the overture ends. Hero and Claudio are betrothed, in spite of Don John's attempt at mischief; the feud between Benedick and Beatrice is aggravated to quarrelling-point; and the plot against them is concocted. Little fresh light is thrown on any character except Claudio's; but every line breathes that atmosphere of gaiety which emanates especially from Beatrice, and in which the play moves for the next two Acts.

1. Leonato's question shows that Don John had not been intentionally overlooked.

3, 4. I never can see him. Yet she has seen him but once that we know of. Shakespeare juggles with our sense of time to make us feel that the company has been long together.

4. heart-burned. Heart-burn is said to be caused by acidity in the stomach, an effect which Beatrice, with characteristic exaggeration, attributes to Don John's sour looks. Hero's gentler comment shows less insight. With comic irony Don John's future victim is made his apologist.

7. Apropos of Don John, Beatrice drags in Benedick, just as she did when Claudio was the subject of conversation.

8, 9. my lady's eldest son: proverbial for a spoilt child. "Sons-and-heirs, and fools and gulls, and ladies' eldest sons" (*The Puritan*, i. 2).

18. curst, bitter; quite the same as *shrewd*, and by the same process. Antonio is a feebler Leonato, without his kindly humour. See what is said on Dogberry and Verges in iii. 3.

22. In vain the easy uncle attempts to scold. He is taking part in Beatrice's nonsense again before he knows it.

24. Just, exactly. There is the usual play on 'horns'.

25. This picture of herself as the importunate maiden is one of Beatrice's most audacious flights.

27. lie in the woollen, between the blankets, which would be no worse than a bearded husband. Some editors think that the phrase means 'lie in my shroud', and refer to an act of Charles II's reign enjoining that corpses should be buried in woollen. But that act was meant to encourage the use of English woollen stuffs, and proves, if anything, that wool was *not* previously used for shrouds.

35. bear-ward, bear-keeper. The spelling *berrord* of Q. and F. (corr. Collier) represents the pronunciation, and points to *bear-ward* rather than the *bear-herd* of F 3, F 4, which Schmidt asserts is the Shakespearian form. But *bear-herd* would rather become *berrerd*; cf. *hoggerd*=hogherd in Peele's *Jests* (p. 330, Dyce).

lead his apes into hell. To lead apes in (for which Beatrice substitutes 'into') hell was the proverbial fate of an old maid. Cf. *London Prodigal*, i. 2—

"But 't is an old proverb, and you know it well,
    That women, dying maids, lead apes in hell".

Perhaps, as Wright suggests, the punishment was thought appropriate for those who had escaped the plague of children in this life.

41. The punctuation is Pope's. It gives a better point than that of Q. and F., which have a colon at 'Peter', making "for the heavens" an exclamation, as in *Merchant of Venice*, ii. 2. 12, "'for the heavens, rouse up a brave mind', says the fiend".

42. Beatrice has no objection to bachelors in heaven, where there is no marriage.

merry, happy; a more decorous word in E.E. than now.

45. curtsy. The spelling of Q., *cursie*, no doubt represents the colloquial pronunciation.

46. please is subjunctive; common in E.E. in indefinite relative clauses. F. omits " Father ".

51. Beatrice's dislike to marriage arises partly from her love of independence, her ' wild heart ', which cannot abide the idea of calling any man master; partly from a sense of intellectual superiority, which tells her she is at least as good as any man she has met.

metal, material: same word as *mettle*, and not distinguished from it in Shakespeare either in meaning or in spelling.

53. F., *make account*.

54. marl, a rich clay, now used as a fertilizer.

55. Adam's sons. *Genesis*, ii. 7—" God formed man of the dust of the ground "—reveals the connection of thought.

56. match in my kindred: alluding to the ' degrees ' of kinship within which marriage is prohibited.

57. Remember that Leonato expects the Prince to woo Hero for himself. Her docile readiness now to accept an utter stranger blunts our sympathy with her hereafter.

58. in that kind, to that effect, in the way of marriage.

60, 61. There is a pun on **time and measure.** The measure was a stately dance, like a minuet.

60. important. Shakespeare uses this word (*a*) in its modern sense, (*b*) in the sense of ' importunate '. There is no etymological connection between the words: ' importunate ' is from Lat. *importunus*. It seems to be a confusion of Shakespeare's: he uses ' importing ' for ' importuning ' in *Hamlet*, i. 2. 23.

67. This fantasia on the theme, " Marry in haste and repent at leisure ", reminds us of Rosalind. But Beatrice's wit runs more to ' base comparisons ', and is most fluent on the one subject of marriage.

67, 68. For **cinque pace** see Glossary. Dauney (*Ancient Scottish Melodies*, p. 300) says: " The ' bad legs ' refers to the tottering fabric of the tune; the ' faster and faster ' to the acceleration of the movement towards the close; the ' sinking into his grave ' to the slow and solemn strain of the finale ".

68. F., *sinks*.

73. We are to suppose that the previous conversation took place while the guests retired to dress for the masked dance.

74. **friend,** lover; and like that word applied by Shakespeare to either sex.

75. **So,** provided that—'(if it be) so (that)'.

83. Jupiter and Mercury, in mortal guise, were hospitably received by Baucis and Philemon in their cottage, which was

> " Parva quidem, stipulis et canna tecta palustri ".
> —Ovid, *Metamorphoses*, viii. 632.

Golding translates:

> " The roofe thereof was *thatched* all with straw and fennish reede ".

Lines 83-86 form a rhyming couplet in Golding's metre, and many editors arrange them as such. Don Pedro's mock-heroic metaphor may well have been meant to fall into that metre; but I incline to think that the second heptameter (which is divided between two speakers and ends seriously) and the rhyme are accidental.

87-108. These scraps of dialogue do nothing to forward the action, but much to create the atmosphere.

90. **Which,** of what sort. O.E. *hwilc*=wha-like, Lat. *quale*.

96. **clerk.** The clerk used to utter the responses in the English Church service.

100 seq. Ursula's impertinence is characteristic of the spirit that pervades the play. The guests have arrived elated from the field of victory. In this Saturnalia servants make fun with their masters; and Ursula and Margaret are not menials but 'gentlewomen'. To the elation of victory succeeds the excitement of the wedding. Borachio's condition in iii. 3 is evidence that wine is flowing in abundance.

102. **do him so ill-well,** play a bad part so perfectly.

103. **A dry hand** was the sign of cold blood; Antonio's blood is cold with age.

up and down. Shakespeare elsewhere uses 'up and down' for 'thoroughly, all over, to the life'; *e.g.* "For up and down she doth resemble thee" (*Titus Andronicus*, v. 2. 107). But here there is a play on the literal sense; his hand 'waggles' like his head: and so in *Two Gentlemen*, ii. 3. 31, when Launce says, "Here's my mother's breath up and down", he heaves a sigh.

110. **shall,** must, will have to: a polite imperative.

114. **the 'Hundred Merry Tales':** the 'Joe Miller's Jest-book' of the sixteenth century. It was first printed by John

Rastell in 1526, and is said to have been a favourite with Queen Elizabeth. This slander on her 'good wit' has evidently stung Beatrice, and she proceeds to revenge herself in kind.

122. only his gift is, his gift is only. Adverbs of limitation are often transposed in Shakespeare.

impossible, incredible.

124. He pleases men by slandering others, **and angers them** by slandering themselves. F., *pleaseth*.

126. fleet, company. The nautical metaphor is kept up in 'boarded'.

129. break a comparison: as braggarts do their blades v. i. 181).

131. Such a valiant trencherman would scarcely sup off a partridge wing: it is part of Beatrice's joke to represent Benedick's appetite as slender.

133. the leaders, the 'top couple' in the dance. The play on words is continued in 'turning'.

137. amorous on: cf. line 144. We still say 'to dote on'. If these words are addressed to Borachio they cannot mean "My brother is in love with Hero", for Don John knows that this is not the case. They must mean "My brother is making love to Hero". But possibly this sentence is spoken aloud and is meant to be overheard by Claudio, while the aside begins at "The ladies follow her".

143 seq. For this abortive attempt at mischief Shakespeare found no precedent in his originals. Its introduction serves a threefold purpose. (1) It makes a complication in this long scene, which thus becomes a miniature of the whole play. (2) It lends probability to the main plot, by taking away its singleness and making us feel that we are in a world where such things happen not once but often. (3) It gives a foretaste of Claudio's quality. The man who so readily distrusts his friend will readily discard his mistress.

151. banquet, dessert, as often in E.E. The supper is over.

152. Claudio, left alone, expresses his emotion in blank verse. Here, where he thinks his patron the offender, his resentment evaporates in generalities.

155, 156. On the usual interpretation of the Sonnets, Shakespeare must have known this from his own experience. Cf. especially *Sonnet* xli; and *Two Gentlemen*, v. 4. 53, where Proteus, an earlier Claudio, defends himself by the question, "In love Who respects friend?"

157. use: subjunctive used imperatively.

159, 160. The imagery is founded on the superstition that witches made and melted wax figures of those whose love they wished to procure. This practice is known to us from Theocritus (*Idyll* ii), and is said to survive to this day in remote parts of this country. *Blood* here = passion, and in this sense is often contrasted with judgment and the like. "Honour dissolves in passion when exposed to the witchcraft of beauty."

161. **an accident of hourly proof,** an incident of which we have evidence every hour.

167. The willow was, and is, the emblem of unhappy love.

168. **county,** count. Though F. has *count* here, the form *county* is quite common even in serious passages.

177. **blind man:** spelt *blindman* in Q. and F., and so pronounced, as still in 'blindman's buff'. In E.E. the adjective in such combinations had a stronger accent than the succeeding noun.

A somewhat similar incident occurs in the Spanish picaresque romance of *Lazarillo de Tormes*, chap. i (1554); but there the beggar takes Lazarillo's sausage, who in revenge makes him jump against a post. It was apparently a popular anecdote pretty widely diffused in various forms. *Lazarillo* had been translated into English in 1586.

179. **If it will not be,** if my request is vain. Abbott (§ 321) thinks that 'will', not 'shall', is used because 'it' (*i.e.* fate) is personified. "If things refuse to be as I wish, &c." Cf. iv. 1. 208.

180. A fine instance of Shakespeare's sympathetic observation of animals.

181. Benedick's penetration fails him when Beatrice is concerned. We are thus prepared for the success of the trick played on him.

182. "This sarcasm sunk deeper into the mind of Benedick than all Beatrice had said before. The hint that she gave him that he was a coward, by saying she would eat all he had killed, he did not regard, knowing himself to be a brave man: but there is nothing that great wits so much dread as the imputation of buffoonery, because the charge comes sometimes a little too near the truth" (Mary Lamb). This is parallel to Beatrice's vexation about the Hundred Merry Tales.

185. **the base, though bitter, disposition.** Beatrice, while bitter enough to invent slanders, is base enough to ascribe them to others. The implied inconsistency between bitterness and baseness is odd: Johnson read 'the base, the bitter'. Perhaps Benedick thinks them inconsistent, being himself outspoken in raillery.

185, 186. **puts the world into her person**, takes on herself to speak for the world.

Stage-direction. Q. has *Enter the Prince, Hero, Leonato, John and Borachio, and Conrade*: at 234 simply *Enter Claudio and Beatrice.* This arrangement would seem to be borne out by line 193, where Benedick speaks of Hero as 'this young lady'. On the other hand, it is unlikely that Benedick would speak as he does before Leonato and Hero, and it is clear from the next scene that Don John is not present: 'this young lady', then, means only 'the young lady you wot of'.

191, 192. **a lodge in a warren**, a gamekeeper's lodge, whose loneliness would beget melancholy. F. omits 'I' before second 'told'.

193. F. omits 'good'.

195. F. omits 'up'.

198. **flat**, downright, as still in 'That's flat'—a vulgarism which Shakespeare uses three times.

203. Benedick's persistence, after his slip on 'transgression', and the freedom of his language to the Prince, betray how Beatrice's taunts are rankling in him.

210. 'If it prove so, you have acted honourably.' The apology and the reservation are equally characteristic.

211. **a quarrel to you**: *to* denotes motion against (Abbott, § 187).

214. **misused**, abused. In Mod. E. these two words have partly exchanged meanings. Cf. *misuse*=deceive (ii. 2. 25).

214-233. This brilliant speech marks the climax of the feud between Benedick and Beatrice. It is now a *dignus vindice nodus*. Benedick's wit is most voluble in the absence of its object—a plain confession of discomfiture.

218. F., *and that I.*

219, 220. **impossible conveyance,** incredible dexterity (Staunton). For *impossible*=incredible, see line 122 above. *Conveyance* implies both rapidity and unfairness. Scot (*Discovery of Witchcraft*, bk. 13) uses *convey* of a juggler='to pass'; and it is Pistol's euphemism for 'steal'. The noun is common in the sense of 'underhand dealing'.

220. Benedick's 'comparisons' smack of the soldier.

223. **terminations**, terms. Is Benedick thinking of her *pointed* utterances? The word occurs only here in Shakespeare. F. omits 'her' before 'terminations'.

224. **the north star**, the pole-star, supposed the most remote.

I would not marry her. Thus does Benedick call on himself the Comic Nemesis.

226–229. He is thinking ⸲ ⸲ the three years which Hercules had to pass in the service of Omphale, who dressed him as a woman and made him spin.

226, 227. have turned. This form (preserved in 'ought to have done') probably arises from a desire to express the un-fulfilled nature of the action in the infinitive as well as in the auxiliary.

229. Ate is represented by Shakespeare as the Goddess of Discord.

some scholar. Latin, the language of the church, was used in exorcising spirits. So Dominie Sampson uses it on Meg Merrilees.

230. while she is here: on earth, that is. Hell is Ate's home (cf. "the infernal Ate" above, and *Julius Cæsar*, iii. 1. 271, "With Ate by his side come hot from hell"). But now she is on earth in the person of Beatrice, and hell therefore becomes an asylum to which men flock for escape.

231. sanctuary, an asylum, like the Sanctuary of Whitefriars in Scott's *Fortunes of Nigel*.

In this outburst, as in Othello's description of his adventures (*Othello*, i. 3. 140 seq.), we hear the contemporary of Raleigh and Drake.

239. Prester (*i.e.* Presbyter, Priest) **John,** a legendary monarch, supposed to maintain a Christian court in the Far East. Purchas, however, identifies him with the Prestegian or King of Abyssinia.

240. the great Cham, the Khan of Tartary.

241. the Pigmies, a mythical race of dwarfs, located by Milton "beyond the Indian Mount", by others south of Ethiopia. Both Prester John and the Pigmies figure in Marco Polo, who had been translated into English by Frampton in 1579.

245. F., *this Lady Tongue.*

In spite of Don Pedro's mischievous request, Benedick flees. His departure here is dramatically necessary that the plot against him may be concocted. For the same reason Beatrice is dismissed at line 304.

248–251. These lines seem to imply some passages between Benedick and Beatrice to which Shakespeare has given us no clue. They serve, as usual, to heighten the illusion of a length-ened intercourse. There may be a pun on 'double' in the sense of deceitful; and on 'single' in the sense of unmarried. Marshall thinks they refer to some game like Philippine; Furness that they are relics of an earlier play.

249. use, interest. F., *a single one.*

262. civil: with a pun on 'Seville'. Cotgrave gives 'a civil orange' (clearly a familiar colloquialism) as the equivalent of *aigre-douce*. It means, therefore, something both sweet and sour, and in this sense is applied to Claudio, who is neither merry nor well.

263. that jealous complexion: yellow is the hue of jealousy. F., *a jealous complexion*.

264. blazon, description; with a reference to its use as an heraldic term. See Glossary.

271. Note again the allusion to Leonato's fortune.

all grace, God, who is the source of grace. There is the same play on the word in *Macbeth*, v. 8. 72, "by the grace of Grace".

273. cue. Shakespeare, though not proud of his calling, naturally abounds in theatrical metaphors. See Glossary.

278. Beatrice is charmingly excited and happy at her cousin's engagement. The woman is too much for the wit. Claudio is formal; Hero is silent.

281. poor fool. *Fool* in E.E. may be a term of endearment.

282. the windy side: a nautical metaphor. Care is an enemy of whom we must keep the weather-gauge.

285. Good Lord, for alliance! Malone's explanation is correct—"Claudio has just called Beatrice *cousin*. I suppose, therefore, the meaning is, 'Good Lord, here have I got a new kinsman by marriage'." Other editors think it means much the same as 'heigh-ho for a husband'; but *alliance* never means marriage in Shakespeare. In the instances which Schmidt quotes to support this view the word always refers to the relationship established by marriage between two families, not between man and wife. So Bacon (*New Atlantis*) distinguishes 'marriage' and 'alliance'—"what is marriage to them but a very bargain; wherein is sought alliance, or portion, or reputation".

285, 286. goes to the world, gets married. In this expression 'the world' is perhaps contrasted with the church.

286. sunburnt: and therefore neglected. So Hamlet complains that he is "too much i' the sun" (i. 2. 67); "out of heaven's benediction to the warm sun" is quoted by Kent as a common saw (*Lear*, ii. 2. 168). These phrases, as B. Nicholson points out, are the imported produce of other climes. He compares *Psalm* cxxi. 6, "The sun shall not smite (in the old version 'burn') thee by day"—a Psalm then read at churching. Also *Song of Solomon*, i. 6, "I am black, because the sun hath looked upon me". In native metaphor Beatrice would say

that she was 'left out in the cold'. The contemporary prefer-
ence for blondes determines the choice of metaphor.

287. **heigh-ho for a husband** was the name of a popular
tune.

292. In Bandello, Re Piero is a married man.

296. **matter**, sense.

298. F., *out of question*; and so frequently.

As Conrade was born under Saturn, so was Beatrice
born under a dancing star. Wright notes that the sun was
believed to dance on Easter day.

300. How prettily Beatrice retracts her jest at Claudio's
'cousin', by her use of the plural embracing him and Hero!

304. **cry you mercy**, beg your pardon. She then apologizes
to the Prince for quitting his presence.

306. **the melancholy element.** In Shakespeare's physiology, a person's temperament depends on the mixture (*tem-
peramentum*) of the four humours, bile, blood, black bile, and
phlegm, which correspond to the four elements, fire, air, earth,
and water. Temperaments are choleric, sanguine, melancholy,
or phlegmatic according to the humour which preponderates.

309. **unhappiness.** The ordinary force of the word gives an
excellent, even a profound, sense. In sleep sad dreams may
visit Beatrice, but even in sleep her mirthful spirit is too strong
to yield to sad impressions; she knows they are only a dream,
and wakes herself with laughing. For the psychology of dreams
see *Romeo and Juliet*, i. 4. 53 to end. Schmidt and others
make *unhappiness* = mischief, which it can hardly do in this
context, if at all. *Unhappy* and *unhappiness* are certainly
used actively; but they connote malice rather than mischief:
they are applied to Richard III, to Tarquin, and if to Cupid
(*Love's Labour's Lost*, v. 2. 12), only by a lady whose sister he
has killed.

312, 313. **out of suit**: with a play on the legal sense. 'She
nonsuits her suitors with mockery.'

321. The time of the action is thus precisely marked. See
Introduction, § 12.

322. **just**, exact; Lat. *justus* often means 'regular'. This
sense survives only in the adverb.

seven-night, week. We still say 'fortnight', and 'se'n-
night' survived into this century, though the way in which Mr.
Collins employs it in *Pride and Prejudice* seems to show that it
was already (1812) felt to be old-fashioned.

The dramatic reason for this delay is, of course, to give
time for the plot against Benedick and Beatrice.

323. F. omits 'my'.

325. breathing, delay.

326. The Prince is a born matchmaker. He had proposed of himself to woo Hero by proxy, and now the idea of a match between Benedick and Beatrice comes from him, and the plan for bringing them together.

328. **a mountain of affection** is as natural a metaphor as 'a sea of troubles'.

328, 329. **th' one with th' other.** In E.E. *one* was pronounced *ōn*; as still in *only*.

332. **I am for you, I'll make one.** Old Leonato enters into the frolic with the zest of youth.

336. **any modest office,** anything required of me consistent with modesty. New votaries are said to be eager to make proselytes.

339. Don Pedro's praise of Benedick is not uncalled-for. We have, so far, seen little but his levity. We are now prepared for the good feeling which he is to display at the crisis.

340. **strain,** lineage; still so used by breeders of stock.

343. **practise,** use stratagems. The noun is similarly used in iv. 1. 187.

Scene 2

While the Prince and his allies are concocting the comic plot, a real plot is being concocted by the villains. Don John's first speech shows that he has just heard of the engagement; his last, that he does not yet know the date of the wedding. This scene must therefore follow immediately on the preceding. It offers no scope for dialogue or characterization; it is part of the machinery of the play, and the machinery here creaks a little.

1. **shall,** is going to: not confined to the first person in E.E.

5. **medicinable,** medicinal. In E.E. adjectives, especially those in *-ble*, *-less*, *-ful*, and *-ive*, are used both actively and passively. This particular adj. is always active in Shakespeare.

6. **affection,** wish: not limited to love. 'Whatever crosses his wishes runs parallel with mine.'

12. Another of those touches by which Shakespeare gives perspective to his action.

19. **temper,** to bring into condition, by mixing (of poison), by melting (of wax), or by hardening (of metal). We still 'temper' mortar as well as steel.

22. estimation, worth.   The transition is from (1) what you think, to (2) what is thought of you, to (3) your value.

hold up, maintain.

25. vex, afflict (like Lat. *vexare*).   The word has now lost much of its force.

30. F., *draw on Pedro.*

32. intend, pretend.   It lessens our apprehension to observe that all these suggestions proceed from Borachio of the re-assuring name.   Don John is the tool of his tool.

33. F., *in a love.*

37. instances, facts cited in proof.   Lat. *instantiæ.*

39. hear Margaret term me Claudio.   The explanation of this difficult passage is to be found in the genesis of this episode.   In making Borachio talk with the maid in her mistress's apparel, Shakespeare is following Ariosto, not Bandello.   Now Ariosto's villain is a suitor to the Princess Genevra.   Her maid, Dalinda, is his mistress.   This maid he induces to dress in Genevra's clothes by pretending that he wishes to sate his love with the make-believe that she is Genevra.   Shakespeare could not use this pretext, for his villain is not a rival lover.   But it suggested to him the simple plan of doubling the make-believe.   Margaret is induced to per-sonate Hero (in fun) by Borachio personating Claudio.   Nor will Shakespeare blacken his canvas by making her, like Dalinda, an accessory after the fact.   Why then does she not exculpate Hero?   Shakespeare blandly ignores the difficulty he has created, by keeping her out of the Fourth Act!

It looks simpler to say that Borachio merely wishes to escape detection.   But does he?   In line 31 above he says, "tell them that you know that Hero loves me"; and his own words in iii. 3. 145, "chiefly by my villany, which did confirm any slander that Don John had made", and v. 1. 229, "The lady is dead upon mine and my master's false accusation", taken with the Prince's in iv. 1. 90, "Who hath indeed, most like a liberal villain, Confess'd the vile encounters they have had", imply that he was seized and confessed on descending from the window. Yet it is not expressly said that he was recognized.   The fact is, that these difficulties exist rather for the reader than for the spectator, and Shakespeare is not careful of details not actu-ally represented.   [Many editors follow Theobald in reading *Borachio* for *Claudio.*]

41, 42. for in the meantime . . . absent.   Nothing more is said of this.   It is simply a difficulty which presents itself to Shakespeare's mind in sketching the plot.   This strongly con-firms the interpretation offered above.

43. disloyalty: in E.E. of infidelity in general, especially of infidelity in love.

44. jealousy . . . assurance, suspicion shall seem certainty. F., *truths*.

47. the working this. Such expressions are the result of a M.E. confusion of the verbal noun in *-ing*, the participle in *-ende*, and the gerund in *-enne* (Abbott, § 93).

49. F., *Be thou constant*. But Borachio would hardly address his master so even in the familiarity of conspiracy. Adam's use of *thee* to Orlando (*As You Like It*, ii. 3. 69) is not a true parallel, being in a rhymed passage; he reverts to *you* in ii. 7. 169. F. has the converse misprint in v. 1. 53.

51. their day of marriage. The two nouns joined by 'of' are treated as one compound noun.

Scene 3

The plot against Benedick's single blessedness is now put in execution. This is the only scene which cannot be precisely dated. Shakespeare does not mean that it should. The previous scenes fell on a Monday; the rest of the play occupies the Sunday, Monday, and Tuesday of the week following. Here we are made to feel that the engagement is several days old; yet in iii. 2 Benedick has been exhibiting love-symptoms for some time.

On Spedding's arrangement the third Act should begin here.

4. Shakespeare loves to lay his comic scenes out of doors.

5. The boy means, 'No sooner said than done. You may consider it brought.' Benedick reproves him by taking him literally.

7-33. The swan-song of the bachelor. This soliloquy is in designed contrast to that at the end of the scene. In declaring his independence, he defines the terms on which he is to capitulate.

Q. and F. mark exit after l. 5.

10. argument, subject. See Glossary.

14. tabor, tambourine. The tabor and the pipe are the instruments of peace. Cf. Wither's *Merry Christmas*, "Our lasses have provided them A bag-pipe and a tabour". For the sentiment cf. Lyly's *Alexander and Campaspe*, ii. 2, "Is the warlike sound of drum and trump turned to the soft noise of lyre and lute?"

15. armour, suit of armour.

16. carving, planning. The metaphor is suggested by 'cutting out'.

19. **orthography**: abstract for concrete, like 'villany' in iii. 3. 105. This figure, which identifies a person with one quality, is suited to the expression of indignation or contempt. By *orthography* (spelt *ortography* in Q.) Shakespeare appears to mean 'euphuist'. See note on *epithet*, v. 2. 59. In *Love's Labour's Lost*, v. 1. 22, the word is more correctly used.

19, 20. Cf. *Love's Labour's Lost*, v. 1. 39—

"*Moth*. They have been at a great feast of languages, and stolen the scraps.

"*Costard*. O, they have lived long on the alms-basket of words."

25, 26. **fair, wise, and virtuous** are Benedick's demands; and Beatrice is "fair, virtuous, and wise" (ll. 212–14). If he stipulates for riches now, he forgets that when his heart is touched.

30, 31. **noble . . . angel**: a familiar pun. The noble was worth 6s. 8d., the angel 10s. F. omits 'I'.

31. **an excellent musician**. It is a very natural touch that Benedick, himself unmusical, should stipulate for music in his wife. In the same way, Othello does not care for music (iii. 1. 17); yet he reckons it among his wife's chief graces that she is "an admirable musician" (iv. 1. 199).

32. **her hair . . . God**. This is thought to be a hit at the practice of dyeing the hair or of wearing false hair. Shakespeare certainly detested the practice, and attacks it again and again. But here it gives a better point to suppose that Benedick, having specified his requirements in a wife, graciously leaves the colour of her hair to Nature.

34–71. This little interlude, with the song it leads up to, makes a pretty transition from the soliloquy to the plot. Inspired by the music and the stillness, the style rises for a little to blank verse.

35, 36. For the sentiment cf. *Merchant of Venice*, v. 1. 56, "soft stillness and the night Become the touches of sweet harmony". Claudio speaks here, as does Romeo in *Romeo and Juliet*, ii. 2. 166, "How silver-sweet sound lovers' tongues by night, Like softest music to attending ears". But in both cases the speeches have descriptive rather than dramatic value. The poet, having created a beautiful situation, steps back from the picture and exclaims on it with pleasure. We feel no incongruity, so perfectly does he echo our own thought.

39. **We'll fit . . . pennyworth**, we'll give him his money's worth (Furness).

kid-fox: said to mean fox-cub, but no parallel is quoted. Others refer to M.E. *kidde*, shown (p.part. of *kythen*, to show),

and render 'detected'. Perhaps we should read 'hid fox'.
Hamlet (iv. 2. 33) says, "Hide fox, and all after", in allusion
to a game like hide-and-seek, in which one person (the 'fox')
hid, and the rest looked for him. Pegge (*Alphabet of Kenticisms*) defines 'hide fox' as "hide and seek, a child's play"
(Dowden).

    Stage-direction. F. omits, having given above, "Enter
Prince, L., C., and Jack Wilson". See Appendix on the Text.

    44. 'To disguise one's accomplishments, by miscalling them.'
Singers seem to have shown this foible since Horace's day.
Cf. the Tigellius of *Satire*, i. 3, "Omnibus hoc vitium est
cantoribus, inter amicos Ut nunquam inducant animum can-
tare rogati".

    52. There is the same pun on 'nothing' and 'noting' in
Winter's Tale, iv. 4. 624, "no hearing, no feeling, but my sir's
song, and admiring the nothing of it". And 'nothing' rhymes
to 'a-doting' in *Sonnet* xx. Pun and rhyme passed (1) because
the *o* was long in E.E., (2) because *t* and *th* were sometimes
interchanged, especially in words of Romance origin.

    55–58. Lorenzo's description of "the man that hath no music
in himself" (*Merchant of Venice*, v. 1. 83), as "fit for treasons,
stratagems and spoils", must not be taken as Shakespeare's
last word. Benedick is unmusical; so is Hotspur; so is Othello;
so, apparently, is Prince Hal. All these have this in common,
that they are soldiers and men of action, not of sentiment.

    59. The song gives a mocking echo to the theme of the play.
Both Benedick and Claudio are inconstant, though not in this
sense. The first line may have suggested Milton's "Weep no
more, woful shepherds, weep no more".

    66. Hey nonny, nonny: the burden of many a gay old
song, like Shakespeare's own "It was a lover and his lass"
(*As You Like It*, v. 3. 17).

    67. For **more** and **moe** see Glossary. *Moe* is used only with
plural nouns (expressed or understood), or with nouns of plural
meaning. Here supply *ditties*. This proves that **dumps** means
melancholy, not (as it might otherwise do) a melancholy song.

    70. leavy: the only form in Shakespeare.

    73. If Balthasar is fishing for a compliment, he catches a
well-earned rebuke.

    76. been: spelt *bin* in Q., and so pronounced.

    should have. The unreal nature of the assumption is
expressed in the subordinate clause. Cf. ii. 1. 226, and note
there.

    79. night-raven: a poetical bird, unknown to ornithology.
It cannot be the owl, for they are mentioned together—"The

dismal night-raven and tragic owl" (Peele's *Battle of Alcazar*); "Night-ravens and owls to rend my bloody side" (Peele's *David and Bathsabe*). Cf. also Spenser, *Epithalamion*—

> "Let not the shriech Oule, nor the Storke be heard,
>   Nor the night Raven, that still deadly yels".

Some identify it with the night-heron (*Ardea nycticorax*). Goldsmith, apparently from personal knowledge, says that the bittern was so called: "I remember in the place where I was a boy with what terror this bird's (*i.e.* the bittern's) note affected the whole village. . . . If any person in the neighbourhood died, they supposed it could not be otherwise, for the night-raven had foretold it."

81–83. Another of those unused touches which lend concreteness to the picture.

86–202. These lines should be compared, point by point, with the scene which follows. Here the plotters dwell chiefly on Beatrice's passion and suffering, aiming artfully alike at Benedick's masculine vanity and at his manly compassion. Detraction is thrown in jestingly, and qualified by the Duke's "I love Benedick well".

93. "Is that how things stand?"

100. life, reality.

discovers, reveals.

104. The first **you** is ethical dative; the second is addressed to Claudio.

108, 110. would, says Abbott (§ 331), is not = should, but means 'I was ready to'. But 'would' is certainly sometimes used for 'should' even in the first person.

112. gull, trick; more usually of the person tricked, in which sense it survived into this century. See the parody of Crabbe in *Rejected Addresses*.

115. hold it up, keep it up.

128. told us of. *Q., told of us.*

130. between can be used with the sing. of a bipartite noun. The sheet would be folded. So in *Hamlet*, iv. 5. 119, the reading of Qq. and F1, "between the chaste unsmirched brow", is probably sound.

131. That, that was it.

132. halfpence. The halfpenny was a better symbol of smallness when it was made of silver, whether it was half of the silver penny or a separate coin. In 1600 Elizabeth contracted with the mint-master for the coinage of silver halfpence. Silver halfpence were first issued by Edward I; copper halfpence not till Charles II's reign.

146. F., *he would but make.*

148. an alms, a good deed. Originally a singular noun, f. *elmesse*, Gk. ἐλεημοσύνη; and probably singular everywhere in Shakespeare. Cf. 'riches'.

156. and her guardian. It is implied that Beatrice is an orphan.

158. daffed ... respects, put aside all other considerations. It does not diminish the value of a prize to know that our betters covet it.

168. contemptible is often used by Shakespeare for 'contemptuous', and *vice versâ*. For the indifference of such adjs. with regard to voice see note on ii. 2. 5.

170. a good outward happiness, a handsome exterior.

171. F., *'Fore God.*

173. wit corresponds to **wise.** The gradual limitation of its sense dates from the Restoration.

174. F. assigns to *Leon.*

176. F., *you may see.*

178. F. omits 'most'.

183. large, broad. See Glossary.

187. counsel, reflection. We can take counsel with ourselves as well as with others. So 'on advice'=on reflection.

193. unworthy so good. F. inserts *to have* needlessly.

194. dinner. But the time is evening, and the Elizabethans dined at noon or earlier. This is a mere slip on Shakespeare's part.

200. and no such matter, and there is nothing of the sort. (Lamb, whose style is impregnated with Elizabethan idiom, uses this phrase in *Tombs in Westminster Abbey*.)

201. dumb-show: because both would be tongue-tied. There is an allusion to the primitive dramatic practice of exhibiting the subject of an act first in dumb-show. See the play-scene in *Hamlet*.

203-226. In this matchless soliloquy, in its thoughts and the succession of its thoughts, we feel the very pulse of the masculine heart. Abrupt sentences enforce, not against his will, the amazed conviction that Beatrice loves him. He must return the compliment. Ah, but he must make the advances; then he must pocket his pride: it has brought him censure anyway. As he reviews Beatrice's charms in the light of others' judgment, his jauntiness returns. He will be as great a fanatic for love as he has been a heretic against it. Not till then does he think of the gauntlet of jeers that he must run. But he cares little; his line is taken.

204. sadly borne, seriously conducted. Benedick's astonishment expresses itself in abrupt repetitions, very different from the airy antitheses of his former soliloquy.

206. have their full bent: like a bow strained to the utmost. For the metaphor cf. iv. 1. 185. F., *the full bent.*

211, 212. This manly utterance shows that Benedick's vanity is but skin-deep, unlike the irritable egotism of Claudio. It should be set off against his chagrin at being called jester; together they betoken a core of seriousness.

212–220. Observe how, as his determination settles, his style regains its elasticity.

214. reprove, disprove. 'Reprove' and 'reproof' are used by Shakespeare either of refutation or of reproach.

217–222. The metaphors are soldierly. *Broken* and *career* are both drawn from the tilt-yard. Cf. v. 1. 134, 135. Benedick will not expose his *tendresse* to his friends. Caprice, which has hitherto shielded him from love, shall now protect him from satire.

221. sentences, saws. Lat. *sententiæ.*

229. Benedick's new-born passion expresses itself in blank verse.

235. withal: an emphatic 'with' at the end of a clause. Beatrice's manner shows a trace of resentment from their last encounter. Of course the 'marks of love' and the 'double meaning' are due to Benedick's fancy.

Act III—Scene I

The plot against Beatrice is now carried out. This scene resembles the preceding in general plan, as is proper from the similarity of the feats to be performed; but the details are varied, partly to avoid sameness, partly because Beatrice is a woman. (1) The use of blank verse indicates a higher level of feeling, as women talk of love more seriously than men. (2) There is no introductory soliloquy; there are no asides from Beatrice; and her final speech is in a style even more heightened than the body of the scene. (3) Hero dwells less on Benedick's sufferings than on Beatrice's pride. (4) The whole scene is much shorter; Beatrice's nature is simpler than Benedick's, and the trick is being played for the second time.

The time is Sunday (l. 103).

1. Scan **Margaret** as dissyllable, **parlour** as trisyllable. See note on Elizabethan Pronunciation, (γ) (1).

run thee. Cf. iv. 1. 21, " Stand thee by ". Abbott (§ 212) thinks that *thee* is used as being less emphatic than ' thou ' after an emphatic verb. The substitution of ' you ' (originally objective) for ' ye ' is first noticed with imperatives and interrogatives, *i.e.* when it follows the verb (Kellner, § 212).

3. **Proposing,** talking. See Glossary.

4. **Whisper her ear.** This dative construction is common with persons, rare with things. Ursula: Q. *Ursley.*

7. **It is another garden scene.** Hero's pretty descriptive touch matches Claudio's exclamation in ii. 3. 35.

9–11. Critics have thought that this simile was pointed at some contemporary — Essex or Cecil. Dr. Furnivall indeed suggests that these lines were interpolated after Essex's rebellion in 1601. But they occur in the Quarto of 1600. No such allusion is meant; if Shakespeare thought of any real favourite, it was surely Wolsey. The simile is not unnatural. In this poetic scene, Hero's mood of quiet mischief naturally brims over into similes.

12. **propose,** conversation. Cf. l. 3 above. F., *purpose*: but there is no evidence for the accentuation *purpóse*, and to read *púrpose* brings two stress-inversions together and gives an intolerable rhythm.

14. Margaret is thus quietly excluded from the delicate trick played on Beatrice. She is too boisterous, and too nearly concerned in a more dangerous plot.

23. **only** belongs to ' hearsay '.

24. **like a lapwing.** The lapwing runs with its head down to escape notice till it can get to a distance from its nest.

26. These similes are steeped in sunshine, and eke out the scanty descriptions to which Shakespeare was limited by the conditions of his art.

30. **woodbine** is here the same as honeysuckle, though a word of wider application, used of other climbing plants, and even distinguished from the honeysuckle in *Midsummer-Night's Dream,* iv. i. 47, " So doth the woodbine the sweet honeysuckle Gently entwist ".

34. Compare this with Don Pedro's opening words, ii. 3. 85.

41. Scan:

" But I | persuad | ed them, | if they | loved Ben' | dick ".

Or ' persuaded ' may form a dissyllable, as in *Two Gentlemen,* v. 4. 65, " Could have persuaded me: now I dare not say ".

42. **wish** is treated as an auxiliary, and followed by the infinitive without 'to'.

45. **as full as fortunate.** Wright and others render "as fully as fortunate", which is strange English. The meaning wanted is, "Does not Benedick deserve a wife at least as good as Beatrice?" The first 'as' seems superfluous. The editors of the later Folios, feeling this, put a comma at 'full'.

55. **project,** outline, vague idea. The metaphor seems to be, 'She is so cased in self-esteem that she cannot receive any impression of love'.

56. **self-endeared,** in love with herself.

58. **lest she make sport.** The reading of Q., *lest sheele make,* is just possible. 'Lest' is not elsewhere followed by 'will' in Shakespeare, but it is followed by 'would' in *Merry Wives,* iii. 5. 105. Cf. (though not quite parallel), "I drede lest God on us will take venjance" (*Townley Mysteries,* p. 21).

60. **how,** however.

61. **spell him backward,** as witches do their prayers, making his merits faults. Beatrice's 'comparisons' in ii. 1. 7–9, and elsewhere, are humorously exaggerated for her reproof, with a zest that surprises us in the demure Hero. Perhaps, in the new-born superiority of her betrothal, she is paying off a few old scores against her masterful cousin.

63. F., *anticke.*

70. **purchaseth,** earneth, deserveth. See Glossary.

72. **from all fashions,** peculiar: *from* = away from, different from.

76. **press me to death:** alluding to the *peine forte et dure,* the punishment inflicted on one who refused to plead. "Hero means that Beatrice would first reduce her to silence by her mockery, and then punish her for not speaking" (Wright).

79. Q., *It were a better death then* (*i.e.* than) *die;* F 1, *death to die;* F 2, *a bitter death to die,* perhaps under the impression that Hero is speaking of herself. But she is speaking of Benedick, and means that he had better sigh to death than be mocked to death. 'To' is often omitted with the infinitive after 'better'.

84. **honest slanders,** slanders that will not touch her reputation. This feminine threat depends for its success on the assumption that Beatrice does not wish Benedick cured. There is some irony here. Hero herself is to be the victim of slanders by no means honest.

90. **prized,** esteemed.

93. For the order cf. *Cymbeline*, i. 1. 87, "Always reserved my holy duty".

96. **argument,** reasoning power. See Glossary.

100, 101. Ursula means, "When are you going to be married?" Hero, in high spirits over the ruse, chooses to take her literally, and answers, "Why, every day", *i.e.* 'Once married, always married'; then, dropping her levity, says seriously, "To-morrow".

104. **limed,** caught with bird-lime. Beatrice has been compared to a lapwing (l. 24), her spirits to haggerds (l. 36). The metaphor is kept up in **traps.** The editor of F 1, not seeing this, read *she's tane*.

105, 106. Rhyme marks maxim and exit.

107–end. As the body of the scene is in blank verse, a still higher level of emotion can only be indicated by rhyme. A similar sequence of quatrains and couplets is used in *Locrine*, iv. 1, to express intense emotion.

107. **What fire is in mine ears?** It is a common belief that a person's ears burn when he is being talked of behind his back. That this belief is referred to is clear from l. 110. But Shakespeare transmutes the commonplace; the fire in Beatrice's ears burns contempt and pride out of her heart. Beatrice has not indeed been talked of in absence, but she believes that her presence is unknown.

Can this be true? Beatrice, unlike Benedick, suspects no trick. A man is more accustomed to hoaxing and to being hoaxed.

110. 'Such qualities are never praised in their owner's absence.' Beatrice thinks only of Benedick's love and her own misdeeds. Her repentance is alloyed by no touch of complacency, no fear of ridicule, no care for consistency.

112. The metaphor of the "haggerds of the rock" is still ringing in her ears.

116. **better than reportingly,** on better evidence than hearsay—a shy admission that Benedick's merits had already impressed her.

Scene 2

This scene falls into two vividly contrasted parts, the 'chaffing' of Benedick and the accusation of Hero. In the height of their triumph, the merry plotters are themselves tricked, and fall into Don John's snare as easily as Benedick has fallen into theirs.

This scene follows close on scene 1 (see l. 68); the time is Sunday afternoon (see ll. 72 and 79).

1–66. Beatrice, who had feared no ridicule, gets off with little. Margaret's covert gibes in scene 5 are all that correspond to this cross-fire of banter.

1. See note on i. 1. 135. It may be, however, that Don Pedro's resolve and Claudio's offer are mere pretence, contrived to put Benedick in a dilemma between love and courtesy.

1, 2. consummate: here p. part., now adj. Dr. Murray thus explains the history of such forms:—M.E. following French formed adjs. direct from Latin p. parts., those in -*ate* being from verbs of the first conjugation. From some of these adjs. identical causative verbs were formed, which then developed regular participles in -*ed*, the original words then becoming obsolete or surviving as adjs., *e.g.* 'separate'. 'Situate' is the only participle of this form admitted in Mod. E., though Mr. Meredith ventures on 'dedicate' and Mr. Pater on 'deteriorate'.

3. bring, escort.

3, 4. vouchsafe me, give me leave. Only here is the verb used absolutely, but 'to bring' is easily supplied. See Glossary.

5, 6. new gloss, untarnished lustre. The metaphor suggests the simile, rather than exactly matches it, though a new dress would doubtless lose some of its splendour in a child's eyes when he was forbidden to wear it. The simile is a prose version of Juliet's exclamation in the same circumstances—"so tedious is this day As is the night before some festival To an impatient child that hath new robes And may not wear them" (*Romeo and Juliet*, iii. 2. 28–31).

7. only goes with Benedick.

be bold with Benedick, venture to ask him.

10. the little hangman. The name of this loathed office ('hangman' in E.E. stands for 'executioner') would easily pass into a general term of opprobrium, a sense in which I have heard it used in Scotch. Similarly, Cupid is called "a shrewd unhappy gallows" in *Love's Labour's Lost*, v. 2. 12. And so doubtless "the hangman boys" in *Two Gentlemen*, iv. 4. 60.

11. Wright proves conclusively that there is no allusion to the proverb "As the fool thinketh So the bell clinketh", which means, not that the fool speaks as he thinks, but that he reads his own thoughts into the sound of the bell.

16. The word truant may have suggested true, as in *Sonnet* ci, "O *truant* Muse, what shall be thy amends For thy neglect of *truth* in beauty dyed?"

18. A fair inference from Benedick's own boast, i. 1. 223.

19. Steevens quotes Beaumont and Fletcher's *The False One*, ii. 3, to show that lovers suffered, or affected to suffer, from toothache—"You had best be troubled with the toothache too, For lovers ever are".

22. A punning allusion to the punishment of traitors by hanging, drawing (*i.e.* disembowelling), and quartering.

25. Q. and F., *cannot master*; corr. Pope.

28, 29. For the play on the two meanings of **fancy**, see Glossary.

30–33. or in the shape . . . doublet: omitted in F. See Appendix on the Text. To "wear strange suits" was a characteristic of the fantastic Englishman. See Portia's description of her English suitor (*Merchant of Venice*, i. 2. 79), "I think he bought his doublet in Italy, his round hose in France, his bonnet in Germany . . ." Among many allusions, there is one in Dekker's *Seven Deadly Sins* (1606) which seems to be a reminiscence of this passage in *Much Ado*: "For an Englishman's suit is like a traitor's body that hath been hanged, drawne, and quartered, and is set up in several places", &c. The odd simile reminds us of Claudio's pun above.

32. slops, wide breeches; originally 'slop-hose'. The word survives in the language of sailors, and the article in the clown's breeches in the pantomime.

35. F., *would have it to appear.*

37. Rosalind pretends that a lover's appearance should demonstrate a careless desolation; but on one who has hitherto affected the plain soldier love has the opposite effect.

39–44. These lines recall Beatrice's avowed aversion to a bearded husband. To such echoes from scene to scene is due some of the wonderful resonance of Shakespeare's style.

50. to wash his face, to use cosmetics, as the next line shows. Our forefathers were not so rude as the literal interpretation of these words would make them, though Erasmus thought it 'nonsense' to wash one's face oftener than once a day.

53, 54. now . . . now does not mean 'at one time . . . at another time', for the 'stops' or 'frets' belong to the lute, being lengths of wire or cord wrapt round the finger-board at intervals of a semitone. The second 'now' may be a misprint. Walker read *new-governed*. The lute was used to accompany love-songs.

56. F. omits second 'conclude'.

62. with her face upwards, in her lover's arms—an appropriate end for one who is dying for love. Theobald would read, "with her heels upwards"; and his view, though ridiculed by modern editors, is supported by Beaumont and Fletcher's *Wild Goose Chase*, i. 3:

> "love cannot starve me;
> For if I die o' th' first fit, I am unhappy,
> And worthy to be buried with my heels upwards".

Suicides appear to have been buried face downwards. Don Pedro may have had this in mind.

63. Such a charm for the toothache is given by Chettle—

A AB ILLA HVRS GIBBELLA.

65. hobby-horses, laughing jackasses. The hobby-horse was one of the parts in the morris-dance. As a term of contempt it is elsewhere in Shakespeare applied only to women.

67. But from v. 4. 21 it does not appear that Benedick had broached the subject.

68. Hero and Margaret: a natural mistake on Claudio's part. From Ursula's question in iii. 1. 100, and from scene 5 of this Act, it is clear that Margaret, not Ursula, is Hero's immediate attendant. Ursula may have acted as maid to Beatrice.

72. Good den, good even. The greeting shows that it is past noon. By postponing his accusation to the last moment Don John renders investigation impossible. This is the only scene in which Don Pedro speaks to his brother. The curtness of his replies is in marked contrast to the Bastard's clumsy assumption of civility.

82, 83. discover, reveal.

85. aim better at me, form a truer estimate of me.

86, 87. Q. and F. bracket ('I think . . . heart').

90, 91. circumstances shortened, not to beat longer about the bush. *Circumstance* is common in the singular in the sense of 'circumlocution'; cf. *Merchant of Venice*, i. 1. 154, "To wind about my love with circumstance". The plural here may be a misprint due to the following *s*; but cf. *Taming of the Shrew*, v. 1. 27, "To leave frivolous circumstances". The ordinary sense, 'particulars', hardly fits either context.

97. paint out, depict to the full. *Out* added to verbs shows that an action is developed to a finish.

99. fit her to it, show that she deserves it.

101. From the subsequent accounts of this episode it does not appear that Borachio actually enters the room. In Ariosto's version, however, Polinesso does so. Here, as in ii. 2, we see the plot in the making.

102. Q. and F. put comma after 'her'; corr. Hanmer.

103. An artful appeal, as Borachio had suggested, to Claudio's self-esteem.

104. There is no generous reaction in Claudio. The calumny takes him weak with laughter at his own wit; with amazed ejaculations he turns to his patron. His first coherent thought is of revenge.

110, 111. Q. and F. have no comma. Rowe's punctuation brings out the antithesis between *to-night* and *to-morrow*. Moreover, the recapitulatory 'there' implies that 'in the congregation' stands at the head of its clause.

118–120. The Prince's emotion expresses itself in words which form a broken verse, echoed by Claudio and Don John.

Scene 3

It is the height of comic art to introduce the frustration of the plot before its consummation in the church scene. The edge is thus taken off a situation which otherwise would be intolerably pathetic. This is 'comic irony' in the full sense, when the spectators are aware of some happy circumstance of which the actors are ignorant. The ministers of justice are conceived in the same comic spirit. Police duties were discharged in Shakespeare's days by watchmen—a kind of special constables, whose incompetence is a standing joke with Elizabethan writers. How little need Shakespeare had to exaggerate their stupidity is shown by a letter of Lord Burghley to Sir F. Walsingham (1586), in which he tells that at Enfield he came upon twelve constables 'in a plump' waiting to catch three young men, of whom they knew nothing except that one of them had a hooked nose!

Mr. Verity thinks that Lyly's *Endimion* (iv. 2) supplied the germ of this scene; and certainly there are several reminiscences of *Endimion* in Shakespeare's comedies. In turn, Dogberry's charge suggested a scene in May's *Heir* (1620), and in *Lady Allimony* (iii. 5) (published 1659). I have not thought it necessary to explain all Dogberry's blunders.

The time is about 1 A.M. of Monday.

2. Verges is the shadow to Dogberry's substance. He can only echo or amplify, or at most hesitate a doubt. But, like the shadow, his presence adds immensely to the illusion of reality. Shakespeare is very fond of creating such characters in couples.

7. The chief constable had to explain his men's duties to them. So a judge 'charges' a jury.

9, 10. **to be constable**, deputy constable, that is; for Dogberry himself is 'the right master constable' (l. 153).

11. **George Seacole**, not the *Francis Seacole* of iii. 5. 52, who is evidently the same as the *Sexton* of iv. 2, a man of sense. 'Sea-coal' occurs as a common noun in *2 Henry IV*, ii. 1. 95. In some instances, Sarrazin thinks, a common noun in one play suggested a proper name in another of slightly later date.

14. **well - favoured**, good - looking. See Glossary under *favour*. The sentiment is parodied from Lyly, "To be rich is the gift of fortune, to be wise the grace of God".

19. Cf. *As You Like It*, ii. 5. 37, "I give heaven thanks, and make no boast of them".

23. In the ill-lit streets of that day a lantern formed part of the equipment of the watch. The spelling of Q. and F., *lanthorne* (corr. Steevens), is a piece of popular etymology, from the thin lamina of horn which served for glass. The word is really from Lat. *lanterna*.

34. F., *to babble and talk*.

34, 35. **most tolerable and not to be endured.** This famous phrase at once took root in the language. Cf. Heywood's *Fair Maid of the Exchange*, iii. 3 (1607). It may have been suggested by an expression in Northbrook's *Treatise on Plays* (1579), "Plays and players are not tolerable nor to be endured". "Intolerable and not to be endured" occurs in *Taming of the Shrew*, v. 2. 94.

40. Johnson tells us that in 1765 the watchmen of Lichfield still carried bills.

41. F., *them that are*.

46. We gather from Lupton's *London and the Country Carbonadoed* (1632) that this was a familiar excuse of the watchmen in attempts to extort blackmail.

49. **true man**, honest man. Cf. *Measure for Measure*, iv. 2. 46, "Every true man's apparel fits your thief".

50. **meddle or make**: a tautological expression, recommended by its alliteration to characters like Dogberry, Dr. Caius, and Pandarus. *Make* here = have to do with.

50, 51. **the more is for, the better for.**

54, 55. **they that touch pitch**: from the Apocryphal *Ecclesiasticus*, xiii. 1.

60. While Dogberry swells with conscious magnanimity at Verges' admiration, the latter ventures to interject an order of his own, but is at once caught up by his partner. Steevens

thought that this part of the charge might be a burlesque on
The Statutes of the Streets (printed 1595), one of which forbids
any sudden outcry in the still of the night under a penalty of
3*s*. 3*d*.

70. present, represent. This is not a blunder of Dogberry's;
cf. *2 Henry IV*, v. 2. 79, " The image of the king whom I presented "—spoken by the Lord Chief Justice.

74. Q., *statutes*. Conversely in Greene's *Looking Glass*, l.
1547, " The statutes of our gods are thrown down " (Qq. 1, 2, 3).

without, unless. This use of *without* is a vulgarism put
into the mouth of such characters as Speed, Dromio, and Dogberry.

79. Dogberry laughs in the consciousness of superior knowledge and the prompt suppression of Verges' attempt at
criticism. The first *ha* is interrogative = eh?

80, 81. Part of the oath of a grand-juryman still runs—" The
King's counsel, your fellows', and your own you shall observe
and keep secret ".

84. the church-bench. Such benches may still be seen
inside church porches.

85. The sensible and practical tone of this parting injunction
is hardly in keeping with the burlesque style of the rest of
Dogberry's orders; nor is the prompt action of the watch
exactly what we should have expected from them. But these
things are necessary to the action; and it may be said that
Dogberry is not without a vein of racy sense, when the man
is not eclipsed by the magistrate.

88. It is not for nothing that Dogberry and Verges here
retire and leave the arrest to be made by the watch. Had
they overheard Borachio themselves they could hardly have
failed to realize the danger, and to warn Leonato in time. But
now Justice must run its course.

93. Mass. See note on iv. 2. 47.

my elbow itched: apparently (like the 'pricking of the
thumbs' in *Macbeth*) an omen of some ill neighbourhood. Cf.
Yorkshire Tragedy, i. 1—

> " *Ralph*. Now my nose itches for news.
> *Oliver*. And so does mine elbow."

94. scab: a term of contempt.

97. pent-house, shed, lean-to.

98. like a true drunkard: alluding (1) to his name, for which
see *Dramatis Personæ* and Glossary; (2) to the proverb, *In
vino veritas.* This expression makes it probable that the word

borachio was already in use in the sense of 'drunkard', though no instance is known before 1607.

103, 105. villany. Conrade means 'act of villainy', Borachio means 'villain', using the abstract for the concrete, a figure of which Shakespeare is very fond. His point is, 'You need not wonder that an act of villany should cost so much, but rather that any scoundrel should be able to afford it'.

108. unconfirmed, inexperienced. A pedantic word so used by Holofernes (*Love's Labour's Lost*, iv. 2. 19). With the rest of this scene compare *Othello*, ii. 3; *Antony and Cleopatra*, ii. 7 (on board Pompey's galley); above all, *2 Henry IV*, v. 3 (in Shallow's orchard). Drink makes Borachio argumentative, as it makes Cassio quarrelsome, Lepidus inquisitive, and Silence a mere sounding-board. In all cases, Shakespeare observes that it numbs the power of actively correlating ideas, and leaves its victim at the mercy of a single train of association.

116. This has been supposed to refer to Amorphus or the Deformed, a character in Ben Jonson's *Cynthia's Revels*. But that play was not acted till 1600, and Amorphus is a fantastic traveller and lady-killer.

117. this seven year: F., *years*. In O.E. certain neuter nouns, *e.g.* 'year', 'night', &c., had the same form in both numbers. This usage is common in Shakespeare after numerals, especially in the language of vulgar persons. Cf. 'a thousand pound', iii. 5. 23 (Dogberry *loquitur*).

124. Pharaoh's soldiers: perhaps in a picture of the passage of the Red Sea.

reechy, smoky. Reechy : reeky :: church : kirk.

125. god Bel's priests: presumably a representation of the story of Bel and the Dragon, from the apocryphal *Daniel*.

126. the shaven Hercules. Hercules is usually represented with a beard; cf. "The beards of Hercules and frowning Mars" (*Merchant of Venice*, iii. 2. 85). Some picture of him without this appendage had caught Shakespeare's eye; hence the epithet. But in what scene could he be so represented? The editors follow Steevens in referring to his servitude with Omphale (see on ii. 1. 226). But I find no authority for this view; in fact, Sidney's allusion (also to a picture) would prove the contrary: "Hercules, painted *with his great beard* and furious countenance, in woman's attire, spinning at Omphale's commandment" (*Apology for Poetry*). And here he is plainly in man's attire. A grotesque episode, first mentioned by Lycophron (*Cassandra*, 35), may be put forward in competition with Warburton's *Samson* and Brae's *Hercules Gallus*. There it is implied that Hercules killed the sea-monster to which Hesione was exposed by jumping down its throat, but lost his hair from the heat of its belly!

129. F. omits second 'I'.

135. leans me: ethical dative.

136, 137. I tell this tale vilely. See note on Borachio's drunkenness above.

138. possessed: intermediate in meaning between 'influenced', as in "possessed with a Fury" (i. 1. 172), and 'informed', as in "Possess the people in Messina here How innocent she died" (v. 1. 268).

141. they: F., *thy*.

148. temple: in Shakespeare of any church.

151 seq. In spite of Gifford, it is hard to believe that Jonson was not alluding to this scene in the Induction to *Bartholomew Fair* (1614): "and then a substantial watch to have stolen in upon them, and taken them away, with mistaking words, as the fashion is in stage practice". The speaker is the Stage-keeper, a *laudator temporis acti*. No doubt there are other such scenes in Elizabethan drama, but none so famous as this. The same Induction contains a gibe at 'tempests' and 'servant-monsters', which can hardly refer to anything but Caliban.

157. a lock, a love-lock, "often plaited and tied with riband, and hanging at the ear" (Schmidt).

158. Conrade, who is sober, attempts to protest. Borachio's levity is another proof of his condition.

164-165. A triple pun. Commodity=(1) goods, (2) a bargain, a handful; **taken up=**(1) got on credit, (2) apprehended; **bills=**(1) bonds, (2) halberts.

166. A commodity in question, a doubtful bargain, with a quibble on the meaning 'under examination'. Cf. *Winter's Tale*, v. 1. 198, "Has these poor men in question".

Scene 4

Except for the glimpse it gives of the wedding preparations, this short scene does nothing to advance the action. But it has a dramatic value far beyond its apparent importance. It shows us the spirit in which our two heroines advance to the great crisis of Act iv, so that we enter the church, as it were, by their side. Hero is heavy with vague forebodings; Beatrice is sick of Benedick's malady: it is Margaret who fills the scene in boisterous spirits, ignorant of the mischief she has done.

The time is almost 5 A.M. of Monday.

6. Q. and F., *rebato*; corr. Hanmer.

8. **'s.** The pronoun is most frequently omitted with *is, was, has*, where an appellative or oath precedes, as here and in line 18 below (Abbott, § 400).

10. Hero's depression makes her answer testily to Margaret's persistence.

12. **the hair**, the false hair which formed part of the tire and was attached to the cap.

16. **exceeds**, is surpassing; used absolutely, like 'excels' and 'passes'.

17. **a night-gown in respect of**, a dressing-gown in comparison with. Many of the terms which follow are obscure; we may be forgiven for doubting if Shakespeare himself was so familiar with dress-making as this glib enumeration would imply.

18. **cuts**, indentations on the edge of a gown, showing an inlay of different material. (Distinguished from 'slashes', which were in the body of the garment.)

19. **down sleeves, side sleeves.** "Beside a sleeve which fitted more or less closely to the arm and extended to the wrist, there was another, for ornament, which hung from the shoulder, wide and open" (Grant White). The latter is certainly the 'side sleeve'. *Side* is O.E. *síd*, long, used of clothes, in which sense it still survives in Scotch. The E.E. use is proved by 'side-coats' in *Lingua*, iii. 2 (1607). 'Down sleeves' should then mean the ordinary close sleeves; but there is no apparent connection between name and thing, and Steevens was perhaps right in reading "set with pearls down sleeves".

19, 20. **round underborne**, edged on the inside, so as to stiffen the skirt.

20. **quaint**, dainty, *recherché*. See Glossary.

22. Cf. *Richard III*, ii. 3, 42, "By a divine instinct men's minds mistrust Ensuing dangers". Whether Shakespeare believed in presentiments or not, he employs them frequently with great dramatic effect. The pity inspired by the sight of a fellow-being advancing on his doom is enhanced by his vague apprehension of evil. The ground of this lies in the sympathy between our knowledge and the victim's apprehension, producing the desire to impart that 'little more' which would avert the catastrophe. Here pity is kept within the bounds of comedy by the further knowledge that the plot is out.

28. Cf. *Hebrews*, xiii. 4, "Marriage is honourable in all".

30. '**saving your reverence**', *sauf votre respect*. The phrase, often corrupted to 'sirreverence', regularly introduces

some offensive expression. Margaret means that Hero is so prudish that she considers even 'husband' an offensive expression. This is brought out by the punctuation in the text, which is practically that of Q. and F.

31. wrest, misinterpret.

34. light. The play on the sense 'wanton' is kept up in the dialogue with Beatrice.

37. Beatrice's greeting is very natural and touching. Hero answers a little brusquely, perhaps remembering the part she had played in the garden.

40. Clap 's into, start off, please: 's is for 'us', ethical dative.

'**Light o' love**', an old dance tune, first noticed in 1578. The music was recovered by Hawkins, and is given in Boswell's Variorum Edition. The "very proper dittie: to the tune of Lightie Love", printed in Chappell, p. 224, is probably the original ballad, for the words 'lightie love' recur frequently. Its author was Leonard Gybson.

40, 41. without a burden, without bass, "there being no man or men on the stage to sing one", as Capell says. See Glossary. Margaret's unnatural exaltation would have a tragic cast, but for our knowledge that all will end well.

43. you'll see: F., *you'll look.*

44. barns, bairns: a provincialism used by the old shepherd in *Winter's Tale*, and by the clown in *All's Well* in the proverb "Barnes are blessings".

45. There is the same joke in *Merchant of Venice*, ii. 2. 9, "Scorn running with thy heels".

47. 'T is almost five o'clock. To anticipate the disclosure of Borachio's plot, Shakespeare is obliged to put the wedding at the earliest possible hour after sunrise. It was not till the Act of 4 George IV that the hours of celebration were fixed from 8 A.M. to noon; there is no mention of hours in the earlier statute of 26 George II: and that five was not an impossible hour appears from *The Puritan*, v. 1: "Hie thee; 'tis past five; bid them open the church-door; my sister is almost ready". Morning marriages are a relic of the Roman Catholic practice of taking the nuptial mass after the ceremony; the mass was taken fasting.

49, 50. Margaret's proverbial question and Beatrice's answer are explained by the couplet in *Wit's Recreation* (1654):

"Nor hawk, nor hound, nor horse, those letters h. h. h.,
But *ach* itself, 'tis Brutus' bones attaches".

The noun 'ache' was then pronounced like the name of the letter (the verb was pronounced and even written 'ake'); Beatrice plays both on this and on 'For', which in Margaret's question means 'for desire of', in her answer 'because of', as in 'sick for fear'. This pronunciation of *ache* seems to have survived into this century, to judge from *Pendennis*, ch. vii : "Lady Brouncker . . . never wanted medicine certainly, for she never had an *h* in her life ".

51. turned Turk, become a pervert (from your vows of celibacy).

52. the star, the pole-star.

53. trow. There is an ellipse, not of 'you', but of 'I', as appears from *Merry Wives*, ii. 1. 64, "What tempest, I trow, threw this whale ashore?" *Romeo and Juliet*, ii. 5. 64, "marry come up, I trow." With imperatives and interrogatives, 'I trow' forms an ironical parenthesis, referring either to some word used—"What tempest (I trow it must have been a tempest) . . ."—or to some thought unexpressed. Cf. the use of "I declare ".

56. Gloves were a common present between lovers. Scented gloves were introduced from Italy by the Earl of Oxford about 1574 (Stowe). "Gloves as sweet as damask roses " formed part of Autolycus's pack.

58. I am stuffed, I have a cold in my head—due to the same cause as Benedick's toothache.

62. professed apprehension, set up for a wit. See Glossary under *apprehend*.

65, 66. wear it in your cap: as a knight his lady's favour?

67. Carduus Benedictus, holy-thistle, then thought a cure for all ills, but especially for affections of the heart.

71. moral, hidden meaning, like the moral of a fable. Margaret (l. 72) uses the word as an adjective.

75–80. By a familiar figure, Margaret insinuates the charge which she disclaims.

81. he eats his meat without grudging. *Grudging* is grumbling: "to eat one's meat with grudging" was proverbial for "to grumble at one's lot ". Here the phrase is clearly parallel to "and now is he become a man ": it means that, in spite of his resolution not to marry, he acquiesces in the common lot of man. A more definite interpretation would spoil the intentional vagueness of the phrase.

81, 82. how you may be converted recalls Benedick's " May I be so converted " (ii. 3. 20).

82, 83. look with your eyes: and love is engendered in the eyes.

84. Another echo, this time of Benedick's gibe in i. 1. 128.

85. false gallop, a forced or unnatural pace, between trot and gallop, identified by Bradley with the canter. The expression is said to be still used in horsemanship.

Scene 5

In this admirable little scene the 'blundering Bumbledom' of Dogberry and Verges, which might otherwise seem a mere trap to catch a laugh, is wrought into the very structure of the plot. Only such a pair—and only the pair of them—could have wasted a whole scene without conveying a hint of their information. Coleridge's remark that any other pair of constables would have done equally well is thus very wide of the truth. With comic irony, Leonato's own impatience and easy-going delegation of duty becomes a main instrument in preventing that disclosure which would have forestalled disaster.

The time is about 5 A.M. of Monday.

1. Leonato's 'honest neighbour' indicates the genial discipline of Messina's government.

3. that decerns you nearly. Dogberry has some inkling of the object of the plot. But the intelligence has grown dim in its passage through the minds of the watch.

9, 10. a little off the matter, beside the point. Q. and F., *of*; corr. Steevens after Capell.

11, 12. honest as the skin between his brows: a homely simile of frequent occurence in E.E. The brow is regarded as an open page on which the mind is charactered. Observe Dogberry's two styles—the magisterial, with its malapropisms; the colloquial, abounding in those racy similes and proverbs, not always very pertinent to the matter in hand, with which uneducated talkers bedeck their conversation. Dogberry's mind is a rag-bag of such patches.

15. Comparisons are odorous: improved in *Sir Giles Goosecap* (1606) into "Caparisons are odorous". Did Sheridan filch this for Mrs. Malaprop? Cf. *The Rivals*, iv. 2: "No caparisons, miss, if you please. Caparisons don't become a young woman."

palabras: presumably for *pocas palabras*, 'few words', a scrap of Spanish disguised by Christopher Sly as "paucas pallabris" (*Taming of the Shrew*, Induction, 1. 5).

18, 19. the poor duke's officers. Elbow makes the same blunder in *Measure for Measure*, ii. 1. 186; cf. also ii. 1. 47.

Elbow is a kind of sapless Dogberry; one of the few instances
in which Shakespeare has spoiled a character in the rehandling.
Who is the duke? Don Pedro is elsewhere called 'the Prince';
in iii. 3. 70, the constable is told that he 'presents the prince's
own person'. The precise relation of Don Pedro to Messina is
left vague.

21. bestow it all of. This construction is used even by
Olivia in *Twelfth Night*, iii. 4. 2, and is therefore not a blunder
of Dogberry's. Interchange of *of* and *on* (cf. line 35 below)
may have been facilitated by the practice of representing both
by *o'*.

23. pound: F., *times*. See Appendix on the Text.

29, 30. excepting your worship's presence. Verges means
'saving your reverence', but contrives to imply that Leonato
is the arrantest knave in Messina.

30. ha': F., *have*.

33. When the age is in, the wit is out: a variant of the
proverb, "When the wine is in, the wit is out", or rather of the
version "When ale is in, wit is out".

34. a world to see, a wonderful sight.

35. God's a good man. This phrase recurs in contemporary literature, and Halliwell says is still heard in the pro-
vinces, but no definite meaning need be attached to it in
Dogberry's mouth. The whole of this speech is an extrava-
gant example of that proverbial style remarked on in the note
to l. 11, 12 above. Wurth compares the German, "Gott einen
guten Mann sein lassen".

a, one: cf. iv. 2. 28 and Glossary. In stage practice,
Dogberry illustrates the proverb by planting himself in front of
Verges.

43. This is Dogberry's magisterial paraphrase of Verges'
"ta'en a couple of arrant knaves". In *A Mad World my
Master* (1608) Middleton makes his constable say, "May it
please your worship, sir, here are a company of *auspicious*
fellows".

45. By this ill-timed compliment in delegating the enquiry,
Leonato himself stifles any lingering sense that Dogberry may
retain of the importance of his intelligence.

46. F., *as may appear*.

52. Francis Seacole: the sexton. See note on iii. 3. 11.

54. examination: F., *examine*. The reading of F. has been
preferred by many editors on the ground that Dogberry does
not confuse the parts of speech. But this cannot be maintained
in the face of 'suffigance' (l. 47).

56. We will spare for no wit, there shall be no stinting of wit.

56, 57. here's that: tapping his forehead.

57. noncome. Dogberry means *non plus*, but confuses it with another scrap of Latin, *non compos mentis*.

Act IV—Scene I

This great scene falls naturally into two parts: (1) the repudiation, which forms the climax of the serious plot; (2) the prose after-piece, which forms the solution of the comic plot. The first part is a great rhetorical set-piece, rivalling the finest declamatory scenes of *Julius Cæsar* or the *Merchant of Venice*. In spite of our foreknowledge of the issue, the passion rises dangerously near the level of tragedy.

This scene follows immediately on the preceding.

1–20. The formal preliminaries are sketched in prose.

2. To expedite the action, the customary address on the responsibilities of marriage is to be deferred.

10–12. In the English marriage service the words now run: "I require and charge you both . . . that if either of you know impediment, why ye may not be lawfully joined together in matrimony, ye do now confess it".

20. F. omits "not knowing what they do". See Appendix on the Text.

19, 20. Benedick's speech is a quotation from a school grammar. Cf. Lyly's *Endimion*, iii. 3: "An interjection, whereof some are of mourning; as *eho, vah*".

21. With "Stand thee by, friar", ceremony is put aside, and the style rises at once to verse. Claudio's 'Father' grates on our ears, though betrothal established a more formal connection then than now. So Paris says "My father Capulet" (*Romeo and Juliet*, iv. 1. 2).

28–30. Even at this crisis Claudio takes his cue from the Prince. This preconcerted effect agrees well with the theatricality of Claudio's whole performance.

34. Note the cross alliteration, "*c*unning *s*in *c*over it*s*elf".

37. were: subjunctive of grammatical dependence.

39. luxurious, lascivious. See Glossary.

42, 43. For the scansion see Appendix on Prosody, ii (*a*) (*β*).

Leonato does not doubt the charge for a moment; he only
seeks to give it the least odious interpretation.

43. in your own proof, by the strength of your temptation.

45. made defeat of, overcome.

48. the 'forehand sin, the sin of anticipation. See note on
i. 3. 11, 12.

50–52. With Claudio's quick sense of self-respect there is
associated a moral delicacy, for which he does not fail to take
credit by contrast.

53. At this sudden crisis of her fate Hero can only ejaculate
a helpless question.

54. Q. and F., *Out on thee seeming, I will write against it,
you seem,* &c.; corr. Seymour.
Seymour's punctuation is borne out by *Cymbeline,* ii. 5. 32,
where Posthumus in similar circumstances utters the same
threat, "I'll write against them", *i.e.* women. It is against
women in general, against seeming in general, that Posthumus
and Claudio will write. We must therefore reject Pope's "Out
on thy seeming!"

55. You seem. The present is right, though Hero said,
"And seem'd I". Claudio means, "What though you did?
Even *now,* when I know you false, you still *seem* chaste."

Dian, Diana, the goddess of chastity and of the moon;
hence orb = orbit.

56. ere it be blown, "before the air has tasted its sweet-
ness" (Johnson). So Posthumus thought Imogen "as chaste as
unsunned snow" (*Cymbeline,* ii. 5. 13). But for the superlative
of such similes see Coriolanus's description of Valeria:

> "The moon of Rome, chaste as the icicle
>   That's curdied by the frost from purest snow
>   And hangs on Dian's temple" (*Coriolanus,* v. 3. 65).

58, 59. That moral nicety which we have noted keeps Claudio
from descending, like Lear, to a more particular comparison.
(Cf. *Lear,* iv. 6. 110 seq.)

61. Some editors give this speech to Claudio, but Don
Pedro's answer is clearly not addressed to him.

65. Note the unrhythmical line. Don John's harsh accents
contrast with Claudio's, melodious even in denunciation.

66. nuptial. Shakespeare generally, perhaps always, uses
the singular. The exceptions are *Pericles,* v. 3. 80, which may
not be his, and the Q. of *Othello,* ii. 2. 8, where F. has singular.

True? O God! This is not an assent to Benedick, but
an echo of Don John. Hero is in no condition to attend to

the comments of by-standers; her unreflecting mind is simply stunned by the catastrophe. Her bearing at this crisis should be compared with that of Desdemona, of whom she is an early sketch. (See Mr. Rose on 'Sudden Emotion', *N. S. S. T.*, 1880-82, p. 1.)

71. **move one question**, put one question. Cf. 'move a resolution'.

72. **kindly**, natural. See Glossary.

74. F. omits 'so'.

77. Possibly, as Deighton suggests, Claudio's answer is prompted by the word 'catechizing', the first question in the English Catechism being "What is your name?"

80. **Hero itself**, the name 'Hero'. His proof of Hero's guilt is that he heard Borachio address the woman at the window by the name of Hero.

85. Don Pedro's reasoning is, "Since you deny what we know to be true, we must believe the worst". F., *Why then you are.*

90. A reminiscence of this line occurs in *The Fair Maid of Bristow* (1605):

> "But Vallinger, most like a liberal villain,
>   Did give her scandalous ignoble terms".

93-95. See note on ii. 2. 39, and cf. Borachio's words in v. 1. 230, "upon mine and my master's false accusation".
These three speeches are most characteristic; Don Pedro, like a great prince, stating but not dwelling on the fact, not without some regard for Leonato; Don John gloating in hypocritical commiseration; and Claudio improving the occasion with emotional rhetoric.

94. F., *spoken.*

101. Observe the lingering spondaic rhythm.

102. A fine example of the figure called oxymoron, of which Tennyson's "And faith unfaithful kept him falsely true" is the stock instance.

103-106. Compare this with Claudio's words at i. 1. 273 if you would estimate the nature of his love by his own conception of the passion. With him love is an invasion of the fancy rather than an outgoing of the heart.

> "Young men's love then lies
>   Not truly in their hearts, but in their eyes".
>   —*Romeo and Juliet*, ii. 3. 67.

With this generalization against love compare his generalization against friendship in ii. 1. 155. It is this power of gene-

ralizing under stress of wounded feeling that gives us what
George Eliot calls our "superiority in mistake over the dumb
animals".

107. This line may have been suggested by the action of
Girondo in the novel, who on confessing proffers his poniard
to Timbreo.

110. Don John withdraws his dupes to avoid further enquiry.
The Friar's scheme can then be propounded.

121. **The story that is printed in her blood**, "the story
which her blushes discover to be true" (Johnson). To this
interpretation it is objected that Hero had fainted; but from
ll. 117, 118 it is clear that she has revived. In any case,
Leonato would regard the pallor of her swoon equally with her
blushes as evidence of guilt.

124. **shames.** The use of the plural is due to the corre-
sponding plural, 'spirits'.

125. **rearward.** F., *reward*. There is a similar metaphor
in *Sonnet* xc: "Come in the rearward of a conquer'd woe".
Reproach and *woe* are regarded as hostile armies.

127. **frame**, mould. Cf. *Winter's Tale*, ii. 3. 103, "The very
mould and frame of hand, nail, finger"; also *Coriolanus*, v. 3. 22,
"the honour'd mould Wherein this trunk was framed".

132. **Who smirched thus**, *quâ sic pollutâ*—relative in abso-
lute construction. F., *smeered*.

135-137. As an expression of intense emotion, repetition is
as primitive and as natural as the rhythmic sob.

137. "That she was more myself than my own self."

142-144. Q. and F. print Benedick's speech as prose.

143. **attired in wonder:** a bold metaphor, more familiar in
Greek and Hebrew than in English.

145. While Benedick, honestly anxious to believe the best,
still stumbles amid the pitfalls of false evidence, Beatrice's
womanly instinct, inspired by heart knowledge, carries her
clear to the truth.

146-148. Question and answer were suggested by Bandello.
After the repudiation, Timbreo reflected that Fenicia, sleeping
with her sister in a chamber within that of her father and
mother, could not have come through their chamber to this
side.

148. **this twelvemonth** recalls Borachio's words, "I told
your lordship a year since how much I am in the favour of
Margaret" (ii. 2. 12).

153. Wash'd. The subject of a subordinate clause may be omitted when it is the same as that of the principal clause.

154-156. Q. and F. print these lines as prose. Two arrangements have been suggested: (1) The Cambridge editors think that the passage was thrown down and reset as prose, half a line or a line and a half being lost in the process; (2) Mr. Daniel thinks that there is no lacuna, and that the passage was set up in prose simply to get it into the page, the next page having already been set. He therefore arranges:

> " *Friar.* Hear me a little:
>
>> For I have only been silent so long
>> And given way unto this course of fortune
>> By noting of the lady: I have marked ", &c.

This arrangement gives *by* a force which it cannot bear; and I believe with the Cambridge editors that there is a lacuna, though I doubt their theory of dislocation. The lost words would give the Friar's reason for his silence.

158. apparitions, appearances.

160. In angel whiteness beat away those blushes. F., *beare away*, which spoils the image. The modern reader thinks of Mephistopheles pelted with roses by the angels. Precisely the same picture occurs in the Morality of the *Castell of Perseverance*, where the Virtues pelt the Deadly Sins with roses. Shakespeare may have seen this in his boyhood, and appropriately transferred the image to the memory of the Friar.

161-163. The princes are heretics in the despite of Hero's chastity. The fire in her eyes is to consume their heresy. The metaphor, appropriate to the Friar, is expanded in *Romeo and Juliet*, i. 2. 93:

> " When the devout religion of mine eye
> Maintains such falsehoods, then turn tears to fires,
> And these, who often drowned could never die,
> Transparent heretics, be burnt for liars ".

165. experimental zeal, the confirmation of experience.

doth. The singular is due to the intervention of the singular noun 'zeal'.

185. the very bent. The metaphor, originally from archery (cf. ii. 3. 206), is extended to aim, inclination, or propensity of any kind.

187. practice. This noun often has a bad sense in E.E.

lives, operates; cf. ii. 2. 17.

188. frame, framing. Shakespeare freely uses verbs (but generally those of French origin) as verbal nouns; cf. ' make

prepare for war' (Abbott, § 45).   Benedick's penetration reveals
the very nerve of Don John's being.

189–199. The rhythm, ending in a crescendo of reiterated
'nors', marks the ebb and flow of Leonato's emotion through
despair to the thought of revenge.

196, 197. This couplet is very unlike Shakespeare's mature
style. It does not mark a maxim, nor an exit, nor is it syntactically complete in itself. The offence is heightened by the
mid-line rhyme on 'find'. Heuser thinks that the rhyme here
is unintentional—a mere outburst of the poet's lyric speech.
But accidental rhymes, where they do occur, as in v. 1. 236–
37, 248–49, are so weak as to be unnoticeable; here the
rhymed words have a strong accent. Wright points to lines
214–15 below; but that is not a rhyme. I believe that there
is a printer's error, of the kind due to 'parablepsy'. No
restoration can therefore be certain; but Capell's *cause* is as
good as any. [Of such 'imbedded' couplets syntactically in-
complete there are two instances in *2 Henry IV*, viz. iii. 1.
54–58, iv. 5. 228–230: the first is of the nature of a maxim, in
the second the rhyme is doubtful. There is no clear case in the
serious verse of *Henry V*.]

201. Q. and F., *Your daughter here the Princesse* (*left for
dead*): corr. Theobald.

203 seq. The plan in its essentials is from Bandello. But in
assigning it to the Friar, Shakespeare may have acted on a
hint from Ariosto, when Ariodante, repenting of suicide, "halted
at a hermit's humble cell", and there stayed until he should
hear how Genevra bore the news of his death.

204. **a mourning ostentation**, a show of mourning. In E.E.
the word does not imply pretentiousness. It is regularly used
of funeral ceremonies. Cf. *Hamlet*, iv. 5. 215, "No noble rite,
nor formal ostentation".

205, 206. It was not unusual to attach eulogistic verses to
the hearse or tomb of a deceased person. The most famous
of such encomia is Ben Jonson's on the Countess of Pembroke:
"Underneath this sable hearse Lies the subject of all verse".
This suggestion is repeated by Leonato to Claudio (v. 1. 271),
and is carried out in v. 2.

208. **shall...will**. Abbott (§ 321) thus explains the change:
"The indefinite unknown consequence is not personified, the
definite project is personified. 'What *is destined to result* from
this project? What does this project *intend to do* for us?'"

210. **remorse**: used by Shakespeare (1) in the modern sense
of 'compunction'; (2) as here, in the wider sense of 'compassion'.

212. Yet it cannot be said that the Friar's project amounts to anything more. He has no scheme to prove Hero's innocence. At most, he only gives chance time to work.

218. lack'd and lost. This may be a hysteron proteron for 'lost and lack'd'; but *lack* in E.E. = *carere* (to be without) as well as *egere* (to feel the want of).

219. rack, strain to the utmost, exaggerate. Cf. *Merchant of Venice*, i. 1. 181, "(my credit) shall be rack'd". Still closer is the difficult passage in *Love's Labour's Lost*, v. 2. 828, "your sins are racked".

222-232. These exquisite lines show a marvellous insight into the nature of such love as Claudio's. See note on lines 103-6 above.

222. upon, immediately after, and so in consequence of, the idea of *post* passing easily into that of *propter*.

224. his study of imagination, his imaginative broodings. Cf. 'brown study'.

230. This peculiar expression seems to echo Lyly, *Endimion*, ii. 2, "I defy time, who hath no interest in my heart", and to be echoed in *The Puritan*, iii. 5, "If ever pity had interest in the blood of a gentleman". In Shakespeare's physiology the liver is the seat of passion, as the heart of emotion and the brain of thought. "Liver, brain, and heart" sum up the human faculties (*Twelfth Night*, i. 1. 37).

233. success, the issue, not necessarily prosperous in E.E.

236. levell'd, aimed. The noun is used as a technical term for the direction in which a gun is 'laid'.

239-242. It is characteristic of the churchman that the only practical issue which he definitely contemplates is the withdrawal of Hero to a nunnery.

244. inwardness, intimacy.

245. much, great; an adj.

248. Being that, it being the case that. So we still use 'seeing that' without a noun. (Abbott, § 378.)

I flow in grief, am dissolved in grief. Leonato's emotional nature has exhausted itself in outcries; his powers are unstrung, and he wearily lets others think for him.

250-253. The high-strung emotion of the scene passes off in a solemn quatrain at the close. Cf. iii. 1. 107-116.

253. prolong'd, postponed. "*Prolongyn*, put far away" (*Prompt. Parv.*, 417). Note the alexandrine.

254-end. This welding of the comic into the serious plot is a masterpiece of constructive skill. It is not the Prince's ruse but the villain's machination 'which finally brings Beatrice and Benedick together. The heat of generous emotion which Hero's fate evokes dissolves the barriers reared by wit and pride. The plot to ruin one match achieves another. When Beatrice and Benedick are left alone together, though pity remains its object is withdrawn, and their old relation so far reasserts itself that the dialogue drops at once to prose.

262. even, plain, forthright.

271 seq. Benedick's use of *thou* and *you* is a delicate index of fluctuating hopes—confident, rebuffed, reviving.

272. F., *Do not swear by it and eat it.* But Beatrice means, "Do not swear and eat your oath".

282. And, then, marking the consequence, as often in Shakespeare. καί can be similarly used in Greek, "Lord, it is good for us to be here, *and* let us make three tabernacles (καὶ ποιή σωμεν τρεῖς σκήνας)" (*Mark*, ix. 2).

286. Kill Claudio. After her bewitching confession of love these words come like a flash of lightning, revealing depths of passionate indignation and blasting Claudio with scorn.

288. to deny it, by denying it. In such cases the infinitive with *to* represents various cases of the gerund; here the ablative, *negando.* F. omits 'it'.

290. Benedick tries to detain her: she struggles to free herself, declaring that though her hand is held, her spirit is gone already.

298. Q. and F., *Is a not approved*; corr. Rowe. The form 'a', though not confined to vulgar persons, seems too colloquial for this context. Yet I am not certain that such a colloquialism is not in the nature of such indignation as Beatrice's.

300. bear her in hand, delude her. Dowden compares Fr. *maintenir.*

312. a goodly count. Grant White sees a play on 'count' =*conte*, a story. After 'a princely testimony' it seems that there must be a play on 'count', but it is rather on the legal sense of accusation: cf. *Hamlet*, iv. 7. 17, "Why to a public count I might not go".

Count Comfect, "My Lord Lollilop" (Staunton). *Confect* is E.E. for comfit. The bitter word-play, expressive of intense indignation, is kept up in 'a sweet gallant', and by one of those echoes to which attention has already been drawn, recalls Beatrice's words about Claudio in happier circumstances, viz. ii. 1. 261-63.

313. Repeated in Chapman's *Monsieur d'Olive* (1606).

315. Q. and F., *cursies.*

316. **only goes with tongue**, to which also **ones** refers, in spite of the change of number.

trim, rare, ironical; their 'trimness' consists in lying and swearing.

320. Benedick's somewhat formal 'good Beatrice' emphasizes a purposeful tone, which commands her attention. This is marked by the change of pronouns. His profession of love he must repeat with 'thee', but having repeated it he drops the loverly.

326. **engaged**, pledged, *i.e.* to do your will.

327. F. omits second 'I'.

By this hand: not his own this time, but Beatrice's which he is kissing.

329, 330. **I must say she is dead**. Benedick repeats his lesson to reassure Beatrice of his purpose. The blended comedy and passion of this dialogue forms an admirable transition from the pathos of the repudiation to the broad fun of the next scene.

Scene 2

Hardly has Hero been accused in the church when her innocence is proved elsewhere. Dogberry, elated by his commission, is *in excelsis*; but further mistakes are prevented by the presence of the sensible sexton. The time is still Monday.

Stage-direction. Q. and F. have, *Enter the Constables, Borachio, and the Toune Clearke in gownes.* The Town Clerk is the sexton: a parish-clerk might more naturally have united the offices. Conrade's name is omitted. Throughout the scene Dogberry's speeches are marked *Kemp* and Verges' *Cowley.* See Appendix on the Text. It is very singular that, except for the name *Jacke Wilson* in F. at ii. 3. 33, this form of error should be exhibited only in this scene. Perhaps, as Marshall suggests, the original MS. was here defaced, and the scene printed from the actors' parts. There is a similar error in the 3rd and 4th Quartos of *Romeo and Juliet*, where *Will. Kemp* is printed for *Peter.*

4. Dogberry takes the long Latin word for a term of honour, and appropriates it. Contrariwise, in *Measure for Measure*, ii. 1. 50, Elbow speaks of "two notorious benefactors".

5. **exhibition**: a legal term, which Verges takes to mean 'commission' or the like. The verb is technically used for promulgating a bill (*Merry Wives of Windsor*, ii. 1. 29): the noun occurs repeatedly in the sense of 'allowance', in which sense it survives in the universities.

9. The duties of examining magistrate are new to Dogberry, and (like many of his successors) he relies on the clerk.

12. sirrah implies inferiority in the person addressed, and so is resented by Conrade.

16–19. F. omits. See Appendix on the Text.

18. defend, forbid. See Glossary.

24. go about with him, circumvent him (Deighton). The expression has a slightly different sense in i. 3. 11 and iv. 1. 62. In *Hamlet*, iii. 2. 361, "Why do you go about to recover the wind of me, as if you would drive me into a toil?" the metaphor is from hunting.

28, 29. they are both in a tale, both say the same. For *a* = one, see Glossary. Dogberry (attempting a cross-examination) puts to one of the prisoners in a whisper the question he had put to both aloud, and is amazed to find the answers agree.

41. promise, assure. See Glossary.

47. by mass. F., *by th' masse.* This relic of Roman Catholicism survived in stage language till Sheridan's day. See David in *The Rivals*.

57. This shows that some little time has elapsed since the previous scene.

62. opinioned, pinioned.

63, 64. Q. and F., *Let them be in the hands of Coxcombe*, Q. giving the words to *Couley*, F. to *Sex*. The text is Malone's. Verges meant to say, "Let them be in the hands of justice", or the like, when Conrade throws off the watchman who attempts to bind him, shouting, "Off, coxcomb!". This is not quite convincing, and the Cambridge editors suggest that Verges' words may be the corruption of a stage-direction [*Let them bind their hands*].

65. God's my life, God save my life. 'God save me' is contracted into 'God sa' me' (so I would restore Jonson, *Poetaster*, i. 1. 5, for "Gods a' me" of the edd.), then into 'God's me' (*1 Henry IV*, ii. 3. 97).

67. Thou naughty varlet is addressed to Conrade: 'naughty' = worthless, wicked, still retaining in E.E. its original sense as the adj. of 'naught'; cf. Lat. *nequam*. Q. and F. have only a comma at 'then'.

69-end. The Act, which began almost tragically, thus ends in an explosion of wounded vanity the most comic in literature. Conrade's insult is a terrible blow to one whose self-conceit has battened so long on applause, and has just been crowned with an honour to which he has hardly shown himself equal.

76. Cf. *Twelfth Night*, i. 5. 30, "as witty a piece of Eve's flesh as any in Illyria". F. here reads (as in *Twelfth Night*) "as any in Messina", but the construction is the so-called omission of the relative. See note on i. 1. 17.

77. one that knows the law: cf. iii. 3. 73, "Five shillings to one on 't, with any man that knows the statues".

78, 79. a fellow that hath had losses. In iii. 5. 25 Dogberry modestly calls himself "but a poor man" (in comparison, that is, with Leonato); and though here he declares that he is "a rich fellow enough", he holds it an addition to his consequence that he had once been richer. See Scott's delightful comment in Introduction to *Quentin Durward*.

80. See Introduction, § 2.

Act V—Scene I

The climax having been delayed till Act iv, the solution must follow hard upon it. But Shakespeare has first to show the effect of the catastrophe on the chief characters, and bring home the need of a solution, in the impossible situation created by the church scene, the straining or disruption of the old kindly ties between host and guest, between friend and friend. This state of things cannot last. A tragic solution, we know, will be averted: meantime feeling is kept below the pitch of tragedy by Antonio's senile inconsistency, by the manly but sober tone of Benedick, and by Claudio's incurable levity.

This scene follows on iv. 2 without interval.

1. Observe how this single line fills up for our imagination the interval since Leonato left the stage.

3. Leonato's careless but unseasoned kindness breaks down under stress of trouble. His passionate Italian nature surrenders itself to grief till it is diverted to the thought of revenge.

4, 5. as profitless As water in a sieve: a classical simile, expanded into a myth in the story of the Danaides, which may have been in Shakespeare's mind. The 'sieve' is first alluded to in Aristotle, *Oeconomics*, i. 6. 1: τῷ γὰρ ἠθμῷ ἀντλεῖν τοῦτ' ἐστι καὶ ὁ λεγόμενος τετρημένος πίθος.

6. comforter. F., *comfort*.

7. suit, match. F., *doth suit*.

10. A broken line, natural in passionate speech. There is no need to suppose any words lost.

12. **answer every strain for strain**, correspond, pang for pang. In *strain* two meanings lie near together: (1) a strain on the feelings—"other strains of woe" (*Sonnet* xc); (2) a strain in the blood, a trait. That this latter force is felt here appears from line 14.

16. **Bid sorrow wag**, bid sorrow begone. Q. and F., *And sorrow, wagge*; corr. Capell. Emendations of this difficult passage may be classified according as they assume that 'wag' is noun or verb. Of the latter, Capell's is the best; it involves a change of but two letters. 'Wag' is a jocular word for 'go' (like 'trot' or 'toddle'), used elsewhere in this sense only by mine host of the Garter, and highly appropriate in this contemptuous speech. Of emendations which make 'wag' a noun, Steevens's "And, sorry wag, cry hem", though withdrawn by him, has been adopted by Marshall, and makes fair sense. Corrections like 'sorrow-wrung' need not be considered: 'wag' at least is sound. Schmidt alone defends Q. and F., and renders "And if sorrow, a merry droll, will cry hem". But 'he' shows that this is impossible.

17, 18. **make misfortune drunk With candle-wasters**, numb grief with philosophy. *Candle-wasters* are students, burners of the 'midnight oil'. B. Jonson uses the word as a synonym for 'book-worm' (*Cynthia's Revels*, iii. 2. 3).

18. What is the precise force of 'yet' here? Cf. iii. 3. 100. Furness interprets, "It will be very hard to find such a man, *yet* if you do, bring him to me".

20–30. These lines should be compared with Adriana's speech on the same topic (*Comedy of Errors*, ii. 1. 34–37):

"A wretched soul, bruised with adversity,
    We bid be quiet when we hear it cry;
But were we burden'd with like weight of pain,
    As much or more we should ourselves complain".

The idea is the same; but the treatment is flat compared to the nervous power and imaginative insight here displayed. The difference of style is most felt when the imagery is most alike, as in line 28, "To those that wring under the load of sorrow".

22. **tasting it**. A pronoun is easily supplied from **Their** (l. 23)=of them (Abbott, § 379).

23. What a weight of experience is in these words, compared with which Adriana's seem bookish!

24–26. These lines afford a good instance of that peculiarity of Shakespeare's rich style which Ten Brink thus describes: "If he has used a word or a figure which does not satisfy him, and then employs another, he does not efface the first, but leaves it undisturbed in its place, and allows himself to drift on upon the swelling current of his thoughts". But such redundancies, it should be added, have generally a dramatic propriety.

24. preceptial medicine, the medicine of precepts. Q.'s *medcine* suggests an alternative scansion:

"Would give' precep'tial' med'cine to rage'".

26. Note the vowel-alliteration.

28. wring, writhe—intransitive.

30. moral, moralizing. Cf. i. 3. 11. The verb is similarly used in *As You Like It*, ii. 7. 29, where Schmidt thinks it an adj. as here.

32. My griefs cry louder than advertisement, my grief cries so loud that I cannot hear your exhortation (Marshall). Antonio takes 'cry' literally, and retorts, "Such behaviour is childish". For *advertisement* = admonition, see Glossary. Neither the verb nor the noun in Shakespeare implies 'proclamation', or has any meaning but that of 'information, instruction'.

36. This is an echo of iii. 2. 19–26, as "charm ache with air", above, is an echo of iii. 2. 63. Such touches link the serious and the comic scenes together.

37. writ the style of gods, affected superiority to human weaknesses.

38. made a push at, pooh-poohed. *Push* is the same word as *pish*, an exclamation of contempt. For the phrase compare Day's *Law Tricks* (1608), "you that *make a pish* at the black art".

sufferance, suffering.

39. That the suggestion of revenge comes from Antonio should prepare us for his vigorous outburst, which yet comes as a surprise. To prepare the spectator, and still to surprise him, is the secret, as Brandes says, of all dramatic effect.

46. The Prince, who had shown some consideration for Leonato, is now more embarrassed than Claudio.

49. Are you so hasty now? reminds the Prince of his promise to stay "at the least a month" (i. 1. 135).

all is one, it is all one, no matter.

53. Leonato addresses Claudio with the contemptuous 'thou'.

54. Claudio's instincts are egotistical. He is a gentleman upon reflection.

57. meant nothing to. We could still say "meant nothing with"; 'to' is here preferred because of the motion implied—"my hand meant nothing in moving to my sword".

62. to thy head: an expression still used in East Anglia for "to thy face".

63. F., *my innocent child.*

65. bruise of many days. This touching phrase suggests the battered veteran forced to resume arms he had laid by.

66. trial of a man, the judicial "trial by combat".

69. Realistic criticism has objected to this hasty burial. But Juliet's is even more hasty: cf. the "two and forty hours" of *Romeo and Juliet,* iv. 1. 105, with the "two days buried" of v. 3. 176.

72. My villany? In his resentment the news of Hero's death actually seems to pass unheard.

81. But that's no matter: cf. 100 below, "Come, 'tis no matter". Antonio catches up his brother's "all is one" (l. 49) as he catches up and enforces his taunting 'boy'.

82. Win me and wear me: a proverbial expression, but usually of winning a lady.

answer me, meet me. The noun was a technical term of the duello, as Osric explains (*Hamlet,* v. 2. 176–79), for "the opposition of one's person in trial".

86. The travesty of his own rage brings Leonato back to his senses. His attempts at interruption remind us of Benedick's (iv. 1. 292, &c.). See note on l. 36 above.

89. a man indeed, a real man, as in l. 80.

91. Q. and F. have *Anthony* here and *Anthonio* in l. 100. This is the English form of the name: cf. the readings *Don Peter* (i. 1. 1) and *Ursley* (iii. 1. 4).

96. Q. and F., *Go anticly and show:* corr. Spedding. The old reading is not metrically impossible. For *anticly =* grotesquely, see Glossary. Antonio means that such carpet-knights affect "a horrid suit of the camp" (*Henry V,* iii. 6. 81).

97. Q. and F., *speak of:* corr. Theobald.

dangerous, threatening.

102. wake, rouse. Cf. "awake Your dangerous lenity" (*Coriolanus,* iii. 1. 98–99). They have not indeed shown patience, but the Prince means to be conciliatory.

105. full of proof, fully proved.

106–8. Perhaps we should read:

" *Leon.* My lord, my lord—
    D. Pedro.   I will not hear you.
    Leon.   No?
Come', | bro'ther; | away' !"

See Prosody, ii. (*a*) (*β*).   As they stand ll. 106, 107 are two broken lines.

110. With Benedick's entrance the style drops to prose.

111, 112. Claudio, eager to change a disagreeable situation, is the first to hail Benedick, who ignores him and greets the Prince.

113, 114. " You have come almost in time to part what was almost a fray."   The repeated 'almost' marks the Prince's amusement.   Cf. *Love's Labour's Lost*, i. 1. 161, " I am the last that will last keep his oath".

115. The contrast between Claudio and Benedick and the reversal of their positions is marked very strongly in the dialogue which follows.   Claudio as at first wants Benedick's sympathy, but now to make fun of an encounter in which he has had the worst.   It is Benedick's turn to be serious.

123. high-proof melancholy: spirits which contain more than a certain percentage of alcohol are still said to be 'above proof'.

125. Benedick's retort is suggested by Claudio's 'beaten'.

128. draw: variously explained, of drawing the bow across a fiddle, or of drawing instruments from their cases.

134-137. The metaphors are from the tilt-yard.   **staff=** spear-shaft.   **broke cross:** the tilter tried to carry his spear fair upon his opponent's shield, so that if broken it split lengthways.   To break it across implied clumsiness.

138, 139. I think he be.   *Be* (in O.E. generally future, then exclusively subjunctive) implies a shade of doubt (1) in questions, (2) after verbs of thinking.   The *locus classicus* is *Othello*, iii. 3. 384, " I think my wife *be* honest, and think she *is* not " (Abbott, §§ 298, 299).

140. he knows how to turn his girdle: a proverbial expression best rendered by the vulgarism, " If he doesn't like it he can lump it ".   That this is the true meaning appears from a remark of Cromwell's (Sept. 17, 1656): " If any man be angry at it—I am plain and shall use an homely expression: let him turn the buckle of his girdle behind him!   If this were to be done again I would do it."   Cromwell means simply, " He may occupy his hands till he cools ".   And so Scott understood the phrase; cf. *Rob Roy*, ch. xxv., " Nay, never look gash or grim at me, man—if ye 're angry ye ken how to turn the buckle o' your belt behind you."

142. bless, preserve.

145. Do me right, give me satisfaction.

  protest, proclaim before witnesses.

152. **curiously,** carefully, nicely. In Shakespeare 'curious' always retains its original sense of 'care' (Lat. *cura*), and never means merely 'peculiar'.

152, 153. **a woodcock** was supposed to have no brains. Cf. Ford, *Lover's Melancholy*, ii. 1.

Claudio is at least quite fearless. He accepts his friend's challenge and the news of Hero's death with equal nonchalance. But something must be allowed for the soreness of one in such a situation.

160. **a wise gentleman,** a wiseacre, wittol.

161. **hath the tongues,** is a linguist.

This recalls Beatrice's nonsense in ii. 1. 248 seq.

165. **trans-shape,** turn the wrong side out, as Hero said.

173. The reference is to *Genesis*, iii. 8.

179. Benedick recurs to Leonato's taunt of 'boy'; but in manner the two challenges are sharply contrasted.

181. Is Shakespeare thinking of his own braggart Falstaff hacking his sword? Such a reminiscence is not unlikely when we remember that *Henry IV* had been printed about a year earlier.

192, 193. "What an inconsistent fool is man, when he covers his body with clothes, and at the same time divests himself of his understanding" (Steevens). There may be, as Mr. Herford thinks, a sub-allusion to the custom of taking off the cloak before fighting a duel, in which case "to go in doublet and hose" will mean not to be dressed but to be partially undressed. But Don Pedro seems to be referring not to the folly of duelling but to the infatuation of love.

194, 195. "He is then as much inferior to an ape in sense as he is superior in stature." **to,** compared to; **doctor,** man of learning. Capell remarks: "The replier's comparisons bear a little hard upon the ladies; and upon men too, whom they hold in their chains".

196. **let me be,** leave me alone, give me time to think.

pluck up, rouse thyself.

199. **reasons:** perhaps with a pun on 'raisins'. The words were then similar in sound, and sometimes identical in spelling, and are played on certainly in *1 Henry IV*, ii. 4. 264, "if reasons were as plentiful as blackberries", and probably in *As You Like It*, ii. 7. 100, "An you will not be answered with reason, I must die".

200. **once,** *i.e.* now. Cf. Greene's *Friar Bacon*, sc. 6: "Lord Lacy, yield. I'll be your jailor once." Abbott, however, puts

the comma at 'hypocrite' and renders 'positively'. See on i. 1. 289.

207, 211, Q. and F., *sixt*; corr. F. 4.

215. well suited, "put into many different dresses" (Johnson).

217. bound: with a pun on the sense of 'going to a destination'.

222. This is indeed the *raison d'être* of Dogberry and Verges.

224. incensed, instigated; see Glossary.

226. in Hero's garments. This important touch is added for the first time in this, the last account of the midnight episode.

230. upon mine and my master's false accusation. For the implication of these words see note on ii. 2. 39.

235. The Globe editors seem to reckon this speech as prose. But it is a blank verse. The change of feeling in the Prince and Claudio is marked at once by the rise to blank verse; their emotion envelops Borachio, who speaks in blank verse for the rest of the scene: Dogberry alone, preoccupied with Conrade's insult, is impervious to emotion, and finally brings Leonato down to prose.

236, 237. Here, and in 248, 249 below, the rhyme is accidental. The Prince's words recall Benedick's description of Don John, iv. 1. 188.

238, 239. That revulsion of feeling which the Friar had anticipated from the news of Hero's death is wrought only by the proof of her innocence.

239. loved it first. The preposition, as often, is not repeated.

242. specify. Does Dogberry mean 'testify' or this one hit among all his misses? His suspicious harping on "I am an ass" is as comic as Bottom's "you see an ass-head of your own, do you?" (*Midsummer-Night's Dream*, iii. 1. 119), and for the same reason, though here the ass-head is visible only to the mental eye.

250, 251. F. repeats 'thou' and prints Leonato's speech as prose.

260. Impose me to, impose on me. The construction, not elsewhere found, follows the analogy of other verbs of commanding; cf. l. 265 below.

268. Possess, inform.

270. invention, poetic composition, as often.

271, 272. This penance was suggested by the Friar's advice,

iv. 1. 206. A similar observance is implied in *Winter's Tale*, iii. 2. 239:

> " Once a day I 'll visit
> The chapel where they lie ".

273 seq. This is from Bandello, though for dramatic purposes Shakespeare has shortened the period of mourning to one night. Again compare *Winter's Tale*, where this theme is touched to sterner issues. There Paulina says to Leontes, after his sixteen years of penance, " yet if my lord will marry . . . give me the office To choose you a queen ".

277. In i. 2 mention is made of Antonio's son. But the marked allusions to Hero's fortune (see note on i. 1. 265, 266) make it probable that this is no slip, but an intentional misstatement of Leonato's.

282. poor Claudio. If Claudio turns to a new bride with a fickleness more displeasing than that of Proteus or Orsino, it is to be remembered that all trust in his own judgment is for the moment shattered. The final touch of self-pity sets the seal on our estimate of this young sentimentalist.

284. To-night shows that we have reached the evening of Monday.

286. pack'd, confederate; see Glossary.

287. As he turns to a happy close Shakespeare contrives to give a redeeming touch to Borachio.

290. by, about—a meaning which follows naturally on its original sense of 'near'. Abbott (§ 145) compares *1 Cor.* iv. 4, " I know nothing by myself ". The usage survives in dialect.

294–298. This enlarged version of the " Deformed that wears a lock " is an admirable caricature of the growth of a fiction in uneducated minds.

296. borrows money in God's name, like a professional beggar. Minsheu gives *Pordioséro* as Spanish for a beggar.

300. Leonato still speaks in blank verse, but drops to prose after Dogberry's compliment.

304. God save the foundation! the formula of thanksgiving uttered by those who received alms from a religious house (Herford).

307–309. The ambiguities are in the style of Verges' " excepting your worship's presence " (iii. 5. 29).

314. Antonio has fallen again into his natural place of echo to his brother.

316, 317. Q. and F. print as prose; corr. Pope.

317. lewd, base. See Glossary.

Scene 2

Now that our fears for Hero are allayed we would fain know how Benedick and Beatrice have sped in their wooing. That desire is gratified in the present scene, which adds nothing further to the action, but displays these characters in a new and charming light in their new relation, and fills up the interval between scenes 1 and 3 with an interlude in contrasted tone.

3. We have noted that Margaret, who might have exculpated Hero, is kept out of the fourth Act altogether. Her unabated boisterousness in this scene is meant to disguise that structural flaw, by creating the impression that she has not heard enough of the accusation to connect it with herself and Borachio.

5. style: with a pun on 'stile', for which compare Chaucer, *Squire's Tale*, 97, 98:

> "Al be it that I can not sowne his style,
> Ne can not clymben over so high a style".

6. come over, surpass, with a play on the literal sense which Margaret characteristically catches up. There may be a further pun on 'comely'.

9. keep, stay, in which sense the word is common in Cambridge.

below stairs, in the servants' room. [All the examples collected by Mr. Hart (*N. S. S. Transactions*, 1877–79, p. 471) may be so explained, even Chapman's *Widow's Tears*, i. 4, for Tharsalio had been page to the Count.]

10. The greyhound alone among dogs can seize its prey in full career.

15, 16. I give thee the bucklers. 'To take up the bucklers' = to enter the lists (properly for sword-and-buckler play); so 'to give up the bucklers' = to own one's self beaten.

19. pikes, the spikes in the centre of shields.

vice, screw. See Glossary.

24–27. Q. and F. print as prose; corr. Capell. These lines are the beginning of a song by William Elderton, and are imitated in Heywood's *Fair Maid of the Exchange*, which abounds in reminiscences of *Much Ado*:

> "Ye gods of love that sit above,
> And pity lovers' pain,
> Look from your thrones upon the moans
> That I do now sustain".

28. Leander lived at Abydos, on the Hellespont, and swam the strait to visit Hero. Their story was made famous by Marlowe's *Hero and Leander*, a translation from the Greek of Musæus (?), published in 1598, and completed by Chapman. The story of *Troilus and Cressida* had been told by Chaucer, and forms the subject of Shakespeare's play of that name. Leander and Troilus are stock instances of faithful lovers; see *As You Like It*, iv. 1. 97 and 100.

29. pandars: from Cressida's uncle, Pandarus.

30. carpet - mongers, carpet - knights. The termination *monger* is regularly contemptuous, except when used literally.

34. 'lady' . . . **'baby'**: a rhyme familiar from the nursery song, "Baby, baby, mother's a lady".

37. So Henry V says (v. 2. 137), "Marry, if you would put me to verses or to dance for your sake, Kate, why you undid me". King Henry is a creation of the same time as Benedick, with whom he has much in common.

38. festival terms, spruce holiday language; opposed to the workaday speech of "russet yeas and honest kersey noes" (*Love's Labour's Lost*, v. 2. 413).

39–end. When Beatrice and Benedick meet at last as avowed lovers they meet alone. They are as witty as ever, but now they employ their wit in playing up to each other, not in running each other down. If Beatrice still has the better in repartee Benedick has ceased to care. He knows that she loves him for his manliness, upon which he can retire in fond superiority.

43. with that I came, *i.e.* came for. The omission of the preposition is not parallel to v. 1. 239, for here the prepositions are not the same, but to *Richard II*, i. 1. 26, "As well appeareth by the cause you come".

46–48. A quibbling sorites like Touchstone's argument on manners (*As You Like It*, iii. 2. 41–45).

51. undergoes, is under, has received.

52. subscribe him, 'post him', we should say. The word properly implies a signed attestation.

59. epithet. Cf. *Othello*, i. 1. 14, "Horribly stuff'd with epithets of war". Shakespeare's use, and indeed his spelling, of Greek words shows no feeling for their etymology. He uses 'epithet' for 'expression', and spells it *epithite* both here and in the Quartos of *Othello*.

64. Benedick enfolds Beatrice in his self-complacency, but she asserts her independence by her saucy retort.

67, 68. **in the time of good neighbours,** "when a man had no need to praise himself" (Wright).

70. F., *monuments . . . bells ring.* **Monument,** memory.

71. It is a charming note of Beatrice's changed attitude that she now encourages Benedick to talk.

72. **clamour** refers not to lamentation, but to the clapping of the bell, which by an unexpected turn is made to ring longer than the widow weeps.

73. **rheum,** tears. See Glossary.

74. **Don Worm, his conscience.** The comparison of conscience to a worm seems to come ultimately from *Mark*, ix. 48, "where their worm dieth not".

85. **old coil:** a slang expression, like 'awful row'. For *coil* see Glossary. 'Old' is E.E. slang for something extreme: *vecchio* is so used in Italian.

86. **abused,** deceived: cf. ii. 2. 25 and note on ii. 1. 214.

88. **presently:** clearly 'at once'. See note on i. 1. 78.

92. **uncle's.** Q. and F., *uncles.* The 'moreover' which introduces the anticlimax is peculiarly delicious.

Scene 3

The injunction of v. 1. 271 is now fulfilled. The setting of this scene may have been suggested by Girondo's confession before Fenecia's tomb. The spectacular form of the penance accords well with the theatricality of the repudiation. The whole is highly symbolical: "sorrow may endure for a night, but joy cometh in the morning".

3. **Done to death,** slain. O.E. *dón* can mean 'to put'.

7, 8. **with** is used in two senses. In line 7 it introduces the cause, in line 8 the accompaniment.

9, 10; 22, 23. The first of these couplets is not part of the epitaph nor the second part of the hymn. They are therefore not strictly lyric. Elsewhere, except in lyrics, Shakespeare uses trochaic tetrameters only for the speech of supernatural beings. Here the solemnity of the occasion determines the choice of metre. (Heuser.)

10. **dumb:** Q., *dead.* Note that 'dumb' rhymes with 'tomb', the *u* being still open in E.E.

13. **thy virgin knight.** Diana is addressed: maidens are called in the poetic style 'Diana's knights', as belonging to the Order of Chastity. Cf. *All's Well,* i. 3. 119, "Dian no queen of virgins, that would suffer her poor knight surprised";

and *Two Noble Kinsmen*, v. 1. 140, "thy female knights" (addressed to Diana).

21. **Heavily, heavily:** F., *Heavenly, heavenly.* The interpretations of this difficult passage may thus be classified:—
(*a*) those which make 'death' the subject of 'be uttered';
(*b*) those which make 'death' the object of 'Till'.

(*a*) (1) Halliwell explains: "they invoke midnight, &c. to assist until her death be uttered, *i.e.* proclaimed". (2) Wright: "till death be cast out or expelled, and there is no more death", referring to *Rev.* xx. 13, 14. The meaning then is that midnight and the grave are to assist Claudio in expressing his remorse to the end of time. (3) Others, explaining 'uttered' as 'cast out', prefer F.'s *Heavenly*, and render "till death be expelled by the power of heaven".

(*b*) (1) Schmidt: "the cry of 'Graves, yawn, &c.' shall be raised till death". (2) Delius: "Till death comes to us, let the words 'heavily, heavily' be uttered".

Of these explanations, (*a*) (3) and (*b*) (1) are impossible. It is an objection to Wright's view that the graves are not called upon to 'assist Claudio', but to 'yield their dead' till the resurrection. On the whole, then, Halliwell's rendering is the most likely, and best brings out the parallelism of the stanza.

25. **The wolves have prey'd.** In the spirit of this symbolic scene these words remind us that treason has done its worst on Hero.

26, 27. Of all 'skyey influences' none (as yet) touched the country-bred Shakespeare so much as the sweet approach of morn. This dappled summer dawn should be compared with the still more gorgeous description of a July morning in *Romeo and Juliet*, ii. 3. 1-4, and contrasted with the cirrous spring morning of *Julius Cæsar*, ii. 1. 103, "yon gray lines That fret the clouds are messengers of day"; and with the tragic wintry daybreak of *Hamlet*, i. 1. 166, "the morn, in russet mantle clad, Walks o'er the dew of yon high eastward hill". Many other descriptions are collected by Madden (p. 22), all written before Shakespeare was forty.

32. **speed's**, *i.e.* speed us. Q. and F., *speeds*; corr. Theobald, after Thirlby. The context requires a wish, not an assertion, and a transitive verb, else 'this' (l. 33) is left ungoverned. 'This' refers to Hero, as 'whom' shows.

Scene 4

The formal dénouement is sketched in lightly, as often in Shakespeare's comedies. Don John has fled; Claudio has done penance; bygones are bygones, and gaiety resumes her sway.

Only in Hero's accents is there any trace of the ordeal through which she has passed.

7. sorts. F., *sort*, but Abbott, § 333, shows that this concord is undoubtedly found in E.E.

8. Since the church scene Benedick has ranged himself with Leonato's household, and now appears with them, not with the lords.

17. confirm'd, unmoved.

29. stand, coincide.

30. Scan: 'In the state' | of hon' | ourab' | le mar' | riage''. Note on Pronunciation, (β) (3).

33. F. omits.

34. Scan 'assembly' as four syllables. **Note on Pronunciation**, (γ) (1).

40–42. Benedick's February face is due to Leonato's enigmatical answer.

44–47. The allusion to Europa is suggested by "tip thy horns with gold". Cf. Tennyson, *Palace of Art*:

" And sweet Europa's mantle blew unclasped
    From off her shoulder backward borne:
From one hand dropt a crocus, one hand grasped
    The mild bull's golden horn".

Jupiter changed himself into a bull to carry off Europa. The story is told by Moschus, whom Tennyson imitates. It was known to Shakespeare from Ovid, *Metamorphoses* ii.

46, 47. The rhyme is mock-heroic, to suit the matter. Benedick retorts in kind.

54. Q. and F. give this line to Leonato. But cf. l. 16. The style, moreover, suits Antonio.

59. like of. The 'of' is perhaps due to the impersonal construction 'me liketh'; cf. 'it repents me of' (Abbott, § 177).

63. F. omits 'defiled'. See Appendix on the Text. Hero now meets Claudio with a prompt justification. Attempts to defend F. on the ground that Hero was not defiled are mistaken. The Hero who was defiled, like the Hero who died, was a creature of Claudio's imagination.

67. qualify, moderate.

74. Scan: " Do not' | you love' | me?
                    Why no' | &c.". (Prosody, § II (a) (α).)

75, 76. F. prints as prose.

77. Scan: " Do not you' | love me'?".

80, 81. F. omits 'that' and spoils the rhythm. The scene is in verse down to l. 90, where Benedick, convicted, escapes to prose.

82. **'T is no such matter,** nothing of the sort. F. omits 'such', and spoils both sense and rhythm.

87. Recalls v. 2. 33-38.

97. Q. and F. give to Leonato; corr. Theobald after Thirlby.

100, 120. Benedick's elation is betrayed by the familiar 'thou'. Cf. note on i. 1. 160.

102. Recalls iv. 2. 79.

105. F. omits 'what'.

112. **double-dealer:** used of one who is unfaithful in love.

121. The staves used by elderly people were often headed with a cross-piece of horn.

122, 123. Our sense of justice, which for the last two Acts has been growing for vengeance on the villain, is thus appeased with the promise of a sop 'to-morrow'; and the play concludes with music and dancing. This is the only comedy of Shakespeare's that ends with a dance.

APPENDIX A

ON THE TEXT

The text of *Much Ado* supplies an easy introduction to the textual criticism of Shakespeare. I have therefore recorded the chief variants in the notes. When the reading of Q. is given in the notes, that of F. has been adopted in the text, and *vice versa*. When the readings of both are found in the notes, I have added the name of the critic whose correction has been adopted in the text. All readings in which both Q. and F. are wrong have been recorded, except stage-directions, and minor slips of spelling and punctuation: other variants only when they throw light on the relation of F. to Q., or on interesting points of Elizabethan pronunciation.

Q. is not divided into Acts or Scenes: F. only into Acts. In the division into scenes, and the form of the stage-directions, Capell is usually followed.

The stage-directions at i. 1. and ii. 1. in Q. and F. indicate a character, Innogen, Leonato's wife, who takes no part in the play. See note to i. 1. At ii. 3. 38 F. has, 'Enter Prince, Leonato, Claudio, and Jacke Wilson'. In iv. 2. the speeches of Dogberry are given in Q. and F. to Kemp, except line 4, which is given to Andrew; those of Verges to Cowley. William Kemp and Richard Cowley are known from the list prefixed to F. to have been among the principal actors who appeared in Shakespeare's plays. Jack Wilson was evidently the actor who took the part of Balthazar (at least in ii. 3.); while Andrew (= Merry Andrew) may be a nickname of Kemp, who was famous in low comic parts. Taken along with the known circumstances of its publication, these facts seem to show that Q. was printed from an acting copy of the play, probably without Shakespeare's concurrence, and certainly without his supervision.

An analysis of the recorded variants shows that, setting

aside stage-directions, the printing of verse as prose, and minor points of spelling and punctuation, there are only seven places in the actual text where both Q. and F. are wrong.   These are—

(1) i. 2. 6—'events stamps' for 'event stamps'.
(2) iii. 2. 25—'everyone cannot master' for 'everyone can master'.
(3) iii. 5. 9—'a little of the matter' for 'a little off the matter'.
(4) iv. 1. 201—'Your daughter here the Princesse (left for dead)' for 'Your daughter here the Princes left for dead'.
(5) iv. 2. 63—'Let them be in the hands of coxcomb' for 'Let them be in the hands'—'Off, coxcomb'.
(6) v. 1. 16—'And sorrow, wagge' for 'Bid sorrow wag'.
(7) v. 1. 97—'And speak of half-a-dozen dangerous words' for 'And speak off, &c.'.

To these should probably be added a lacuna at

(8) iv. 1. 156, (see notes *ad loc.*).

Of these (5) and (8) alone present difficulty.   The rest are simple misprints, mostly due to dictation, complicated in two cases by wrong punctuation.   This gives a very high opinion of the traditional text.

A comparison of Q. and F. shows that (with the same exceptions as before) there are only five places in which F. corrects Q.   These are—

(1) i. 1. 86—Q. 'are you'; F. 'you are'.
(2) ii. 3. 128—Q. 'told of us'; F. 'told us of'.
(3) iii. 1. 58—Q. 'lest sheele make'; F. 'lest she make'.
(4) iii. 3. 74—Q. 'statutes'; F. 'statues'.
(5) v. 3. 10—Q. 'dead'; F. 'dumb'.

To these most editors would add—

(6) v. 4. 7—Q. 'all things sorts', but see note *ad loc.*

Of these corrections (4) seems brilliant, but the misprint can be paralleled; (5) is sound, but the rhyme is a guide.

Are these corrections Shakespeare's?   An analysis of the other instances in which Q. and F. differ suggests that they are not.

1. Two important omissions in F. are due to assignable reasons.   At iii. 2. 30 the words, 'or in the shape of two countries at once, as, a German from the waist downward, all slops, and a Spaniard from the hip upward, no doublet', were omitted in F. to avoid offending some foreign dignitary, usually (but I think erroneously) assumed to have been a Spanish ambassador.   At iv. 2. 16–19, a passage in

which the name of God is freely used, was omitted in F. to escape penalties under the statute of 3 James I, c. 21, 'to restrain the abuses of players'.

2. Other omissions in F. are due to recognizable printer's errors. Thus in i. 1. 280-81—

'And I will break with her [and with her father
And thou shalt have her]',

the bracketed words are omitted in F., the printer's eye having caught the second 'her'. So in iv. 1. 17-18, 'What men daily do [not knowing what they do]', and in v. 4. 63, 'One Hero died [defiled]', where 'defiled' is omitted in F. owing to its resemblance to 'died'.

3. There remain several changes, of which it is not easy to say on mere inspection whether they are due to printer or editor, and whether they are right or wrong. I believe them to be mostly due to an editor, and to be wrong.

Omission of epithets, vocatives, and repeated words is hardly arguable, though such a case as v. 4. 80, 81, 82 can scarcely be accidental. But there are several changes and additions which betray the corrector, and four at least which show that the corrector was not Shakespeare. In ii. 2. 49, F. has 'Be *thou* constant' for Q.'s 'Be *you* constant'. Borachio is the speaker. It is contrary to Shakespeare's practice for a dependant to address his master as 'thou'. In iii. 1. 104, for 'she's *limed*', F. reads 'she's *tane*'—obviously a correction, and the correction of an editor who fails to notice that the image of Beatrice as a coy, wild bird (ll. 24 and 35) is still present to the speaker's mind. In iii. 5. 23, for 'Yea, an 'twere a thousand *pound* more than it-is', F. reads 'a thousand *times*'—again an obvious correction, and a poor improvement on Dogberry's racy nonsense. Finally, in iv. 1. 272, F. reads, 'Do not swear [by it] and eat it', but 'it' is Benedick's oath, not his sword.

To this editor, then, we may fairly attribute most of the other changes in F., even when inoffensive in themselves. Now many of these changes consist in the substitution of a literary for a colloquial form in spelling or syntax. Thus, the pronoun *a'* is changed to *he*; the preposition *a'* to *of*; *brings* to *bringeth*; *cursie* to *cutsy*; *Ursley* to *Ursula*; *unworthy so good a lady* to *unworthy to have so good a lady*; *would have it appear* to *would have it to appear*; *all things sorts* to *all things sort*: and with these might possibly be classed the change of *lest sheele make sport* to *lest she make sport.* For what occasion were these changes made?

The latest known performances of *Much Ado* before the publication of the Folio in 1623, indeed the only performances of which we have actual record before that date, took place in 1613. At some date earlier than May 20th, as Lord Stanhope's accounts testify, *Much Ado* was acted before Prince Charles, his sister—the Lady Elizabeth,—and the Prince Palatine Elector; and a play called *Benedicte and Betteris* was acted (apparently) before the King. (See Introduction, § 2.)

It was for these performances, I infer, that the recension was made which has come down to us in the Folio of 1623. Some colloquialisms were removed to suit the taste of the courtly audience, and the uncomplimentary reference *to the Germans*, in iii. 2. 30, was omitted to avoid offending the Elector Palatine.

Two other considerations confirm this hypothesis. (1) The present division into Acts dates from the First Folio. It has been shown (Introduction to Act II) that that division was determined by stage requirements, not by the natural divisions of the action. On the public stages this would be purposeless, for the public stages had no scenery. The division was clearly made for a court performance, where scenery was used.[1]   (2) The court performances of 1613 were managed by John Heming, who afterwards helped to edit the First Folio.

APPENDIX B

NOTE ON SHAKESPEARE'S PROSODY

I. **Definitions: Verse, Prose, Blank Verse.**—In reading any English composition a certain *stress* is laid on syllables at various intervals. The succession of these stresses makes the *rhythm*, or flow, of the composition. When they succeed each other at (more or less) regular intervals, the flow is called *metre*, and the composition *verse*.

---

[1] This hypothesis is consistent with the view that Jack Wilson was the John Wilson, born 1594, who was afterwards Professor of Music at Oxford. He wrote an air to "Lawn as white as driven snow".

Ordinary Shakespearian dialogue is written in a metre which consists of five stressed, alternating with five unstressed syllables, *i.e.* of five dissyllabic feet, in *rising rhythm*, *i.e.* opening on the unstressed syllables, and without rhyme—whence the name *Blank Verse*. *E.g.*—

> Is lit′tle Cu′pid's craf′ty ar′row made′.

II. Variations.—All variations will fall under the head of (*a*) more or fewer syllables; (*b*) more or fewer stresses; (*c*) falling or level rhythm.

(*a*) **Syllables.** (*a*) *Extra syllables.*—An additional (unstressed) syllable may be inserted anywhere in a line. It is most common immediately before a pause, and so is most frequently found at the end of the line. Such endings are called *feminine* endings, and, properly used, impart a peculiar softness and beauty; cf. i. 1. 287–299 with Hero's words, iii. 1. 59–64. Within the line the extra syllable usually comes at the mid-line pause, *e.g.*—

> Be yet my ne | phew: my brother hath a daughter (v. 1. 275),

or with a change of speakers, *e.g.*—

> With any just reproach?
> > Mar | ry, that can Hero (iv. 1. 79).

(Cf. also iv. 1. 169, iv. 1. 248, v. 1. 287; and for 'marry' at beginning, iv. 1. 209, v. 1. 53).

Two extra syllables sometimes appear to be added, *e.g.*—

> Thou pure in piety and impious pur | ity (iv. 1. 102).

But unless there is slurring, such instances should be classed as Alexandrines (III, below).

Extra syllables are also common in proper names, thus—

> But I persuaded them, if they loved Ben | edick (iii 1. 41).

Cf. 'Beatrice' 'Ursula', 'Antony', *passim*.

Indeed, Shakespeare sometimes treats proper names as altogether extra-metrical, *e.g.*—

> Hero! why, Hero!   Uncle! Signior Benedick! Friar (iv. 1. 112).

(β) *Syllables omitted.*—An unstressed syllable is sometimes, though rarely, omitted, *e.g.*—

> Dear′ | my lord, if you, in your own proof (iv. 1. 43);

and so possibly—

> *D. Pedro.* I will not hear you.
> *Leon.*   No?
> Come′, | brother; away!   I will be heard (v. 1. 107, 108).

But see below. This happens especially after a marked pause, hence this omission is most common in the first foot (compare the monosyllabic first feet in Chaucer), and after that in the third. An emphatic monosyllable, often an imperative, generally precedes.

(*b*) Lines of more than five full feet, not being slurred, and lines of less than five feet, not being exclamatory or broken lines, are not mere variations of the ordinary pentameter (see III below). But Shakespeare makes abundant use of *short* or *broken* verses. They occur usually at the beginning or end of a speech, when a speaker leaves off in the middle of a verse, or interrupts another without regard to the metre. They sometimes occur in the middle of a speech, when the speaker breaks off and resumes anew, *e.g.*—

> A thousand times in secret.
> *D. John.* Fie, fie! they are not to be named, my lord,
> Not to be spoke of— (iv. 1. 93, 94)

(breaks off in affected disgust). Cf. also v. 1. 10.

Exclamations and asides belong to this class of broken lines, and present no difficulty. At iii. 2. 118–120, Don Pedro's 'O day untowardly turned!' is echoed by Claudio and Don John, but is probably not meant for verse.

Apparent four-stress lines are sometimes to be explained as two broken lines, *e.g.*—

> *Leon.* My lord, my lord,—
> *D. Pedro.* I will not hear you (v. 1. 106, 107).

(But see (*a*) (*β*) above.)

Sometimes part of a line seems to do double duty, *e.g.*—

> Smother her spirits up.
> *Bene.* How doth the lady?
> *Beat.* Dead, I think. Help, uncle! (iv. 1. 110–111).

Here Benedick caps Don John's line, and is in turn capped by Beatrice. So v. 1. 99, 100.

(*c*) So far I have spoken only of 'stressed' and 'unstressed' syllables. But as grammarians distinguish between Primary and Secondary Accent, we must distinguish in Prosody between strong and weak stress. The three syllables, *e.g.* of 'Ur'sulà', have three degrees of stress: they may be called, in order, strong-stressed, unstressed, weak-stressed. Hence, without actual omission of syllable, a foot may be weakened by the substitution of a *weak* or intermediate for the normal strong stress.

This variation is exceedingly common—not more than one line in fifteen having the normal five full stresses, but is exercised under the following laws:—

(1) The weak stress (ˋ) is most common in the fifth foot, *e.g.*—

> The fairest grant is the necess | ity' (i. 1. 288).

(2) There are never more than two weak stresses in a line.

(3) Two weak stresses rarely come together.

(4) When there are two weak stresses in a line, the loss of weight is made up for in one or both of two ways. Either the other syllable in one foot has also a slight stress—

> He' is' | the only man of Italy (iii. 1. 92),

or, one of the neighbouring feet has two stresses—

> Of the | false' sweet' | bait that we lay for it (iii. 1. 33).

(*d*) *Rhythm.*—(*a*) The order of stressed and unstressed syllables may be inverted in any foot, thus changing the rhythm (for that foot) from rising to falling, *e.g.*—

> (i) Say'ing | I liked her ere I went to wars (i. 1. 275).
> (ii) And so | dies' my | revenge (v. 1. 279).
> (iii) Strike at thy life. | Grieved' I, | I had been one (iv. 1. 126).
> (iv) My love is thine to teach; | teach' it | but how (i. 1. 262).

Stress-inversion, like stress-weakening, is practised within certain limits.

(1) Since inversion brings two stresses together, it is most common after a pause, *i.e.* in the first, and after that in the third and fourth feet; it is not often found in the second.

(2) It is very rare in the last place, because a change of rhythm there produces a halting effect. Hence the name *scazon* ('limping') given to this metre in Greek.

(3) There are never more than two inversions in a line; a majority of inversions would alter the character of the rhythm, not merely of the foot, but of the line.

(4) Two inversions rarely come together.

(*β*) Under the conditions recorded above, the two syllables of a foot may have approximately equal stress, thus giving a level ('spondaic' or 'pyrrhic') rhythm. This is occasionally found even in the fifth foot, *e.g.*—

> But now I am returned and that | war'-thoughts' | (i. 1. 272).
> When I do name him let it be | thy' part' | (iii. 1. 18).

III. Other Unrhymed Measures are occasionally introduced at impressive turns of the dialogue Genuine four-
foot measures are very rare: there is no instance in *Much
Ado*. Six-foot measures (Alexandrines) are probably found
at iv. 1. 159—

> To start into her face, a thousand innocent shames,

and at iv. 1. 102—

> Thou pure impiety and impious purity,

although the reading has been doubted in the first case,
and an alternative scansion is possible in the second [II
(*a*) (*a*)]. This is the regular type of Alexandrine, with
mid-line pause.

IV. Rhyme is used in the form of (*a*) couplets, (*b*) stanzas,
(*c*) lyric measures.

(*a*) (*a*) *Heroic Couplets* differ from normal blank verse
simply in having rhyme. They are used (1) to close a
speech, *e.g.*—

> If this be so, then loving goes by haps,
> Some Cupid kills with arrows, some with traps (iii. 1. 105-6).

(2) to clinch an epigram, *e.g.* v. 4. 46-51. The first use is
closely allied to the second, as appears from the epigram-
matic turn of the couplet quoted. This use of a rhymed
'tag' to cover an exit, or to mark the close of a scene,
survives even in the prose comedy of Congreve.

(β) *Four-stress Couplets* in falling rhythm are found at
v. 3. 9-10 and 22-23. This measure is elsewhere confined
to the speech of supernatural characters. See note *ad loc.*

(*b*) *Stanzas* belong to the conventional form of higher
poetry, and bring a verse scene to an impassioned or
solemn close. At the end of iii. 1. Beatrice's emotion is
expressed in a sequence of two quatrains and a couplet.
The verse part of iv. 1. concludes with a solemn quatrain,
ending in an Alexandrine. The lyric scene, v. 3, is closed
with an imperfect sestet and a quatrain.

(*c*) *Lyric Measures* are represented by the Song (ii. 3.
59-71), the Epitaph (v. 3. 3-8), and the Dirge (v. 3. 12-21).

V. Prose.—Two-thirds of *Much Ado* is in prose. Shakespeare's choice of prose or verse is determined in this play
primarily by consideration of the dominant sentiment of
each situation. Prose represents the language of ordinary
life, it appeals to the intellect, and is therefore used for
formal preliminaries, comic dialogue, and commonplace

conversation, *i.e.* by vulgar persons habitually, and by gentlefolks in matters of business and light or familiar talk.   Verse is a more heightened and conventional mode of speech, and so is used when there is an appeal to emotion or imagination, *i.e.* by gentlefolks in their serious moments.   Hence, generally, the serious parts are in verse, except ii. 2.; the comic in prose, except iii. 1.   The former is a vulgar plot, concocted in cold blood between familiars; the chief speaker is a low fellow.   The latter is in verse, to contrast it more effectively with the parallel scene, ii. 3: a sweeter and more serious tone is assumed: Hero is the chief speaker.   Changes within the same scene are most instructive.   In i. 1. Claudio tells his tale of love in verse; in ii. 1., when he thinks himself betrayed, he soliloquizes in verse; the verse of the poetic interlude in ii. 3. 34-71 marks the passing of a mood inspired by music and evening stillness.   In the church scene formal prose is soon flung aside, and the emotion rises till it passes off in a solemn quatrain.   It breaks out again in v. 1., dropping on Leonato's exit, but rising at once on Borachio's confession, and enveloping Borachio himself, who has hitherto spoken only in prose.   Dogberry alone remains on the pedestrian level, and drags Leonato down to it.   The verse of the last scene balances that of the church scene.   Benedick uses prose even to make love to Beatrice and to challenge Claudio; the former relations of these characters have placed them, as it were, on a prose footing.   Prose is Benedick's natural speech: he abandons it only in iv. 1. and v. 4.: his resumption of it at v. 4. 91 marks that he is himself again.

VI. Pauses.—In § 2 I have enumerated the variations possible within the limits of the single line.   But when we come to consider a sequence of lines, or verse-paragraph, a new source of variation is disclosed in the disposition of the pauses.   Naturally there is a pause at the end of each line, with a slighter pause within the line.   Such is the regular structure of the primitive English pentameter, the mid-line pause falling commonly after the second foot. This monotony Shakespeare breaks up (1) by varying the position of the mid-line pause, (2) by dispensing now and then with the end-line pause, thus producing what are called *enjambed* or run-on lines.   There is enjambement in some degree wherever the end of a line goes more closely *in reading* with what follows than with what goes before. But the closeness of an enjambement depends upon the grammatical connection, the relative importance, and the order of the parts. The enjambements in *Much Ado*, though numerous, are not bold. There are none of those 'light' and 'weak' endings—lines closing on a conjunction, a preposition, a relative, or a copula—which may be found on every page of *The Tempest* or *A Winter's Tale*.

VII. Metre as a Test of Date.—Three of the types or variations mentioned above are occasionally of use in helping to determine the chronology of Shakespeare's writings :—(1) Rhyme, which he affected less and less; (2) double-endings, and (3) enjambement, which he affected more and more. Their value as chronological tests is not equal; it is lowest in the case of rhyme, which we have seen that Shakespeare uses consciously and for special purposes; highest in the case of enjambement, his increasing fondness for which denotes a gradual growth of the rhythmical sense. More valuable than any, perhaps, is (4) the speech-ending test, based on the coincidence of speech-endings with verse-endings, a coincidence which Shakespeare came gradually to avoid.

The versification of *Much Ado* has the general characteristics of the middle period — rhymes are scarce, double-endings common, &c., but the various tests yield no very definite result. This is partly due to lack of data, the bulk of the comedy being in prose. I give the percentages for *Much Ado*, *Love's Labour's Lost* (a typical early play), and the *Tempest* (a typical late play).

	L.L.L.	*Much Ado.*	*Tempest.*
Rhyme	22.2	5.2	.1
Double-endings	7.7	22.9	35.4
Enjambements	18.4	19.3	41.5
Speech-endings	10	20.7	84.5

By the first and third tests, *Much Ado* stands 16th in the list of plays; by the second, 21st; by the fourth, 20th. In fine, with *1 Henry IV*, *Julius Cæsar*, and *The Merry Wives*, it falls between *Richard II* and *Hamlet*.[1]

---

[1] König's figures (*Der Vers in Shakespeare's Dramen*, pp. 130–138) are retained, though they are not absolutely right for *Much Ado*. Under the third head König reckons only such enjambements as are strengthened by close syntactical connection or otherwise.

NOTE ON ELIZABETHAN PRONUNCIATION AS AFFECTING PROSODY.

Difference of pronunciation then and now accounts for many apparent variations.

(*a*) *Accentual Variations.*—There has been little change in the accentuation of *simple* words, but E.E. shows greater laxity in the case of *compounds*. The M.E. struggle between French and English accent ended in the victory of the latter. But the influence of Latin quantity preserved or restored the original accent in many compounds, and by analogy in simple words as well. Thus, in Shakespeare we sometimes find the English accent where we have returned to the Latin, *e.g.* an'tique (iii. 1. 63), and so always; com'mendable (iii. 1. 71, 73), but also commend'-able; con'firm'd (v. 4. 17), but confirm'd' (iv. 1. 149). On the other hand, F. reads purpose' at iii. 1. 12, but the word is not elsewhere so accented. Of change in the accent of Germanic words there is no clear instance in *Much Ado*. König accents be'twixt in iv. 1. 82, but this is doubtful; and always' in iii. 1. 93, but this is wrong.

(*b*) *Syllabic Variations.*[1]—(*a*) (1) The vowel of an unaccented monosyllable is sometimes lost before a consonant, *e.g.* not to knit (2 sylls.), iv. 1. 42. [But cf. § II (*a*) (*a*) above].

(2) Except here and there in early plays, short *e* is always mute in *-es* of genitives and plurals. In the 3rd pers. sing. of verbs *-es*[2] mute, *-eth* sonant is the rule. In *-est* and *-ed* (of verbs and adjectives) there is much variety, but Shakespeare favoured the shorter form as he grew older, *e.g.* beliest (2 sylls.) (v. 1. 252), pleasant'st (iii. 1. 26), pleachèd (iii. 1. 7), couchèd (iii. 1. 30), movèd (iii. 1. 67), unconstrainèd (iv. 1. 22), grievèd (iv. 1. 87) accusèd (iv. 1. 231). But in the past indic. *-ed* mute is the rule, and is sometimes found even after a dental, *e.g.* mistrusted (ii. 1. 162), and possibly *persuaded* (iii. 1. 41). [But cf. § II (*a*) (*a*) above.]

(3) An unaccented vowel is sometimes lost before a consonant in the middle of a word of more than two syllables, *e.g.* med'cine (Q. in v. 1. 24). But in such cases, unless

---

[1] In this section I have followed the order adopted by Professor Herford in the admirable Appendix to his *Richard II* in this series.
[2] The mark (.) under a vowel shows that it is mute.

indicated in printing, it is not always easy to say whether a vowel is lost or an extra syllable is inserted.

(β) Two adjacent vowels may be run into one.

(1) In the same word—*lineament* (v. 1. 14); *being* (iv. 1. 218, v. 1. 61, v. 4. 8); *preceptial* (?) (v. 1. 24); *ruffian* (iv. 1. 89); *friar* (v. 4. 57—but *fri'ar* v. 4. 18); *valuing* (iv. 1. 138).

(2) In adjacent words—*The idea* (iv. 1. 223); *Yea and* (v. 1. 235); *I am* (iv. 1. 86, 97); *many a* (ii. 3. 47). With this may be classed the slurring of the semi-vowel *w*, e.g. *she would* (iii. 1. 62, 75); *virtue would* (iv. 1. 36); *You will* (iv. 1. 47).
In both cases slurring is most common when the first vowel is *i* or *u*, which readily assume a consonantal power =*y* or *w*. But an alternative scansion is often possible.

(3) On the other hand, the terminations: -*iar*, -*ience*, -*ion*, -*ions*, now regularly contracted, are frequently open in Shakespeare, e.g. *famili-ar* (v. 4. 70); *pati-ence* (v. 1. 19, 258); *affecti-on* (iii. 1. 42); *appariti-ons* (iv. 1. 158); *complexi-on* (i. 1. 284); *inventi-on* (iv. 1. 193, v. 1. 270); *ostentati-on* (iv. 1. 204); *graci-ous* (iv. 1. 106). So also *marri-age* (v. 4. 30). In all these cases the open *i-ar*, *i-ence*, &c., is at the end of a line.

(γ) One of the most characteristic differences between Elizabethan and modern pronunciation is the fluid state of the 'vowel-likes': *l*, *m*, *n*, *r*, and perhaps *ng*. These letters may have the force either of vowels or of consonants, e.g. in *little*, the first *l* is consonantal, the second vocalic. The sign (₀) under the letter is used to indicate the sonant (vocalic) value.

(1) A sonant liquid (*l̤*, *m̤*, *n̤*, *r̤*) may form a new syllable, e.g. *assembly* (v. 4. 34); *parlour* (iii. 1. 1); *tickling* (iii. 1. 80).

(2) A liquid may cause the loss of a syllable at the end of a word, either by becoming consonantal before a following vowel, e.g. *given her* (=*givner*), (v. 1. 278); or by being slurred before a following consonant, e.g. *utter them* (2 syllables) (iv. 1. 96); *gentleman* (2 syllables), (v. 4. 84); *stolen from* (2 syllables), (v. 4. 89); *warrant you* (2 syllables), (iii. 1. 14); *impossible: but* (4 syllables), (v. 1. 267); *little, for* (2 syllables), (iv. 1. 154); and perhaps *agent; for* (2 syllables), (ii. 1. 159). In the three last cases there is a pause,

and an alternative scansion is possible. See II (*a*) (*α*) above.

(3) Syncope of an unaccented vowel in the middle of a word, rare before a consonant, is very common before a liquid, *e.g. exçellency* (ii. 3. 43); *ene̦mies* (v. 1. 98); *reckoṇings* (v. 4. 52); *dangeṛous* (v. 1. 97); *inteṛest* (iv. 1. 230); *reveṛence* (iv. 1. 167); *spiṛits* (iv. 1. 124). Contraction before *r* is far the most common. Even when it precedes, a liquid seems to make contraction easier, *e.g. inno̦cent* (iv. 1. 162).

(4) A long vowel or diphthong is sometimes resolved into two syllables before the liquid *r*. So, perhaps, 'De-ar my lord' (iv. 1. 43); but see II (*a*) (*β*) above.

(δ) In *other, whether*, &c., *even, seven*, &c., contraction results after suppression of the consonant, *i.e. e'en* (not ev'n), (iii. 1. 29). So *ta'en* for *taken* (v. 4. 122). This contraction is familiar in Scotch.

GLOSSARY

[I am indebted to Mr. W. A. Craigie for information on *quip, quirk*, and *recheat*.]

a, the indefinite article. O.E. *án*, one, differentiated into *oon*, numeral, and *ǎn*, article. Note the use *a* = one, the same (iii. 5. 35; iv. 2. 28).

advertisement (v. 1. 32), admonition. Fr. *avertissement*, f. *avertiss-* (lengthened stem of *avertir*) + *ment*; ultimately from Lat. *ad*, to + *vertere*, to turn. Meaning (1) the turning of one's mind to anything, attention; (2) the turning of another's mind to anything, calling to attention, admonishing. Murray classes this use with the modern, = announcement. But the sense of the passage is against this. Cf. note *ad loc.*

agate (iii. 1. 65), a sixteenth-century formation from Fr. *agathe*, Gk. ἀχάτης, a precious stone: figuratively, a dwarfish person, in allusion to the small figures cut in agates for seals. Spelt 'agot' in Shakespeare.

an (iii. 5. 35), if. Probably the same as *and* co-ordinate. Spelt *and* before 1600.

ancientry (ii. 1. 66), old-fashioned decorum. From *ancient* + *ry*.

angel (ii. 3. 31), a coin. Originally *angel-noble* (being a new issue of the noble with the archangel Michael on it, first coined in 1465, and worth 6s. 8d., the same as the noble. In the reign of Edward VI its value rose to 10s.

ántique (iii. 1. 63), a grotesque. *Not* from the adj. 'antique', but from It. *antico*, used as = It. *grottesco* (f. *grotta*) and applied to fantastic figures found in exhuming ancient remains at Rome. From this ascription of grotesque work to the ancients, anything bizarre was in English at first called *antique*, the name grotesque not being introduced till a hundred years later. In this sense *antique* is first found in 1548; it is used of a gesture ('antic') in 1529. Hence the adverb **anticly** (v. 1. 96).

apprehend (ii. 1. 69), understand, from Lat. *apprehendere* (not in M.E.), to seize (1) a person, (2) an idea, and so (3) to anticipate something adverse.

arrant (v. 1. 307), notorious Properly pres. part. of Northern verb *argh*, to be cowardly, O.E. *earg*, timid, Sc. *ergh*; but confused with Fr. *errant*. Same root in *arch* with similar change of meaning.

arras (i. 3. 57), tapestry. From *Arras*, a town in Artois famed for this fabric. Familiar instances of such formation (name of manufacture from place of manufacture) are *calico, delf, gouda,* &c.

baldrick (i. 1. 217), belt. Origin and history obscure. In M.E. the form *bawdry* occurs = O.Fr. *baudrei*. The root is perhaps the same as Lat. *balteus*, Eng. *belt*.

beshrew (v. 1. 55), curse. From *be* + *shrew* (v. *shrewd*). Originally 'to make evil' (cf. *befoul*), then 'to wish evil'. Later only as an expletive, in which use it is probably not imperative but elliptical, like 'thank you', 'prithee'.

blazon (ii. 1. 264), description. O. Fr. *blason*. The original meaning is simply 'shield', then a shield in heraldry, armorial bearings. Its metaphorical use shows the influence of the verb *blaze*=to proclaim (Ger. *blasen*, to blow; cf. *blare*), for which see *Mark* i. 45, "to blaze abroad the matter".

Borachio < Sp. *borracho*, drunkard; *borracha*, wine-skin. In the literal sense of 'wine-skin' and the metaphorical sense of 'skinful', 'bellyful', the word occurs in sixteenth-century E.E. There is no instance of the sense drunkard before 1600, and this sense of the common noun *may* have been developed from the proper name. But this is unlikely; see note on iii. 3. 98.

bucklers (v. 2. 17), shields. O. Fr. *boucler*, as if from Lat. *buccularius*, bossed, f. *buccula*, boss, dim. of *bucca*, cheek.

burden (iii. 5. 41), refrain, bass, or undersong. O.E. *byrðen*, < *beran*, to bear. This peculiar sense comes from confusion with M.E. *burdoun*, Fr. *bourdon*, bass [Lat. *burdon-em*, acc. of *burdo*, drone], from the notion that the bass is 'heavier' than the air. Hence the sense of theme.

canker (i. 3. 25), dog-rose. N. Fr. *cancre*, Lat. *cancer-um*, acc. of *cancer*, crab. Originally an ulcer, 'cancer', blight on plants. Applied to the dog-rose apparently because that plant is peculiarly liable to such a blight. The name is still so used in dialect. In Shakespeare also of a blight, literal or metaphorical. In *Midsummer-Night's Dream*, iii. 2. 282, 'canker-blossom' is either the dog-rose, like 'canker-blooms' in *Sonnet* liv, or the first part of the word is a

verb, as in 'mar-plot', 'spoil-sport'.

cheapen (ii. 3. 29), ask the price of. O.E. *cedpian*, to buy, < *cedp*, price. 'Cheap' was still a noun in M.E., the adj. use coming from the phrase *good cheap*, in imitation of Fr. *bon marché*.

cinquepace (ii. 1. 63), five 'steps' of the galliard, the sixth being the *sault majeur* or caper. Fr. *cinq*, five; *pas*, pace.

claw (i. 3. 16), flatter. O.E. *clawian*, Ger. *klauen*. From its figurative use in such expressions as 'claw the back of', 'claw the humour of', 'claw' itself came to mean 'wheedle', and is still so used in Leicestershire dialect.

cog (v. 1. 95), cheat. A sixteenth-century word of unknown derivation. It was a slang word, originally applied to cheating at dice—*not* by loading the dice, as modern use suggests, but by controlling their fall in some way—then to cheating in general.

coil (iii. 3. 87; v. 2. 85), disturbance. Probably a slang word which rose into the literary language. Several words of similar meaning, like 'pother', 'row', 'mob', 'hubbub', have a similar origin in slang.

complexion (i. 1. 284), appearance. Lat. *complexion-em*, acc. of *complexio*, a word originally applied to the combination of the 'humours', the temperament; then of external appearance as index of temperament; finally limited to the hue of the face. For the change of meaning cf. *favour* below.

conceit (ii. 1. 265), idea. An English formation from *conceive*, on the analogy of *deceit* from *deceive*, &c., meaning (1) conception, (2) private opinion, (3) an overweening opinion of one's self. The last, which is now the common meaning, never attaches to the word in Shakespeare,

? cukott !

cousin (i. 2. 1; ii. 1. 69, &c.). From Fr. *cousin*; Late Lat. *cossinus, cossofrenus* < Lat. *consobrinus*, cousin by the mother's side (*con + soror*). But the word was used to translate *consanguineus*, kinsman, and so was extended to other blood-relations, especially uncle, nephew (i. 2. 1), and niece (ii. 1. 69), but also to grandchildren (*Richard III*. ii. 2. 8), and was finally used as a mere term of courtesy (so perhaps i. 2. 22).

cozened (ii. 2. 35), cheated. Usually explained as from *cousin*, and compared with Fr. *cousiner*, 'to claim kindred for advantage' (Cotgrave), and so 'to make a cousin of', 'to sponge on'. But Murray thinks that there is no evidence for the transition, and that the spelling is against this view. (The form 'cosining', however, occurs in Hackluyt's *Voyages* i. 586, quoted by Skeat.) Mr. Palmer suggests It. *cozzonare* < *cozzone*, 'a horse-breaker, a crafty knave' (Florio). But there is no evidence for this.

cue (ii. 1. 273). Sometimes derived from Fr. *queue*, tail, as being the tail of the preceding speech. But never so used in French; the term is *réplique*. As the word is written *Q* or *qu* in old copies, it was explained by seventeenth-century writers as short for Lat. *qualis* or *quando*. Of this there is no confirmation. (Cue=farthing is from *q=quadrans*.)

cunning (v. 1. 218), wise, subtle. Pres. part. of M.E. *cunnen*, to know. The degradation of the word had set in in E.E. Cf. iv. 1. 34.

daffed (ii. 3. 158), put off. A bye-form of *doff*=do off; cf. *don, dup*. In the metaphorical sense the form is always *daff*, not *doff*, except in *Othello*, iv. 2. 176, where, however, F1 has 'dafts', and Globe reads 'daffest'.

defend (iv. 2. 18), forbid. M.E. and O.Fr. *defendre*, Lat. *defendere* = (1) to ward off, (2) to guard. Sense (1) was extended to 'prohibit' and 'forbid', which meanings unite in 'God defend', 'heaven defend', but only in these phrases. Otherwise the E.E. use is like the modern.

deprave (v. 1. 95), slander. Lat. *depravare*, from *de* and *pravus*, bad, perhaps through Fr. *dépraver*. Meaning (1) to make bad, (2) to represent as bad, to defame. For the change from act to thought cf. 'disable', which in E.E. means to disparage.

drovier (ii. 1. 173), drover. The *i*, due to the analogy of French *nomina agentis* in *-ier*, has survived in some words as a glide after semi-vowels and liquids, *e.g.* 'collier', 'bowyer', 'sawyer'; Sc. 'lovyer', 'lawyer'.

ducats (ii. 2. 48), a coin, so called because when first coined (1140 A.D.) in the duchy (*ducatus*) of Apulia, it bore the legend '*Sit tibi, Christe, datus, quem tu regis, iste ducatus*'.

ecstasy (ii. 3. 141), frenzy. Ultimately from Gk. ἐκστασις < ἐκ out of; στῆναι, to stand; so=being beside one's self. The word is now usually limited to transports of joy, but may be used, and in E.E. is often used, of other overwhelming feelings as well, even of a swoon.

eftest (iv. 2. 32), perhaps speediest. Dogberry's mistake for some word unknown, perhaps 'deftest'. The word is unique. The reference to 'eftsoons' is wrong, for any sense of 'soon' which that word may have (and the sense is not apparent in E.E.) comes from its second part; 'eft' is 'after'.

engaged (iv. 1. 326), pledged. Fr. *engager* < *en + gage*, to offer as a guarantee.

fancy. Short for fantasy, through intermediate *fantsy*; ultimately from Gk. φαντασία, imagination. Meaning (1) the faculty of imagination and its objects; (2) individual taste, liking; (3) love. Cf. iii. 2. 28, 29, where there is a play on meanings (2) and (3).

fashion-monging (v. 1. 94), following the fashion. A Shakespearian coinage from E.E.*fashion-monger*. Only here.

favour (iii. 3. 19), looks or good looks. O.Fr. *favor*, Lat. *favor-em*, acc. of *favor* < *favère*, to side with. The transition to the meaning in the text seems to be found in the use of 'favour' for that which conciliates affection, *i.e.* comeliness, and so to the concrete. Similarly 'countenance' has passed from the sense of 'mien' to that of 'face', and 'complexion' from 'temperament' to 'hue'. The verb *favour* is still used in dialect for 're-semble', and the noun for 're-semblance'. Cf. 'well-favoured', 'ill-favoured'.

fleer (v. 1. 58), grin, jeer. Perhaps Scandinavian; *flira* in Norwegian=titter.

flout (i. 1. 258), mock. Dutch *fluyten*, to play the flute, to jeer.

foining (v. 1. 84), fencing. O.Fr. *foine* (Fr. *fouine*), from Lat. *fussina*, a three-pronged spear.

good-year (i. 3. 1), a petty oath. Equivalent to, and perhaps adopted from Dutch *wat goedtjaar*, *que bonne heure*; probably elliptical in origin, 'As I hope for a good year'. Hanmer derived the word from Fr. *goujère*, pox—an explanation which fits the E. E. use singularly, but is etymologically impossible. There is no such word in French.

guerdon (v. 3. 5), recompense. Through O.Fr. from Ital. *guidardone*, Low Lat. *widerdonum*, a hybrid from O.H.G. *wider* (Ger. *wieder*), against. and Lat. *donum*, a gift.

holp (i. 1. 45), helped. O.E. *healp*, *holpen*; M.E. *halp*, *holpen*. Shakespeare uses *holp* both as past indic. and as past part.

horn-mad (i. 1. 242), properly of horned beasts = mad enough to horn one; then with a play on cuckoldry. Survived in Sc., "Miss Grant will be fair horn-mad" (Stevenson).

humour (v. 1. 180), frame of mind; (v. 4. 100), bent. O.Fr. *humor*, Lat. *humor-em*, acc. of *humor*, moisture. Applied specially to the fluids of the body. See notes.

incensed (v. 1. 224), instigated. Not from Lat. *incendere*, the sense of 'fired' being inappropriate here, and out of the question in *Henry VIII*. v. 1. 43, "I have incensed the lords that he is a most arch heretic"; but = *insensed*, which Nares quotes as a Staffordshire provincialism for 'informed'. Shakespeare's use of the word may also have been influenced by 'incentor'=instigator (Foxe's *Book of Martyrs*, ed. 1596).

kind, kindness (i. 1. 25); **kindly** (iv. 1. 72). O.E. *ge-cynde*, native < *cynd*, nature. Both noun and adj. in E.E. frequently retain something of the original sense, which is played on in i. 1. 25.

large (ii. 3. 183; iv. 1. 50), gross. Through Fr. from Lat. *largus*, free, bountiful: this is the common meaning in Chaucer: hence 'too free', perhaps by a kind of euphemism.

learn (iv. 1. 28), teach. M.E. *lernen*, O.E. *leornian*, a neuter form sometimes confused with the causative *leren*, *læran*, to teach. The confusion is reciprocal. (Cf. Ger. *lehren* and *lernen*.)

lewd (v. 1. 317), base. From O.E. *lǽwed*, of the laity, as if from Low Lat. *laicatus*>*<clericatus*, of the clergy. Hence the transition from M.E. 'ignorant', through E.E. 'base', to Mod.E. 'licentious' (Skeat). (But the vowel change is obscure.)

liberal (iv. 1. 90), licentious. Through Fr. from Lat. *liberalis*, becoming a *liber* or freeman. From meaning 'free' it came sometimes in E.E. to mean 'too free', a meaning perhaps helped by association with 'libertine'. Cf. 'large', above.

liege (i. 1.261), sovereign. M.E. and O.Fr. *lige*, *liege*, < O.H.G. *ledic*, 'free': hence properly of the feudal suzerain or *liege-lord*, who alone was free; but also applied to his vassals ("the Queen's lieges"), by supposed derivation from Lat. *ligare*, to bind.

list (iii. 4. 75), choose. O.E. *lystan*, M.E. *lusten*, both used impersonally. For the change to the personal construction cf. 'please'.

luxurious (iv. 1. 39), lustful. This sense of *luxury* and *luxurious* is common in E.E., and is the only sense in Shakespeare. *Luxuria* and *luxuriosus* are similarly used in ecclesiastical Latin. V. Du Cange *s.v.*

meet (i. 1. 43), even; usually= fitting. O.E. *gemet*, fit. Same root as *mete*, to measure. The verb is similarly used in E.E., cf. "I shall meet with you"=I shall be even with you (*London Prodigal*, iii. 3); and Stevens says that in his day the adjective was still so used in the Midlands.

misprising (iii. 1. 52), undervaluing. M.Fr. *mespriser* (Spenser has *mesprize*=contempt) < O.Fr. *mes-*=Lat. *minus*, less, and Lat. *pretiare*, to value, from *pretium*, price.

misprision (iv. 1. 184), mistake.

M.Fr. *mesprison* (Fr. *méprise*), < *mes-*=Lat. *minus*, and *prehendere*, to take. Sometimes confused with *misprise* (*q.v.*), and hence used in the sense 'neglect', as in 'misprision of treason'; *e.g.* "Proud, scornful boy, That dost in vile misprision shackle up My love and her desert" (*All's Well*, ii. 3. 159).

modest (ii. 1. 336); **modesty** (iv. 1. 178). Fr. *modeste*, Lat. *modestus*, measurable < *modus*, measure. In E.E. specially, though not exclusively, of female chastity.

moe, more (ii. 3. 67). *Moe* is from O.E. *ma* (adv.), *more* from *mára* (adj.) = greater. *Ma* was used as neut. noun followed by gen., *i.e.* more of so-and-so. Hence Alexander Gil's dictum that *moe* is comparative of 'many', *more* of 'much'. In Shakespeare *moe* is used only with plurals (expressed or understood) or with nouns of plural meaning.

nice (v. 1. 75), finished, finical. Properly from Lat. *nescius*, ignorant; but confused with E. *nesh*, delicate (still in dialect). Hence the change of meaning from M.E. 'foolish' to Mod.E. 'delicious'. The common meaning in E.E. is 'precise', 'finical'.

pack'd (v. 1. 286), confederate. From the noun *pack*: cf. Sc. 'thrang' and 'thick', both=intimate: "unco pack and thick thegither" (Burns).

pent-house (iii. 3. 97), shed projecting from a building. Properly spelt 'pentice' or 'appentice', being from Lat. *appendicium*, an 'annexe', but confused with Fr. *pente*, a slope, as if it meant 'a house with a sloping roof'.

pleached (i. 2. 8; iii. 1. 7), interwoven. O.Fr. *plessier* < Lat. *plectere*, to plait. Also spelt 'plashed'.

promise (iv. 2. 41), assure. Fr. *promesse*, Lat. *promissa*, past part. of *promittere*. In this sense only in the phrase 'I promise you'.

proper (i. 3. 48; ii. 3. 169; iv. 1. 305), handsome. M.E. and Fr. *propre*, Lat. *proprius*, one's own. Hence 'suitable', 'just', and (externally) 'comely'. Used literally by Claudio (ii. 3. 169), ironically by Don John and Beatrice.

purchaseth (iii. 1. 70), winneth. M.E. *pourchasen*, to acquire, from O.Fr. *purchaser*, to pursue. Now of acquisition by payment; but in law all land other than inherited is still said to be acquired by 'purchase'.

quaint (iii. 4. 20), dainty. Through Fr. *coint*, from Lat. *cognitus*, known (hence its common sense in M.E. 'famous'); but influenced by *compt*, from Lat. *comptus*, neat. In E.E. the element of 'delicacy' is more prominent, in Mod.E. that of 'oddity'.

queasy (ii. 1. 344), squeamish. Scandinavian *kveis*, squeamishness.

quips (ii. 3. 220), jokes. Lat. *quippe*, forsooth. Formerly spelt *quippy*. (Skeat.) [But the word may be a mere 16th-cent. coinage on the analogy of *nip*, *whip*, &c.]

quirks (ii. 3. 217), gibes. Origin uncertain.

quondam (v. 2. 30), ere-while. A Latin adverb used as an adjective.

rabato (iii. 4. 6), either a ruff or the wire support for a ruff. The *-o* "seems to be an English addition, as the word is not Spanish or Italian, but French". Fr. *rabat*, from *rabbatre*, to lessen = *re-abbatre*, < Fr. *battre*, to beat; ultimately from Lat. *batuere*.

recheat (i. 1. 216), a set of notes on the hunting-horn used to rally the hounds. M.E. *rechete* (vb.),

answering to O. F. *rechater* (Godefroy gives *racheter*), to reassemble, used as a term of venery, and representing pop. Lat. *recaptāre*. As sb. the word appears first in Malory's *Morte Arthur*; the spelling 'rechete' is preserved in Q. and F.; the form 'recheat' does not occur before 1550.

rheum (v. 2. 73), tears. Gk. ῥεῦμα < ῥεῖν, to flow.

sad (i. 1. 165), serious. O.E. *saed*, sated. In M.E. and even in E.E. the sense is much wider than now, ranging from 'serious' to 'solid'.

scambling (v. 1. 94), pushing, scrambling (?). Possibly same word as 'scramble', the *r* in which may be excrescent.

shrewd (ii. 1. 17), **shrewdly** (ii. 1. 69), biting, keenly. Properly past part. of *shrewen*, to curse, < *shrewe*, bad. The fundamental sense is 'biting', as in 'shrew-mouse', and this is still felt in E.E., though the second instance shows the transition to the modern sense.

smirched (iv. 1. 132), besmeared. A weak form of *smerk*, extended from M.E. *smeren*, O.E. *smerian*, to smear.

sort (i. 1. 7, 31), kind or rank. Fr. *sorte*, Lat. *sortem*, acc. of *sors*, lot. From meaning (1) lot, it passed through the meaning of (2) lot in life, condition, quality, to that of (3) a group of persons or things in the same condition, *i.e.* 'kind'. But in E.E. two other meanings attach: it is used (4) of a *distinguished* lot in life, *e.g.* 'gentlemen of sort and suit' (cf. 'rank' and 'the Quality'); and it is applied (5) to a group of persons or things connected locally, without implying likeness in the members, *i.e.* = company—"a sorte of shepherd groomes" (Spenser). Cf. **'lot'**.

tax (i. 1. 42; ii. 3. 41), O. Fr. *taxer*, to assess, Lat. *taxare* = *tactare*, to handle < *tactus*, touch. Meaning (1) to charge, to 'task' (ii. 3. 41); (2) to charge with crimes, &c., and so, (3) absolutely, to censure, satirize (i. 1. 42).

tire (iii. 4. 12), head-dress. Short for *attire*. For the limitation to head-gear, cf. 'toy'.

trow (iii. 4. 53), suppose, deem true. O. E. *treowian*, < *treowe*, true. For the elliptical use see note *ad loc.*

varlet (iv. 2. 67), low fellow. O. Fr. *varlet* for *vaslet*, dim. of *vassal*. Same word as *valet*. Cotgrave notes that in old time it was a more honourable title. 'Vassal' was similarly, but not permanently, degraded.

vice (v. 2. 19), screw. Fr. *vis* < Lat. *vitem*, acc. of *vitis*, vine. Properly 'male screw', a female screw being *écrou*.

warrant (iii. 1. 14; iii. 4. 8), assure, guarantee. O. Fr. *warant*, *guarant*, protector: cf. Ger. *wehren*.

weeds (v. 3. 30), clothes. O. E. *waéd*. Common in the sing. in E. E.; now chiefly in 'widow's weeds'.

winded (i. 1. 216), blown. Verb from noun *wind*. This is the proper form: Scott has 'wound' (*Lady of the Lake*, i. 1. 17).

INDEX OF WORDS

GENERAL INDEX

Abbott, *Shakespearian Grammar*, i. 1. 17, 160, 272; ii. 1. 179, 211; ii. 2. 47; ii. 3. 108; iii. 1. 1, 3, 4, 8; iv. 1. 188, 208, 248; v. 1. 22, 138, 200, 290; v. 4. 47, 59.

Actæon, i. 1. 179.

adjectives in -*ate*, how formed, iii. 2. 1.

adverbs, the position of, ii. 1. 122.

Alexander and Campaspe, Lyly's, ii. 3. 14.

alliteration, cross, iv. 1. 34; vowel, v. 1. 26.

Alphabet of Kenticisms, Pegge's, ii. 3. 39.

Angelos, whence introduced into English drama, i. 1. 1.

Apocrypha, references to, iii. 3. 54, 125.

Apology for Poetry, Sidney's, allusion to shaven Hercules, iii. 3. 126.

apparel of Englishmen in Shakespeare's time, iii. 2. 30.

Ariodante, iv. 1. 203.

Ariosto, iv. 1. 203.

Aristotle, *Oeconomics*, v. 1. 4.

Ars Amandi, Ovid's, i. 1. 234.

astrology, influences of planets on a man's disposition, i. 3. 11.

Ate, how represented by Shakespeare, ii. 1. 229, 230.

Bacon, use of *its*, i. 1. 92; use of start-up, i. 3. 61; distinction of marriage and alliance, ii. 1. 285.

Bartholomew Fair, Induction to, Jonson's, iii. 3. 151.

Battle of Alcazar, Peele's, ii. 3. 79.

Baucis and Philemon, ii. 1. 83.

Beaumont and Fletcher, *The False One*, iii. 2. 19.

Bell, Adam, i. 1. 231.

Blakeway, Mr., and Tale of Mr. Fox, i. 1. 194.

borachio, use of in sense of drunkard, iii. 3. 98.

Boswell, Variorum Edition, iii. 4. 40.

Brae's *Hercules Gallus*, iii. 3. 126.

brother, sworn, i. 1. 64.

bruderschaft, i. 1. 64.

Bullokar, definition of model, i. 3. 42.

burying suicides, mode of, iii. 2. 62.

Cambridge editors' opinions on text, iv. 1. 154-156; suggestion as to origin of corrupt passage, iv. 2. 63.

Camden, reference to, i. 1. 45.

Capell, corrections by, iii. 5. 9; iv. 1. 196; v. 1. 16; remarks on comparisons in, v. 1. 194.

Castell of Perseverance, a morality, iv. 1. 160.

Cecil, reference to, iii. 1. 9, 11.

Chalmers, opinion on reference, i. 1. 45.

Chapman, *Monsieur d'Olive*, iv. 1. 313.

Chappell, iii. 4. 40.

204

A BRIEF LIST OF BOOKS ON ENGLISH LANGUAGE & LITERATURE

PUBLISHED · BY · BLACKIE · AND · SON · LIMITED

*Complete Detailed Catalogue of English Language and Literature
publications post free on application*

THE WARWICK LIBRARY OF ENGLISH LITERATURE

General Editor—PROFESSOR C. H. HERFORD, LITT.D.

Each volume deals with the development in English literature of *some special
literary form*, is illustrated by a series of representative specimens, slightly
annotated, and preceded by a critical analytical introduction. In crown 8vo
volumes, decorated cloth boards. Price 2s. 6d. each.

English Tales in Verse. Edited by Prof. C. H. Herford, Litt.D.

English Pastorals. Edited by Edmund K. Chambers, M.A.

English Literary Criticism. Edited by C. E. Vaughan, M.A.

English Essays. Edited by J. H. Lobban, M.A.

English Lyric Poetry (1500–1700 A.D.). Edited by Frederick Ives Carpenter, M.A.

English Masques. Edited by H. A. Evans, M.A.

English Satires. Edited by Oliphant Smeaton, M.A.

English Historians. Edited by Prof. A. J. Grant, M.A.

"The Warwick Library is valuable to teachers and students as it provides at moderate
prices access to masterpieces which are often difficult to obtain, and just those portions of
the masterpieces which are best worth reading."—Journal of Education.

THE WARWICK SHAKESPEARE

General Editor—PROFESSOR C. H. HERFORD, LITT.D.

As You Like It. Edited by J. C. Smith, M.A. 1s. 6d.

Coriolanus. Edited by Edmund K. Chambers, M.A. 1s. 6d.

Cymbeline. Edited by A. J. Wyatt, M.A. 1s. 6d.

Hamlet. Edited by Edmund K. Chambers, M.A. 1s. 6d.

Henry the Fourth. Part I. Edited by F. W. Moorhead, B.A., Ph.D. 1s. 6d.

Henry the Fifth. Edited by G. C. Moore Smith, M.A. 1s. 6d.

Henry the Eighth. Edited by D. Nichol Smith, M.A. 1s. 6d.

Julius Cæsar. Edited by Arthur D. Innes, M.A. 1s.

King John. Edited by G. C. Moore Smith, M.A. 1s. 6d.

King Lear. Edited by D. Nichol Smith, M.A. 1s. 6d.

Macbeth. Edited by Edmund K. Chambers, M.A. 1s. 6d.

The Merchant of Venice. Edited by Prof. H. L. Withers. 1s. 6d.

A Midsummer-Night's Dream. Edited by E. K. Chambers, M.A. 1s. 6d.

Much Ado About Nothing. Ed. by J. C. Smith, M.A. 1s. 6d.

Richard the Second. Edited by Professor C. H. Herford. 1s. 6d.

Richard the Third. Edited by George Macdonald, M.A. 1s. 6d.

The Tempest. Edited by F. S. Boas, M.A. 1s. 6d.

Twelfth Night. Edited by Arthur D. Innes, M.A. 1s. 6d.

Reviewing *Richard the Second*, The Times says: "Perhaps the most intelligent
schoolbook ever contrived out of a play of Shakespeare's".

THE PICTURE SHAKESPEARE

Frontispiece in colours and numerous black-and-white Illustrations.   1s. each

As You Like It.	King John.	Midsummer-Night's
Hamlet.	Macbeth.	Dream.
Henry the Fifth.	Merchant of Venice.	The Tempest.
Henry the Eighth.	Richard the Second.	
Julius Cæsar.	Twelfth Night.	

"The Picture Shakespeare is decidedly attractive, the illustrations maintaining a high level throughout."—Athenæum.

THE JUNIOR SCHOOL SHAKESPEARE

F'cap 8vo, cloth, each (with a few exceptions) price 8d.

As You Like It. Edited by Prof. Lionel W. Lyde, M.A. 8d.

Coriolanus. Edited by W. Dent. (10d.)

Cymbeline. Edited by W. F. Baugust. (10d.)

Hamlet. Edited by Prof. Lionel W. Lyde. (10d.)

Henry the Fourth. Part I. Ed. by J. V. Saunders, M.A. 8d.

Henry the Fifth. Edited by W. Barry, B.A.(Lond.). 8d.

Henry the Eighth. Edited by George H. Ely, B.A. 8d.

Julius Cæsar. Ed. by W. Dent. 8d.

King John. Edited by F. E. Webb, B.A. 8d.

King Lear. Edited by H. A. Evans, M.A. 8d.

Macbeth. Edited by Henry C. Notcutt, B.A.(Lond.). 8d.

Merchant of Venice, The. Edited by George H. Ely, B.A. 8d.

Midsummer-Night's Dream, A. Edited by W. F. Baugust. 8d.

Richard the Second. Edited by W. Barry, B.A.(Lond.). 8d.

Richard the Third. Edited by F. E. Webb, M.A. (10d.)

Tempest, The. Edited by Elizabeth Lee. 8d.

Twelfth Night. Edited by Elizabeth Lee. 8d.

"The excellence and thoroughness of the general plan upon which Blackie's *Junior School Shakespeare* has been projected meets with unqualified approbation."
—Educational News.

THE PLAIN-TEXT SHAKESPEARE

THE GREATER PLAYS—TEXT ONLY—NO NOTES

In limp cloth cover, price 4d. each

As You Like It.	Julius Cæsar.	Richard III.
Coriolanus.	King John.	Midsummer-Night's
Hamlet.	Macbeth.	Dream.
Henry IV. Part I.	The Merchant of	The Tempest.
Henry V.	Venice.	Twelfth Night.
Henry VIII.	Richard II.	King Lear.

"Messrs. Blackie are to be congratulated on the issue of these tasty little texts in limp cloth cover."—School Guardian.

Introduction to Shakespeare. By Edward Dowden, Litt.D., LL.D. Illustrated. 2s. 6d.

THE PLAIN-TEXT PLAYS

Short Introduction.   No Notes.   Cloth limp, 6d. each

GOLDSMITH. — She Stoops to Conquer.

GOLDSMITH. — The Good-Natured Man.

SHERIDAN.—The Rivals and The School for Scandal.

2

LITTLE PLAYS FOR ACTING OR CLASS READING

The Rose and the Ring (Thackeray). Arranged for acting by E. E. Ohlson. 4d.

"When did you last see your Father?" and Just Eighteen. By M. F. Hutchinson. 4d.

The Australian Cousin. For Girls. By M. F. Hutchinson. 4d.

The Masque of the Woodlands. By M. F. Hutchinson. 4d.

Scenes from "Cranford". For Girls. By M. F. Hutchinson. 6d.

In the Days of Chaucer. A Pastoral Interlude. By E. E. Ohlson. 4d.

The Masque or Pageant of English Trees and Flowers. By M. F. Hutchinson. 4d.

The Baron of Brandean. An Historical Play of the Reign of King John. By Margery Barfield and Eleanor Trotter. 1s. net.

BLACKIE'S ENGLISH CLASSICS

ADDISON — Selected Essays from the Spectator. Edited by the Rev. Henry Evans, D.D. 2s.

ADDISON — Sir Roger de Coverley. From the *Spectator*. Edited by Frances Wilcroft. 8d.

AYTOUN—The Burial-March of Dundee and Edinburgh after Flodden. One vol. 4d.

BACON — Essays. Edited by E. H. Blakeney, M.A. 1s. 6d.

BACON — Eight Essays. 6d.

BROWNING—Strafford. Ed. by Miss Agnes Wilson. 2s.

BYRON—Childe Harold's Pilgrimage. Cantos II and III (one vol.). Edited by John Downie, M.A. 6d. Canto IV, Edited by D. Frew, B.A. 6d.

BYRON — The Prisoner of Chillon. Edited by the Rev. Dr. Evans. 4d.

CAMPBELL—The Pleasures of Hope. Edited by W. Keith Leask, M.A., and George H. Ely, B.A. 8d.

CARLYLE—Essay on Burns. With Introduction and Notes. 1s.

CHAUCER—The Prologue to the Canterbury Tales. Edited by E. F. Willoughby. 1s.

DICKENS—A Tale of Two Cities. Edited by Wm. Magennis, M.A. 1s. 6d.

DRYDEN—Essay of Dramatic Poesy. Edited by D. Nichol Smith, M.A. 2s.

GOLDSMITH—She Stoops to Conquer, and The Good-Natured Man. Edited by H. Littledale, M.A. 1s.

GOLDSMITH—The Citizen of the World. Selected Letters. Edited by W. A. Brockington, M.A. 2s.

HOLMES — The Autocrat of the Breakfast-Table. Edited by E. H. Blakeney, M.A. 1s.

JOSEPHUS — Autobiography and Selections from the Jewish War. Edited by S. E. Winbolt, M.A. 1s. 6d.

KINGSLEY — The Heroes. Ed. by E. H. Blakeney, M.A. 1s.

LAMB — Select Tales from Shakspeare. Edited by David Frew, B.A. 1s. 6d.

LONGFELLOW—The Courtship of Miles Standish. Ed. by the Rev. H. Evans, D.D. 1s.

LONGFELLOW — Hiawatha. Ed. by P. T. Cresswell, M.A. 1s.

LONGFELLOW — Saga of King Olaf. Selected and Ed. by Beatrice E. Clay, B.A. 6d.

MACAULAY — Essay on Addison. Ed. by C. Sheldon, D. Litt., B.Sc. 2s.

MACAULAY—**Essay on Horace Walpole.** Edited by John Downie, M.A. 2s.

MACAULAY—**Essay on Warren Hastings.** Edited by John Downie, M.A. 2s.

MACAULAY—**Essay on Clive.** Ed. by John Downie, M.A. 2s.

MACAULAY—**Essay on Milton.** Ed.by John Downie, M.A. 2s.

MACAULAY—**Essay on Pitt.** Ed. by C. J. Battersby, M.A. 2s.

MACAULAY — **Lays of Ancient Rome, with Ivry, The Armada, and Naseby.** 10d.

MACAULAY — **Lay of Horatius, Lake Regillus, and Prophecy of Capys.** Edited with Notes, &c. 8d.

MACAULAY—**Lives of Johnson and Goldsmith.** Edited by John Downie, M.A. 2s.

MACAULAY—**England in 1685** (The Third Chapter of Macaulay's History). Edited by H. Clement Notcutt, B.A. 2s.

MACAULAY—**History of England** (Chapters I, II, III). Ed. by W. H. D. Rouse, Litt. D. 6d. each.

MILTON—**Comus.** Edited by Rev. E. A. Phillips, M.A. 1s. 6d.

MILTON—**Samson Agonistes.** Ed. by E. K.Chambers, M.A. 1s.6d.

MILTON—**Paradise Lost.** Books I, II, and III. Edited by F. Gorse, M.A. 1s. each.

MILTON—**Paradise Lost.** Books IV, V, and VI. Edited by A. E. Roberts, M.A. 1s. each.

MILTON—**Lycidas.** Ed. by H. B. Cotterill, M.A. 1s. 6d.

MILTON—**Nativity Ode, L'Allegro, Il Penseroso, and Lycidas.** Paper, 6d.; cloth, 8d.

MOORE —.**Paradise and the Peri.** Edited by the Rev. Dr. Evans. 4d.

POPE—**Essay on Criticism.** Ed. by Fred. Ryland, M.A. 1s. 6d.

POPE—**Rape of the Lock.** Ed. by Fred. Ryland, M.A. 1s. 6d.

REYNOLDS — **Discourses on Art.** A Selection. Edited by Prof. J. J. Findlay. 2s. net.

SCOTT—**Marmion.** Complete, 1s. Cantos I–III, 8d.

SCOTT—**The Lay of the Last Minstrel.** Complete, 1s. Cantos I–III, 9d., Cantos IV–VI, 9d.

SCOTT—**The Lady of the Lake.** Edited by W. Keith Leask, M.A. Complete, 1s. Cantos I–III, 8d.

SCOTT — **Kenilworth.** Edited by W. Keith Leask, M.A. 1s. 6d.

SCOTT—**The Legend of Montrose.** Edited by W. Keith Leask, M.A. 1s. 6d.

SCOTT—**Old Mortality.** Edited by W. Keith Leask, M.A. 1s. 6d.

SCOTT—**The Talisman.** Edited by W. Keith Leask, M.A. 1s. 6d.

SCOTT — **Quentin Durward.** Ed. by W. Keith Leask, M.A. 2s.

SPENSER — **The Faery Queene.** Book I. Edited by W. Keith Leask, M.A. 2s.

TENNYSON — **The Princess.** Edited by Edith Fry. 1s. 6d.

BLACKIE'S SMALLER ENGLISH CLASSICS

Selections from Standard Authors. Edited with Biographical Sketch and Explanatory Notes. Paper, 2d.; Cloth, 3d. each.

ARNOLD.—**Sohrab and Rustum.**

AYTOUN.—**The Burial-March of Dundee, &c.**

AYTOUN.—**Edinburgh after Flodden.**

BROWNING.—**The Pied Piper of Hamelin.**

BROWNING.—**Select Poems.**

BURNS. — **The Cotter's Saturday Night, &c.**

BYRON.—**Childe Harold.** Cantos II and III, separately.

BYRON.—**The Prisoner of Chillon.**

BYRON.—**Ode to Napoleon.**

CAMPBELL.—**Songs and Ballads.**

CAMPBELL.—**The Pleasures of Hope.**

CHAUCER.—**The Squieres Tale.**

COLERIDGE.—**The Ancient Mariner.**

COWPER.—**John Gilpin,** and other Poems.

COWPER.—**Expostulation.**

COWPER.—**The Task.** Book V.

CRABBE.—**The Village.**

EMERSON.—**Select Poems.**

GOLDSMITH.—**The Deserted Village.**

GOLDSMITH.—**Retaliation.**

GOLDSMITH.—**The Traveller.**

GRAY.—**The Elegy, Eton College Ode, and The Bard.**

GRAY.—**Ode on Spring.**

HOGG.—**The Queen's Wake.**

JOHNSON.—**London and Vanity of Human Wishes.**

KEATS AND SHELLEY.—**Select Poems.**

LONGFELLOW.—**Evangeline.**

LONGFELLOW.—**Select Poems.**

LONGFELLOW.—**The Falcon of Ser Federigo and King Robert of Sicily.**

MACAULAY.—**Armada, Ivry, Naseby.**

MACAULAY.—**Battle of Lake Regillus.**

MACAULAY.—**Prophecy of Capys.**

MACAULAY.—**Lay of Horatius.**

MACAULAY.—**Lay of Virginia.**

MACAULAY.—**Essay on the Pilgrim's Progress and John Bunyan.**

MILTON.—**L'Allegro and Il Penseroso.**

MILTON.—**English Sonnets.**

MILTON.—**Nativity Ode.**

MILTON.—**Lycidas.**

MOORE.—**The Fire Worshippers.**

MORRIS.—**Writing on the Image, &c.**

POPE.—**The Rape of the Lock.**

ROSSETTI—**Goblin Market.**

SCOTT.—
Marmion. Cantos I, II, III, IV, V, VI, and Selections from Canto VI, separately.
The Lay of the Last Minstrel. Cantos I, II, III, IV, V, VI, separately.

The Lady of the Lake. Cantos I, II, III, IV, V, VI, separately.

The Lord of the Isles. Cantos II and VI, separately.

SHAKESPEARE.—

As You Like It: Selections.

Henry the Fourth: Selections.

Henry the Fifth: Selections.

Henry the Eighth: Selections.

Julius Cæsar: Selections.

Richard the Second: Selections.

The Merchant of Venice: Selections.

SHELLEY.—**Adonais.**

SHELLEY.—**Lines written among the Euganean Hills, &c.**

SHERIDAN.—**The Rivals** (slight.y abridged).

SOUTHEY.—**Ballads and Other Poems.**

SPENSER.—**Selections.**

TENNYSON.—**The Palace of Art and Ulysses.**

TENNYSON.—**A Dream of Fair Women and Tithonus.**

TENNYSON.—**Morte d'Arthur, The Lady of Shalott.**

TENNYSON.—**Dora, The May Queen, Mariana.**

TENNYSON.—**The Day-Dream, The Death of the Old Year, The Charge of the Light Brigade.**

TENNYSON.—**Ode on the Death of the Duke of Wellington.**

WORDSWORTH.—**The Shorter Poems.**

WORDSWORTH.—**Ode on Intimations of Immortality, and Laodamia.**

ENGLISH BALLADS.—**Chevy Chase.**

ENGLISH BALLADS.—**Sir Patrick Spens, and Robin Hood.**

ENGLISH BALLADS.—**Hartleap Well** (Wordsworth) and **The Nut-Brown Maid.**

A Book of Sonnets.

Pindaric Odes.

"Each of these dainty little editions consists of introduction, text, and notes. They are as good as can be desired, a marvel of cheapness."—School Guardian.

THE PLAIN-TEXT POETS

Short Introduction by Experienced Teachers. With Frontispiece. **6d. each**

BROWNING, R.—**Shorter Poems.**

GRAY.—**Poems.**

GOLDSMITH.—**Select Poems.**

LONGFELLOW.—**Evangeline, &c.**

LONGFELLOW.—**Hiawatha.**

MACAULAY.—**Lays, &c.**

MILTON.—**Shorter Poems.**

SCOTT.—**Marmion.**

SCOTT.—**Lady of the Lake.**

SCOTT.—**Lay of the Last Minstrel.**

TENNYSON.—**Earlier Poems.**

TENNYSON.—**Princess.**

Historical Lyrics and Ballads. (Two Books). Book I, before 1485. Book II, after 1485.

Scottish Vernacular Poetry.

Scottish Ballads.

"The volumes, both in type and *format,* give wonderful value for the price."
—Guardian.

BLACKIE'S ENGLISH TEXTS. Edited by W. H. D. ROUSE, Litt. D. Brief Introduction. In cloth covers. Price 6d. each.

GENERAL LITERATURE

ANDERSEN, HANS—**Fairy Tales**
Arabian Nights, Tales from the
BACON—**Essays**
BORROW—**Gipsy Stories**
BORROW—**Antonio and Benedict Mol**
BOSWELL—Life of Johnson. (1763-67)
BUNYAN—**Pilgrim's Progress**—Part I
BUNYAN—**Pilgrim's Progress**—Part II
BURKE—**American Speeches**
CARLYLE—**The Hero as Divinity, &c.**
CARLYLE—**The Hero as Poet, &c.**
CERVANTES—**Don Quixote** (abridged)
COWLEY—**Essays**
Decameron, Tales from the
DEFOE — **Captain Singleton's Early Adventures**
DEFOE—**Robinson Crusoe**
DEFOE—**Journal of the Plague Year**
DE QUINCEY—**English Mail Coach**
DICKENS—**A Christmas Carol**
DICKENS—**The Chimes**
DICKENS—**The Cricket on the Hearth**
ERASMUS—**In Praise of Folly**
GATTY—**Parables from Nature**
GOSSE—**Romance of Natural History**
GRIMM—**Fairy Tales**
HAWTHORNE—**Tanglewood Tales**
HAZLITT — **Characters of Shakespeare's Plays**
IRVING—**England's Rural Life, &c.**
IRVING—**Rip Van Winkle, &c.**
KINGSLEY—**The Heroes**
KINGSLEY--**The Water-Babies**
LAMB—**Adventures of Ulysses**
LAMB—**Tales from Shakspeare**
LAMB—**School-Days and other Essays**
Life of Lord Herbert of Cherbury
LUCIAN- **Trips to Wonderland**
MALORY—**The Coming of Arthur**
MALORY- **Knights of the Round Table**
MILTON—**Areopagitica, &c.**
MORE—**Utopia**
POE—**The Gold Bug and other Tales**
RUSKIN—**Sesame and Lilies**
RUSKIN—**Crown of Wild Olives**
RUSKIN — **Byzantine Churches of Venice**
Sindbad the Sailor
Sintram and his Companions
Spectator, Essays from the
SWIFT—**Gulliver's Travels**
WALPOLE—**Letters on the American War of Independence**
WALPOLE — **Letters on France and the French Revolution**
WALTON—**Complete Angler**

TRAVEL

IRVING—**Companions of Columbus**
The French in Canada
DRAKE—**The World Encompassed**
Sir Richard Hawkins's Voyage into the South Seas
Raleigh's Discovery of Guiana
Roe's Embassy to the Great Mogul
Early Voyages to Japan
Adventures of Captain John Smith
The Adventures of Captain James
Anson's Taking of the Galleon
BOSWELL — **Johnson's Tour in the Hebrides**
Captain Cook's Second Voyage
MUNGO PARK—**Travels in Africa**
HUC—**A Sojourn at Lha-Ssa**
HUC—**Travels in Thibet**
DUFFERIN—**Letters from High Latitudes**

HISTORY

1. BRITAIN AND THE BRITISH EMPIRE
Britain and Germany in Roman Times
BEDE — **History of the Church of England**
SCOTT—**Wallace and Bruce**
FROISSART — **Border Warfare**
FROISSART—**The Reign of Richard II**
FROISSART—**Crecy and Poitiers**
COMMINES—**Warwick the Kingmaker**
HOLINSHED—**England in the Sixteenth Century**
The Spanish Armada, &c.
JOHN SMITH—**Early History of Virginia**
ORME—**The Black Hole of Calcutta**
CLARENDON—**Cavalier and Roundhead**
MACAULAY—**First Chapter**
MACAULAY—**Second Chapter**
MACAULAY—**Third Chapter**
MACAULAY—**Essay on Clive**
MACAULAY—**Essay on Warren Hastings**
MACAULAY—**Second Essay on Pitt**
MACAULAY—**Essay on Hampden**
MACAULAY—**Essay on Sir Wm. Temple**
MACAULAY—**Essay on the War of the Succession in Spain**
BURKE—**Speeches on America**
WALPOLE—**Letters on the American War of Independence**
NAPIER—**Battles of the Peninsular War.** Two books. 1. Coruña, Talavera, Badajos. 2. Salamanca, Siege of Burgos, Vittoria, Siege of San Sebastian.
The Battle of the Nile. Letters and Dispatches of Lord Nelson.
Waterloo. Dispatches of Wellington, along with *A Voice from Waterloo* by Sergeant-Major Edward Cotton.
BLAKENEY—**The Retreat to Corunna**

2. General History

Richard Knolles—**Wars with the Turks**
The Adventures of Montluc
Prescott—**The Conquest of Peru**
Prescott—**Montezuma**
Prescott—**The Capture of Mexico**
Motley—**William the Silent**
Walpole—**Letters on France , and the French Revolution**

3. Ancient History

Thucydides—**The Siege of Syracuse**
Plutarch—**Lives of Brutus and Coriolanus; Julius Cæsar; Alexander** (3 vols.)
Livy—**Hannibal in Italy**
Josephus—**The Siege of Jerusalem**
Gibbon—**The Age of the Antonines**
Marcellinus--**Julian the Apostate**

ENGLISH LANGUAGE AND LITERATURE

The Model Classbooks of English. By F. W. Chambers and A. J. Ker. Book II, 3*d.*; III, 3*d.*; IV, 4*d.*; V, 4*d.*; VI, 6*d.* Teachers' Books, I–II, 1*s.*; III, 1*s.*; IV, 1*s.*; V, 1*s.*; VI, 1*s.* 6*d.*

Words: Their Origin and Use. By F. W. Chambers and A. J. Ker. Two Books, 8*d.* each, Teachers' Handbooks, 1*s.* net each.

A New English Spelling and Dictation Book. By T. Bennett, B.A. 1*s.* Word Lists only under title of **A New English Spelling Book.** 4*d.*

English Exercises for Intermediate Classes. By Elizabeth B. Bruce, M.A. 8*d.*

English Exercises for Higher Classes. By E. B. Bruce, M.A. 8*d.*

A First English Course. By Frank Jones, B.A. 2*s.* 6*d.*

First English Exercises. By Frank Jones, B.A. 1*s.* 6*d.*

Picture Composition. By Lewis Marsh. Three books. 6*d.* each.

A Preparatory Course of Literary Reading and Composition. Ed. by Lewis Marsh, M.A. 1*s.* 6*d.*

A Senior Course of Literary Reading and Composition. Ed. by Lewis Marsh, M.A. 2*s.*

Specimens of English Prose. Ed. by Bertha Skeat, Ph.D. 1*s.* 6*d.*

Letters of Great Writers. Spenser to Wordsworth. Ed. by the Rev. H. V. Taylor. 4*s.* 6*d.* net.

Specimens of Scottish Literature. With Introduction, Notes, and Glossary by W. M. Metcalfe, D.D. 2*s.* 6*d.* net.

A Book of Comparative Poetry. By W. Macpherson, M.A. 1*s.* net.

A Book of Comparative Prose. By W. Macpherson, M.A. 1*s.* net.

Graduated Exercises in English Composition. For Class Use. By H. Bendall, M.A. 1*s.* net.

Method of Analysis. By Frances E. Bevan. 1*s.* net.

Elementary Manual of English Etymology. 2*d.*; cloth, 3*d.*

Higher English. By D. Campbell. 1*s.* 6*d.*

Lower English. By D. Campbell 1*s.*

The English Language and Literature. By David Campbell. Cloth limp, 6*d.*; boards, 9*d.*

The Beginner's English. By David Campbell. 1*s.*; limp, 10*d.*

Compendious English Grammar. 1*s.* 6*d.*

Pupil's English Grammar. 1*s.* 6*d.*

The Comprehensive English Grammar. 1*s.*

Selections for Paraphrasing. By W. Murison, M.A. 1*s.*

The Teaching of English Grammar and Elementary Latin. By L. W. Wilsden. 1*s.* net.

The Teaching of English. By A. E. Roberts, M.A., and A. Barker, M.A. 2*s.* 6*d.* net.

Handbook of English Composition Exercises. 1*s.*

Stories and Essays. 1*s.*

A School History of English Literature. By Elizabeth Lee.
Vol. I. Chaucer to Marlowe. 1*s.* 6*d.*
Vol. II. Shakespeare to Dryden. 2*s.*
Vol. III. Pope to Burns. 2*s.*

The Elements of English Prose. By W. A. Brockington. 2*s.* 6*d.*

A Primer of Historical English Grammar. By B. Skeat. 2*s.* 6*d.*

Introduction to the Natural History of Language. By T. G. Tucker, Litt.D. 10*s.* 6*d.* net.

POETRY AND ELOCUTION

A Book of Nature Poetry. Collected and Arranged by William J. Claxton. Illustrated. Cloth, 1s. 6d.; leather, 2s. 6d. net.

A Posy of Pleasant Delights for Children. Gathered from the Golden Garden by A. E. Rouse and W. H. D. Rouse. Cloth, 1s. 6d.; leather, 3s. 6d. net.

Poetica. A Book of English Verse for Repetition, selected by John Ridges, M.A. 1s. 6d.; in four parts, 6d. each.

Songs of Nature and of Home. A Book of Recitations for Young Children. By Margaret Cameron, L.L.A. 1s.

English Poetry for the Young. Selected by S. E. Winbolt, M.A. 1s.

The Call of the Homeland. A collection of English Verse, selected by R. P. Scott, LL.D., and K. T. Wallas. In Two Parts, 1s. 6d. net each. In one volume, suitable for presentation, 4s. 6d. net.

An Introduction to Good Poetry. Ed. by E. F. Davidson, M.A. 1s. 6d.

An Edgbaston Poetry Book. For Girls' Schools. Edited by Edith M. Colman. 2s.

English Narrative Poems. From the Renaissance. Selected and edited by M. W. MacCallum, M.A., LL.D., and E. R. Holme, M.A. 5s.

The Model Poetry Books. Infants, paper, 1d.; cloth, 2d. Junior, with Portraits, 4d.; in two parts, cloth, 2d. each. Senior, with Portraits, cloth, 6d.

Recitations for Schools. Compiled by Margaret Riach, L.L.A. Infants, 5 books, 1d. each. Complete, 8d. Juniors, 4 books. Seniors, 6 books. 1d. each.

Palgrave's Golden Treasury. Book II. With Notes. 6d. net.

Bannockburn. By Louis Barbé. 2d.

How to Speak and Read. By J. Bruce Alston. 2s. net.

The Practical Elocutionist. By John Forsyth. 2s. 6d.

Baynham's Elocution. By G. W. Baynham. 2s. 6d.

Natural Elocution In Speech and Song. By M'Hardy Flint. 1s. net.

DICTIONARIES

Ogilvie's Imperial Dictionary of the English Language. A Complete Encyclopædic Lexicon, Literary, Scientific, and Technological. Revised and enlarged by Charles Annandale, M.A., LL.D. With over 3000 engravings, and numerous plates. In 4 vols., imperial 8vo, cloth, £4 net; or half-morocco, £5 net.

The Student's English Dictionary. Literary, Scientific, Etymological, and Pronouncing. By John Ogilvie, LL.D. Revised by Charles Annandale, M.A., LL.D. With nearly 800 Engravings. Cloth, 4s. 6d. net; half-persian, 7s. 6d. net; half-morocco, 9s. net.

The Concise English Dictionary. Literary, Scientific, Etymological, and Pronouncing. By Charles Annandale, M.A., LL.D. With 16 coloured plates. Cloth, 3s. 6d.; roxburghe, 5s. 6d.; half-morocco, 7s. 6d.

Ogilvie's Smaller English Dictionary. Etymological and Pronouncing. Cloth, 1s. net; roxburghe, 1s. 6d. net.

Blackie's Standard Shilling Dictionary. New Edition, profusely illustrated in colour. 1s.

A New Shakespearean Dictionary. A Glossary to the Plays and Poems. With Definitions and Illustrative Quotations. By R. J. Cunliffe, M.A., LL.B. 9s. net.

BLACKIE & SON, LTD., LONDON, GLASGOW, BOMBAY

Day Dreams of a Schoolmaster
by D'Arcy W. Thompson